MW01378443

Iran and the Global Economy

The relationship between religion and the state has assumed new significance since the Iranian Revolution more than three decades ago. The recent mass uprisings against autocratic rulers in the Arab world have highlighted the potency of Islamist forces in post-revolutionary societies in the region, a force arguably unlocked first by Iran's version of the 'spring' three decades ago. The economic ramifications of these uprisings are of special interest at a time when the possibility of the creation of Islamic states can have implications for their economic policy and performance again. A study of the Iranian experience in itself can offer useful insights whether for its own features and characteristics or for its possible lessons and implications for the region. This book is concerned with the economic aspects and consequences of the Iranian Revolution in general and its interaction with the international economy in particular. Many studies have to date dealt with Iran's economic challenges, policies and performance in the post-revolutionary period but its interaction with the international economy has not received adequate attention. The contributions in this volume by experts in the field address ways in which in the span of three decades, Iran's economy has evolved from a strong aspiration to develop an 'independent economy' to grappling with debilitating international economic sanctions.

Parvin Alizadeh is a Lecturer of Economics and a coordinator of studies at Boston University's study abroad programme in London. She held the position of Principal Lecturer in Economics at London Metropolitan University from 1990 to 2011.

Hassan Hakimian is a Reader in Economics and Director of the London Middle East Institute at SOAS, University of London.

The Routledge Political Economy of the Middle East and North Africa Series

Series editor: Hassan Hakimian

London Middle East Institute, SOAS, University of London

LONDON
MIDDLE EAST
INSTITUTE
SOAS

The aim of the London Middle East Institute (LMEI), through education and research, is to promote knowledge of all aspects of the Middle East including its complexities, problems, achievements and assets, both among the general public and with those who have specialist interests in the region.

The LMEI is based in SOAS, which hosts the largest concentration of Middle Eastern expertise in any European university. The LMEI provides teaching, training, research, publication, consultancy, outreach and other services related to the Middle East. It serves as a neutral forum for the study of issues concerning the region and helps to link individuals and institutions with academic, commercial, diplomatic, media or other specialisations.

Iran and the Global Economy

Petro populism, Islam and economic sanctions

Edited by Parvin Alizadeh and Hassan Hakimian

Routledge
Taylor & Francis Group

LONDON AND NEW YORK

First published 2014
by Routledge
2 Park Square, Milton Park, Abingdon, Oxon OX14 4RN

and by Routledge
711 Third Avenue, New York, NY 10017

Routledge is an imprint of the Taylor & Francis Group, an informa business

British Library Cataloguing in Publication Data
A catalogue record for this book is available from the British Library

Library of Congress Cataloging in Publication Data
Iran and the global economy: petro populism, Islam and economic sanctions / edited by Parvin Alizadeh and Hassan Hakimian.
    pages cm.—(The Routledge political economy of the Middle East and North Africa series; 22)
    Includes bibliographical references and index.
    1. Iran—Economic conditions.   2. Iran—Economic policy.
    3. Iran—Foreign economic relations.   I. Alizadeh, Parvin.
    II. Hakimian, Hassan, 1955–
    HC475.I7155 2014
    337.55—dc23

                        2013020228

ISBN: 978-0-415-50554-3 (hbk)
ISBN: 978-1-315-86720-5 (ebk)

Typeset in Times New Roman
by RefineCatch Limited, Bungay, Suffolk

Contents

Figures

Tables

Contributors

Parvin Alizadeh is Lecturer of Economics at Boston University Study Abroad, London.

Nader Habibi is Henry J Leir Professor of Economics of the Middle East in Crown Center for Middle East Studies, Brandeis University.

Hassan Hakimian is Director of the London Middle East Institute and Reader in the Department of Economics at SOAS, University of London.

M. Hashem Pesaran is Emeritus Professor of Economics, Cambridge University and Fellow of Trinity College, Cambridge; John Elliot Distinguished Chair in Economics, Professor of Economics, and Director, Centre for Applied Financial Economics, Department of Economics, University of Southern California.

Kamiar Mohaddes is Lecturer and Fellow in Economics at Girton College, University of Cambridge, UK.

Sima Motamen-Samadian is Director of the Centre for the Study of Advanced and Emerging Markets (CSAEM), London, UK.

Moaven Razavi is Senior Research Associate at the Heller School, Brandeis University, USA.

Preface and acknowledgements

Ever since the Iranian Revolution more than three decades ago, the relationship between religion and the state has acquired an unprecedented significance in modern times, both on a world scale and especially in the Islamic world. The recent mass uprisings against autocratic rulers in the Arab world – commonly dubbed the 'Arab Spring' – have highlighted again the potency of Islamist forces in relation to the power of post-revolutionary states in the region, a force arguably unlocked first by Iran's version of the 'spring' three decades ago.

The economic ramifications of these uprisings are of special interest at a time when the possibility of the creation of Islamic states can have implications for economic policy and performance emanating from Islamic interpretations of old institutions including private property, its boundaries, functions and enforcement mechanisms. It is our contention that a study of the Iranian experience in itself can offer unique insights whether for its own features and characteristics or for its possible lessons and implications for recent events in the region.

This book is concerned with the economic aspects and consequences of the Iranian Revolution in general and its interaction with the international economy in particular. Many studies have to date dealt with Iran's economic challenges, policies and performance in the post-revolutionary period but its interaction with the international economy – although of growing importance – has not received sufficient attention.

This book is originally the result of a one-day workshop on 'The Iranian Economy at the Crossroads: Future Choices and Prospects' which was held at the London Metropolitan Business School on 24 May 2008 and organized by Parvin Alizadeh. Some of the papers presented in this workshop are included in this book although the passage of time and the relevance of new topics also encouraged us to solicit new work afterwards (such as Chapter 7 on economic sanctions). Those present at the one-day conference were: Sohrab Behdad, Massoud Karshenas, Fatemeh Moghadam, Farhad Nomani and Hashem Pesaran. We are grateful to all of them for their generous support and guidance, without which this book would not have been possible.

This workshop also proved to be important for a new initiative by one of us (Hassan Hakimian) who held discussions about the idea of an 'international association' to promote research on Iran's economy – what later came to be called the '*The International Iranian Economic Association*' or the IIEA for short. The idea of the Association was subsequently widened and received support from 25 eminent 'Founding Members' culminating in its inaugural conference at the London Middle East Institute in December 2011 and co-convened by Hassan Hakimian and Hadi Salehi Esfahani. Several colleagues who presented at the workshop, as well as many others, subsequently helped us in discussions about the Association. These included IIEA's 'Organizing Committee' consisting of: Massoud Karshenas, Hassan Hakimian, Hadi Salehi Esfahani, Djavad Salehi-Isfahani and Hashem Pesaran.

Earlier versions of some of the chapters have also appeared in other conferences and workshops. We are grateful to Hashem Pesaran and Hadi Salehi Esfahani for organizing the Iranian economy conference at the University of Southern California (USC) in September 2009 where earlier drafts of Chapters 1, 4 and 6 were presented. We are particularly grateful to the editors of *Iranian Studies* for permission to include an earlier version of Chapter 4, and also to the World Bank's Commission on Growth and Development for permission to include Chapter 2, which was originally commissioned and subsequently printed as a working paper in the 25 country case studies under the stewardship of Mike Spence, the Commission's Chairman.

We should add that the views expressed, or any errors contained in individual chapters, are the responsibility of their authors and not of the editors or any other institutions and parties. Further, the order in which our names appear as editors of the book is alphabetical and without any prejudice as to our contributions or responsibilities in preparing the book.

And on a personal note, we would like to express our thanks to our family and mentors for their love and support. Parvin Alizadeh's thanks go to Naheed, her sister, for her continuous support and encouragement and Hassan Hakimian's to Mitra, Bijan and Babak for sharing the physical and mental space at home and for providing unlimited and inspiring company.

Parvin Alizadeh and Hassan Hakimian
April 2013

Introduction

Parvin Alizadeh and Hassan Hakimian

More than three decades after the Revolution, the state of the Iranian economy remains the subject of much attention and debate. While interest in the long-term economic consequences of revolutions in general is justified in view of their idealism to improve mass welfare, in Iran's case such interest is tainted by several characteristics and contextual specificities.

Arguably one of the broadest and largest mass-based movements of the last century, the 1979 Revolution brought down one of the strongest and more established monarchies in the Middle East and North Africa (MENA) region. More significantly, perhaps, it also ushered in a new era where the relationship between religion and the state apparatus came to acquire new dimensions and unprecedented significance in modern times, both on a world scale and especially in the Islamic world. The recent uprisings against autocratic rulers in the Arab world – commonly dubbed the 'Arab Spring' – have highlighted again the potency of Islamist forces in relation to the power of post-revolutionary states in the region, a force arguably unlocked first by Iran's version of the 'spring' three decades ago. The economic ramifications of these uprisings are naturally under the spotlight at a time when the possibility of the creation of Islamic states can have implications for economic policy and performance emanating from the Islamic interpretations of old institutions, including private property, its boundaries, functions and enforcement mechanisms. It is our contention that a study of the Iranian experience can offer rare insights whether for its own characteristics, challenges and opportunities, or for its lessons and implications for the more recent religious upsurge in the region.

This book is concerned with the economic aspects and consequences of the Iranian Revolution in general and its interaction with the international economy in particular. Since there is by now a copious literature dealing with the broad economic challenges, policies and performance of the post-revolutionary period as a whole (Mazarei, 1996; Behdad, 2000; Pesaran, 2000; Hakimian and Karshenas, 2000; and Rahnema and Behdad, 1996; Alizadeh, 2003), this book focuses mainly – although not exclusively – on the last decade or so within this period. This is the period that is associated with the reversion of power from the reformist administration of President Khatami (1997–2005) to conservative factions led by Mr Ahmadi-Nejad after 2005. This book is intended as a sequel to an earlier volume edited by one of the co-editors (Alizadeh, 2000) which laid out the salient features of Iran's post-revolutionary economy in its formative years in the 1980s and 1990s. With the passage of time and major new developments since then, we felt time is right for a follow-up volume to present those interested in understanding the Iranian economy and its various turns and twists, specially in the international context, with the opportunity of engaging with the latest research in the form of another collection of articles by experts in the field.

Our interest in focusing on the international aspects of Iran's economy, however, represents more than a mere chronological update. This is partly to do with the fact that, as stated above, other aspects – particularly those dealing with policy challenges and performance in general – have received more attention to date. A second, and complementary, motivation emanates from the very complexities and ambiguities of the Islamist administration's attitude and posture vis-à-vis the international economy, which renders a case study of Iran of special interest.

As is widely known, the post-revolutionary state was from early on shaped by two distinct and inter-related ideals: bringing about 'social justice' and achieving 'economic independence'. Despite their ambiguities, both these ideals have continued to make an imprint on the vision and practice of economic policy in Iran ever since (Pesaran, 2011).

As far as Iran's position in the international economy was concerned, one of the key characteristics of the Iranian Revolution – and arguably one of its differentiating factors from the recent Arab uprisings – was its strong anti-imperialist undertone and standpoint. This in turn arose from the popular rejection of the Shah's dependency on external powers in general and on the USA in particular. A strong and deep aspiration to turn Iran into an 'independent economy' was a distinct element underpinning economic thinking and policymaking throughout the revolutionary process and has lasted – albeit to different degrees – through various administrations at the helm of power during the last three decades. This key characteristic accounts for Iran's pursuit of a generally isolationist development path as well as its suspicion and distrust of greater international economic integration.

However to characterize post-revolutionary Iran's attitude and posture towards the global economy as wholly distrustful, apprehensive or critical would be simplistic since, as various chapters in this book demonstrate, the Islamic regime's approach to the international economy has in reality been more complex and contradictory than may be characterized as 'anti-imperialist', autarkic or disengaging. While it is true that in the main Iran has differentiated herself clearly from the growing club of emerging economies which have – by choice or necessity – tried to ride high on the globalization wave since the early 1980s, it is also true that Iran has at times adopted at best an ambiguous stand combining a critical position with one in search of beneficial opportunities for engagement with the international economy.

So how can we explain Iran's vexed, if not ambiguous and contradictory, position with regards to the global economy?

We believe there are *three key considerations* that need to be addressed. First is the *institutional* setting, namely the Islamic character of the regime and, reflecting this, the type of administration that was installed in Iran after 1979. This feature is arguably Iran's single most distinctive post-revolutionary characteristic, which sets it apart and differentiates it from other developing countries in the MENA region or elsewhere.

Second is Iran's structural characteristic as an oil-exporter, a characteristic which pre-dates the Revolution but has also continued afterwards despite strong revolutionary eagerness for a lasting break with the past.

Third and finally, is the growing international isolation brought about by comprehensive and biting international sanctions against Iran. Though faced with these restrictions in different forms and extent since its inception, the scope and severity of sanctions have escalated markedly posing new challenges for Iran in recent years. In particular, the unilateral EU and US sanctions against Iran's nuclear programme since 2010 have affected her economy in an unprecedented way both in the domestic and international contexts.

These three factors – the *institutional setting* (an Islamic administration), the *structural feature* (of an oil-exporter) and adverse *external environment* (gripping economic sanctions) form our main themes throughout the book and its various chapters. We discuss them briefly below.

Until recently, the role of institutions in explaining economic performance was not well understood. Much of the traditional literature ascribed capital accumulation and growth in different countries to their differences in physical and human capital resources and savings rate (Solow, 1956). With the rise of the 'new institutional economics', the role of institutions in economic growth has been elevated with various cross country studies associating variations in economic performance to a large extent with institutional differences across countries (North, 1990; Acemoglu et al., 2004; Helpman, 2008). From this perspective, institutions are broadly viewed as consisting of both 'formal constraints (rules, laws, constitutions)' as well as 'informal constraints (norms of behaviour, conventions, and self-imposed codes of conduct) ... Together they define the incentive structure of societies and specifically economies' (North, 1993). A prime example of such influence is the existence and effective protection of private property rights which enhances the individuals' incentives to accumulate capital and invest in economic activities. Davis (2009) also distinguishes between *institutions* and *policies* (structure and agency). The former (constitution, property rights and the basic structure of government) are durable while the latter (fiscal, monetary or income policies) are generally discretionary and far less lasting.

Post-revolutionary Iran, in fact, provides a laboratory case where deep-seated and pervasive changes at the institutional level have influenced policies and the performance of the economy too. Here the Islamic nature of the emergent ruling administration – or more specifically, its Shi'ite version – has had a major influence.

First, the Revolution catapulted the clergy to the apex of the political power structure in 1979, hence turning Iran into the world's arguably single theocracy in modern times.

Second, given the novel and unknown character of the emergent state and the absence of a blueprint for an 'Islamic Republic', the new social and economic order had to hinge on broad perceptions, if not vague ideals and promises. As we shall see in Chapter 2, an element of ambiguity has permeated developments in Iran in the post-revolutionary period from the start and has continued to have far-reaching implications particularly in the economic policy area (see also Behdad, 2000; and Behdad and Nomani, 2006).

Third, the particular version of Islam in Iran – Shi'ism – has played its part in shaping the form and function of political and economic institutions. Since various *Marja-e Taqlids* (senior clergy or literally sources of emulation) can provide interpretation on a wide range of legal and jurisprudence matters for their followers (Mohajer and Vahabi, 2011:12–14), the scope for wielding political power has increased markedly. In this way, Iran's political landscape has been transformed from a monolithic structure with the absolute monarch at the helm to a 'polycentric' structure with multiple and often conflicting sources of spiritual and political inspiration. As Chapters 2 and 3 illustrate, such a setting has been especially prone to internal strife and factional politics, which has characterized the contradictory and conflicting cycles of reform and populism witnessed in this period.

Moreover, this diffuse power structure is partly elected and partly unelected (Beeman, 2004). An elected parliament and president operate alongside several unelected political institutions. For instance, the heads of the army (who also preside over the Islamic Revolutionary Guard Corps, the IRGC), the judiciary, radio and television, as well as some members of two powerful conservative religious organizations – namely, the *Guardian Council* and the *Expediency Council* – are appointed by the Supreme Leader. What is perhaps even more significant is that the unelected bodies – normally drawn from the most conservative elements within the leadership – wield veto powers over the elected institutions. As shown in Chapters 2, 3 and 5, this has led to a complex labyrinth of decision-making compounded by additional adjudicating bodies set up to reconcile their decisions.

The result is intense and continuous strife and factional politics with regular spillovers into the economic policy domain. These chapters highlight significant examples from recent times – for instance, the enactment of the foreign investment law, called 'the Foreign Investment Promotion and Protection Act' (FIPPA) in 2002, or more recently in 2005 over the Privatization of SOEs (which required a special decree by the Supreme Leader over Article 44 of the Constitution). In all, these highlight how at different levels, interest groups formed along religious lines constantly exert pressure on the elected institutions because of their close alliance with unelected institutions and their growing economic might (Chapter 3).

A second distinctive element of Iran's economy is its characteristic as an oil-exporter. Whilst reducing oil dependency and diversifying the economy were strong ideals behind the 1979 Revolution, evidence in fact suggests that Iran's dependency on the oil sector has not only continued but increased (Chapters 1 and 2 elaborate on this; Chapter 7 also discusses dependence on oil in the context of the recent sanctions).

With the exception of oil exports, Iran's integration into the international economy has remained limited and disproportionate to its size and economic structure (Chapters 1–4). Compared to other emerging economies which have pursued more liberal open economies (e.g. Turkey, Malaysia or Mexico), Iran's access to international capital flows including foreign direct investment has remained limited, as have its non-oil exports in general and its manufactured exports in particular (Hakimian and Karshenas, 2000).

Whilst oil exports provide the principal mechanism for Iran's integration with the international economy, they also expose her ambivalent and contradictory attitude towards the latter in general (Chapter 4). Whilst pursuing ostensibly isolationist policies in the international arena (especially in the early days of the Revolution), Iran has also tried to maximize its advantages from international oil exports as one of OPEC's largest oil producers.

But oil exports have a significant impact on the domestic economy of oil exporters, too. A copious literature has in recent decades drawn attention to the adverse effects of natural resource booms on economic growth (Gelb, 1988; Frankel, 2010). While the empirical evidence in support of this – the so-called 'resource curse' – literature is at best ambiguous (see Chapter 1 for a comprehensive treatment of this issue), alternative approaches have emphasized political economy factors in general and the 'rentier' nature of the oil states and their monopoly control over the distribution of oil 'rents', in particular (see Mahdavi, 1970, for a classic early statement of this approach). Accordingly, these revenues have propagated unproductive activities with the 'rent-seeking' opportunities generated by them undermining the emergence of an efficient and viable private sector to spearhead sustainable long-term growth in natural resource-rich countries.

The particular form of rentierism in Iran and its intersection with the theocratic institutional framework described above is of special interest in the context of what is described as 'petro-populism' in Chapter 3. Here, we have populist policies financed by growing oil revenues in the context of a 'polycentric' theocratic setting which is germane to adoption of policies aimed at garnering popular support for a particular faction of the political elite against others. In spite of their redistributive objectives in favour of the poor, however, populist policies are ultimately inflationary and erode the purchasing power of lower income groups. This is evident from a comparison of populist policies during the period 2005–11, which benefited from an unprecedented growth of oil income, with the higher rates of economic growth and lower rates of inflation during the reform period of 1997–2005. As Alizadeh observes in the same chapter: 'Ironically, evidence suggests that the cycle of reform in Iran was more conducive to poverty reduction than that of populism.'

And finally, another important aspect of Iran's interaction with the global economy relates to economic sanctions. Whilst contradictory and ambivalent, Iran's attitude to the international economy, and thus her isolationism, has only been partly discretionary or self-inflicted as international sanctions against Iran's nuclear programme have intensified in recent years.

As Chapter 7 shows, the Islamic Republic has operated under some form of sanctions since its inception. For instance, for much of the 1980s and 90s unilateral US sanctions aimed to restrict Iran's international trade. These were followed by restrictions against foreign investment in Iran's energy sector in the 1990s. Overall, however, Iran managed to bypass these, partly because they were not comprehensive and partly because other international players, such as the European Union (EU), did not comply. The result was trade diversification and the rise of third party trade routes (such as the United Arab Emirates (UAE)) which benefited from the diversion of US re-exports to Iran.

The situation has, however, changed markedly after the UN Security Council's multilateral sanctions in 2006 which have targeted Iran's military industries and capability. Since 2010, the scope and severity of these sanctions have escalated in an unprecedented fashion with the US and EU unilateral economic sanctions tightening the noose around Iran's economic lifelines with the rest of the world. These have been widened to target not only Iran's capability to export oil but also embrace now a wide range of sectors, including energy, banking, shipping, insurance, ports, trade, and commodities. In all, these have severed or complicated many of Iran's commercial ties to the rest of the world with severe implications for her position in the global economy.

The structure of the book is as follows.

In Chapter 1, Kamiar Mohaddes and Hashem Pesaran take a long-term view of the Iranian economy and particularly the oil sector and its importance and impact over the past hundred years (1908–2010). They note that although oil has been produced in Iran over a very long period, its importance to the Iranian economy was relatively small until the early 1960s and has grown since. Moreover, in posing the critical question of whether oil income has been a blessing or a curse, they offer a mixed picture: when managed appropriately, oil revenues are a blessing, but their volatility (which in Iran is much higher than the oil price's volatility) can have adverse effects on real output, for instance, through excessively high and persistent levels of inflation.

Moreover, the lack of appropriate institutions and policy mechanisms, which should act as shock absorbers in the face of high levels of oil revenue volatility, has also become a drag on Iran's real output. The chapter ends by suggesting that, in order to promote growth a number of diverse policies should be devized: to control inflation; to absorb the adverse effects of oil revenue volatility; to reduce rent-seeking activities; and to prevent excessive dependence of government finances on oil income.

In Chapter 2, Hassan Hakimian studies the post-revolutionary economy in the first two and a half decades after the Revolution (until 2004). His analysis focuses on Iran's macroeconomic policies and performance in the context of major shocks and upheavals, including oil booms and busts, war, trade sanctions, and internal political strife. Despite Iran's considerable human and natural resource riches, the economic record of the post-revolutionary period is found to be lacklustre, with many Iranians experiencing setbacks to their living standards by regional and international standards.

Hakimian argues that two sets of factors conditioned Iran's performance in this period and are likely to continue to taint her prospects for sustainable growth into the future: limited economic diversification and continued dependence on the oil sector (as discussed above) and the institutional setting in which post-revolutionary economic policies have been formulated and implemented. With regards to the latter, he contends that the Islamic economics 'project' in Iran from start was tainted with ambiguity and ambivalence. Given the novel and unknown character of the emergent state and the absence of a blueprint for an 'Islamic Republic', the new social and economic order had to hinge on broad perceptions, if not vague ideals and promises. Such an element of ambiguity has continued to have far-reaching implications in the economic policy arena during the cycles of populism and reform which characterized the first two and a half decades of the Islamic Republic (this is also exemplified by the experience of free trade zones in Iran, discussed in Chapter 4).

Chapter 3 picks up where Chapter 2 leaves off. Here, Parvin Alizadeh addresses the political economy of 'petro-populism' and reform in the last decade (1997–2011) with a special focus on the period since 2005. In the first phase of this period, during Mr Khatami's Presidency (1997–2005), Iran witnessed a sustained drive for economic reform. In the second phase (after 2005), this drive was reversed in favour of populist policies, when Mr Ahmadi-Nejad took office. She argues that the conceptual framework of 'petro-populism' and 'mature' rentier state are intertwined in this period in Iran. On the one hand, the availability of external rent from the sale of oil enables the state to pursue redistributive policies to ensure its domestic legitimacy or to create popular support for a particular faction of the political elite against others. This is exacerbated by the polycentric structure of governance and political institutions which create a tension between the elected and unelected bodies. Unelected bodies have veto power over elected institutions and are by and large extremely conservative in their interpretation of Islamic law.

Populist policies prove to be inflationary and erode the purchasing power of the lower income groups. The Iranian experience with these policies over the period 2005–11, which benefited from an unprecedented growth of oil income, is a clear example of the failure of populist policies to improve growth and prosperity. By contrast, higher rates of economic growth and lower rates of inflation characterized the period of reform over the period 1997–2005. Ironically, evidence suggests that the cycle of reforms in Iran was more conducive to poverty reduction than that of populism.

Another important example of contradictory and ambivalent economic policy is illustrated in Chapter 4, where Hassan Hakimian offers a study of the experience of free zones in Iran in the context of Iran's contradictory and ambivalent approach to international economic integration in general. Since the late 1980s, Iran has pursued a policy of attracting foreign investment and fostering regional trade by granting favoured status to the so-called 'Free Trade Industrial Zones' (FTZs) and Special Economic Zones (SEZs). The FTZs are strategically positioned for their potential international links with their eyes on markets beyond

Iran, and the SEZs for their value in serving main industries and for improving the country's distribution system and supply network. Hakimian shows that liberal policies pursued in the free zones to attract and benefit from greater international economic presence in 'pockets' of the mainland have been in contrast to Iran's inward-looking policies in general. Indeed, serving mainly as 'back doors' to the international economy, Iran's free zones have stalled mainly because their promotion has been decoupled from, if not at odds with, official attitudes to the international economy at large. As a result, the zones' ability to attract investment has been limited by both adverse external perceptions of Iran as an investment destination and internal complexities discouraging such investment.

In Chapter 5, Sima Motamen-Samadian studies the role of government in the financial and economic development of Iran between 2005 and 2012 and how it has affected the remit of the central bank and the soundness of the banking system as a whole. This sector has gone through considerable upheavals since its nationalization in the early days after the Revolution. Despite partial liberalization and privatization after 2001, government interventions have frequently affected the activity of the banking system. In general, these policies have caused both demand-pull and cost-push inflation, and undermined the independence of the Central Bank in controlling inflation and maintaining the purchasing power of the domestic currency at home and in international markets. Following a sharp downfall in productive activities, the banking system witnessed a significant rise in the level of loan delinquencies followed by several banking scandals. These happened despite the government's earlier promises to eliminate corruption, reduce unemployment and promote industrial development by increasing the availability of funds to small and medium-sized enterprises (SMEs). Two important factors played a major role in the rise of inflation and downturn of economic activities in Iran in this period: the subsidy reform programme and progressive intensification of international sanctions against Iran. The former was a major price reform affecting the products of state-run industries, and in particular energy prices. The second important factor has been international sanctions against Iran's oil exports and international financial transactions, which has seriously affected Iran's ability to earn exports revenue and raised significantly the cost of imports, contributing to cost push inflation and stagflation.

In Chapter 6, Parvin Alizadeh studies Iran's second most important industry after oil and gas – the auto industry – in comparison with those of South Korea, Thailand, Malaysia and Turkey. She highlights their similarities as well as their differences in responding to globalization opportunities, rationalization processes and cost pressures since the 1980s.

The development of the auto industry in emerging markets has been informed by two distinct trends in recent decades. The first trend has emphasized the implementation of a 'national car project' and has been concurrent with substantial government-backed investment to upgrade a country's technological capability. The second path has focused on expansion into the global markets with emphasis on specialization. The two trends are, however, not mutually exclusive and the distinction between them is largely a matter of emphasis placed on any single strategy. The Iranian auto industry, alongside those of South Korea's and Malaysia's, belongs to the first group while the car industries in Thailand, Turkey and Indonesia belong to the second.

This chapter shows that the Iranian auto industry has been one of the fastest growing industries in terms of output and value-added since the mid-1990s. However, the industry is almost entirely state- or parastatal-owned and controlled. Government protection and promotion of this industry in fact typifies its industrial policy of achieving self-sufficiency and autarky since the mid-1990s. However, unlike South Korea's national car project that has managed to break into major global export markets, the Iranian auto industry is primarily oriented towards the domestic market with insignificant levels of exports.

In Chapter 7, Nader Habibi offers a comprehensive study of the economic sanctions on Iran, assessing their impact on the economy. He demonstrates that the impact has been profound and has evolved with the severity and form of sanctions.

Sanctions were initially imposed by the United States, which was Iran's dominant trading partner before the Revolution. These have been justified on a wide range of grounds, such as, the hostage crisis in the 1980s; as part of the United States' dual containment policy against Iran and Iraq; and as punishment for Iran's 'support for terrorism' in general and for Hizbollah in Lebanon, in particular. A new and more important rationale was added in the 1990s, when the United States became alarmed about Iran's nuclear programme. In the 2000s, while the US-sponsored sanctions have become more intense, additional sanctions have been imposed by the EU and the United Nations (UN) as well.

Prior to these new rounds, Iran was generally able to evade sanctions through flexible and dynamic trade diplomacy involving a switch to new trade partners. The impact of sanctions on Iran was thus somewhat limited until recently. However, in the new round since 2011 sanctions on oil exports, financial transactions, the central bank, and cargo insurance have caused severe disruptions on Iran's oil revenues and trade. In addition to economic hardship for the population, they have also caused some deep transformations in Iran's economy. These changes have come about as intended and unintended consequences of the measures that Iranian government has implemented to counter the sanctions.

And finally, in Chapter 8, Moaven Razavi and Nader Habibi address the question of economic and social discrimination against women using Iran's Household Income and Expenditure Survey data to investigate the magnitude of wage discrimination against women in the Iranian labour market. They do this by breaking down the male–female wage differences into differences in human capital (justified) and discrimination (unjustified). This study is important because many urban households now depend on the incomes of both spouses to meet their expenses. Furthermore, in light of the recent increase in the ratio of divorced and unmarried women in Iranian society, wage and employment discrimination against women can have a direct bearing on their standards of living.

Their findings suggest that women face a sizable hourly wage gap in the private sector but not in the public sector. The decomposition of the gender wage gap into contributions of human capital and discrimination reveals that wage discrimination was present in both sectors but it was significantly smaller in the public sector in comparison to the private sector. Taking skills into account, they also find that female scientists and specialists face less wage discrimination than those in lower-skilled categories. The absolute size of the gender wage gap is also smaller for more skilled employment categories, indicating perhaps that highly skilled and specialist female workers have more bargaining power. The high level of wage discrimination in the unskilled service sector is partly due to the fact that in recent years it has become culturally acceptable for young women in larger cities to work in low pay retail jobs.

References

Acemoglu, D., Johnson, S. and Robinson, J., 'Institutions as the fundamental cause of long-run growth', National Bureau of Economics, Working Paper 10481: http://www.nber.org/papers/w10481, 2004.

Alizadeh, P., ed, *The Economy of Iran: Dilemmas of an Islamic State,* London: I.B. Tauris, 2000.

Alizadeh, P., 'Iran's quandary: economic reforms and the "structural trap"', *The Brown Journal of World Affairs*, Winter/Spring, 1X (2), 2003.

Beeman, W., 'Elections and governmental structure in Iran: reform lurks under the flaws', *The Brown Journal of the World Affairs,* X1 (1), 2004.

Behdad, S., 'From populism to economic liberalism: the Iranian predicament', in Alizadeh, ed, 100–141, 2000.

Behdad, S. and Nomani, F., eds, *Islam and the Everyday World: Public Policy Dilemma*, Routledge Political Economy of the Middle East and North Africa Series; London and New York: Routledge, 2006.

Davis, K. E., 'Institutions and economic performance: an introduction to the literature', *New York University School of Law*, NYU Center for Law, Economics and Organization Law & Economics Research Paper Series, Working Paper No. 09–51; available from: http://ssrn.com/abstract=1520515, 2009.

Frankel, J., 'The natural resource curse: a survey', *National Bureau of Economic Research*, Working Paper 15836, 2010.

Gelb, A., ed, *Oil Windfalls: Blessing or Curse?*, Oxford: Oxford University Press, 1988.

Hakimian H. and Karshenas, M., 'Dilemmas and prospects for economic reform and reconstruction in Iran', in Alizadeh, ed, 2000.

Helpman, E., ed, *Institutions and Economic Performance*, Cambridge, MA: Harvard University Press, 2008.

Karshenas, M. and Hakimian, H., 'Dilemmas and prospects for economic reform and reconstruction in Iran', in Alizadeh, ed, 2000.

Mahdavi, H., 'Patterns and problems of economic development in rentier states: the case of Iran,' in Cook, M. A., ed, *Studies in Economic History of the Middle East*, Oxford: Oxford University Press: 428–67, 1970.

Mazarei, A., 'The Iranian economy under the Islamic republic: institutional change and macroeconomic performance 1979–1990', *Cambridge Journal of Economics,* 20 (3): 289–314, 1996.

Mohajer, N. and Vahabi, M., 'Islamic Republic of Iran and its opposition', *Comparative Studies of South Asia, Africa and the Middle East*, 31 (1): 110–19, 2011.

North, D. C., *Institutions, Institutional Change and Economic Performance*, New York: Cambridge University Press, 1990.

North, D., 'Economic performance through time,' Lecture to the memory of Alfred Nobel, December 9, 1993: available from: http://www.nobelprize.org/nobel_prizes/economics/laureates/1993/north-lecture.html

Pesaran, E., *Iran's Struggle for Economic Independence: Reform and Counter-Reform in the Post-Revolutionary Period,* Routledge Political Economy of the Middle East and North Africa Series; London and New York: Routledge, 2011.

Pesaran, M. H., 'Economic trends and macroeconomic policies in post-revolutionary Iran', in Alizadeh, ed, 2000.

Rahnema, S. and Behdad, S., eds, *Iran after the Revolution: Crisis of an Islamic State*, London: I.B. Tauris, 1996.

Solow, R. M., 'A contribution to the theory of economic growth', *The Quarterly Journal of Economics*, 70 (1): 65–94, 1956.

1 One hundred years of oil income and the Iranian economy

A curse or a blessing?

Kamiar Mohaddes[1] *and M. Hashem Pesaran*[2]

Introduction

This chapter examines the impact of oil revenues on the Iranian economy over the past 100 years, spanning the period 1908–2010. It begins with an overview of the history of oil exploration and development in Iran, and considers the quantitative importance of revenues from oil exports for the Iranian economy. Three sub-periods are identified.

In the first sub-period, 1908–1959, oil started to be produced in significant quantities, but Iran's share of profits from exports of oil remained rather limited, despite repeated renegotiations over the oil contracts between the Iranian government and the international (mainly British) oil companies, the nationalization of the oil industry, and the subsequent establishment of the National Iranian Oil Company.

The second sub-period, 1960–1978, saw major changes in the international oil industry and expanding oil revenues for Iran. Iran's revenues from oil exports started to become significant, more or less steadily, from 1960 onwards thanks to increased production and better royalty terms made possible partly due to the increasing importance of OPEC in contract re-negotiations between producers and host companies. But the main factor behind Iran's huge oil revenues in the 1970s was price increases, which were modest initially but then became substantial after the quadrupling of international oil prices in 1973–1974.

The third sub-period, 1979–2010, coincides with the overthrow of the Shah's regime in the February 1979 revolution, the halving of oil exports as an intended policy change by the revolutionary government, and significant volatilities in Iran's oil revenues due to the eight-year war with Iraq (September 1980 to August 1988), US economic sanctions (targeting Iran's oil and gas industry), and the vagaries of international oil markets.

In short, although oil has been produced in Iran for a long time, its importance for the development of the Iranian economy was relatively small until the 1960s. The quadrupling of oil prices in the 1970s and the Shah's policy of spending almost all of the increased revenues domestically substantially increased the country's dependence on oil income, which also happened to coincide with a much higher volatility of international oil prices. Revolution, war and economic sanctions, through their impacts on oil production and exports, have introduced further important sources of variation in Iran's oil revenues. As a result, the Iranian economy has been subject to unprecedented oil revenue volatility. Annual oil revenue volatility has risen from 35.5 per cent per annum during 1960–1978, to 51.1 per cent per annum during 1979–2010, as compared to oil price volatility which rose from 11.3 per cent to 26.1 per cent over the same periods.

In this chapter we argue that it is the volatility in oil revenues and the government's inappropriate economic and political responses to these volatilities that are the curse and not the abundance of revenues from oil exports in itself. To this end we review the literature on resource abundance and growth, as well as the recent macro-econometric evidence on the Iranian economy. Although the early literature showed the existence of a negative relationship between real output per capita and resource abundance, more recent evidence is not so clear-cut. First, the early literature used cross-country analysis that fails to take account of dynamic heterogeneity and error cross-sectional dependence, and this could bias the results. Second, the early analysis ignores the effects of oil revenue volatility on growth, which turns out to be important. Using appropriate econometric techniques and including measures of resource revenue volatility in the analysis, the evidence in fact points to resource revenues having a positive effect on growth, with resource volatility affecting growth negatively. Seen from this perspective, resource revenues can be both a blessing and a curse, and the overall outcome very much depends on the way the negative effects of resource revenue volatility are countered by use of suitable stabilization funds and other policy mechanisms that smooth out the flow of government expenses over time. There are also a number of political economy considerations that are highlighted, such as government accountability, generous subsidy policy, and general rent-seeking activities that often manifest themselves in higher inflation and reduced economic efficiencies.

Turning to the macro-econometric evidence, we first review the historical trends over the period 1937–2010. We show that there are strong positive correlations between growth of real GDP and real oil export revenues over the whole period and a number of different sub-periods. But, at the same time, we observe strong negative correlations between real GDP growth and inflation, again over the full sample period and the same sub-periods. These results are corroborated by the more formal macro-econometric evidence, also reviewed in the chapter. We note that, while oil revenues affect real output positively, inflation has a statistically significant negative effect on real output even in the long run. Based on standard economic theory we would expect inflation to have a significant positive effect on real output only in the short run (through the Phillips curve trade-off), and no effects on real output in the long run. We view the negative long-run relationship between real output and inflation as an indication of the adverse effects of a combination of factors (such as rentseeking, poor institutional arrangements for dealing with oil revenue volatility, and general economic mismanagement) on economic growth.

Econometric analysis also reveals additional insights into the way the Iranian economy functions, which is not apparent from a historical analysis. Using generalized impulse response analysis it is shown that the effects of oil revenue or foreign output shocks work themselves out through the economy within two years, which is much shorter in duration than what is generally obtained (three to five years) in the more developed economies. Such rapid responses to shocks could be due to the relatively underdeveloped nature of money and capital markets in Iran, and the country's relative isolation from the global economic and finance community. Such a fast rate of response to shocks makes it even more important that appropriate stabilization policies are put into effect so that the adverse effects of negative shocks on output and consumption are dealt with in a timely manner.

We conclude that, in order to promote growth, policies should be devised to control inflation, serve as shock absorbers negating the adverse effects of oil revenue volatility, reduce rent seeking activities, and prevent excessive dependence of government finances on oil income.

The rest of the chapter is set out as follows: Section 2 discusses the history of the oil sector and its importance for the Iranian economy during the three sub-periods: 1908–1959, 1960–1978, and 1979–2010. Section 3 reviews the literature on resource abundance and growth, and discusses the relevance of the "Dutch disease" and the "resource curse" literature to Iran. Section 4 considers the macroeconomic trends and reviews the existing macro-econometric evidence on the relationship between oil income, inflation and economic growth, both over the course of a business cycle as well as in the long-run. Section 5 presents the evidence on oil price and revenue volatilities and discusses how they interact and influence the economy. Some concluding remarks are given in Section 6.

Importance of the oil sector in the Iranian economy

It is now over 100 years since oil was discovered in Iran in commercial quantities. But as we shall see, oil export revenues started to play an important role in the Iranian economy only after 1960, largely due to the low levels of royalties that the Iranian government received from foreign oil companies operating in Iran before 1954. The period post 1960 can also be conveniently split into the pre and post-revolution periods. More specifically, we group the years since 1908 into three sub-periods: 1908–1959, 1960–1978, and 1979–2010, and consider each of these periods separately below.

1908–1959

In 1901 William Knox D'Arcy signed an agreement (which became known as the D'Arcy Concession) with Muzaffar al-Din, the Shah of Iran, in which D'Arcy was given the exclusive rights to explore, develop and produce any oil and gas fields in an area that covered three quarters of the country. In exchange for this right, the Shah would receive a lump sum payment of £20,000 in cash and an equal amount worth of shares of the company that was granted the right to explore oil in Iran. More importantly, the Shah would also receive 16 per cent of net annual profits of the company (Article 10 of the D'Arcy Concession 1901 reproduced in Ferrier 1982).

A large number of test wells were drilled in Iran between 1901 and 1904, and while oil was discovered, the amounts found were not commercially viable. As D'Arcy was slowly running out of money, in order to finance further explorations, he was forced to find other sources of funding and finally in 1905 sold most of his right to oil exploration and production to the Burmah Oil Company. By 1908 the cost of exploration had reached over half a million pounds without any viable oil fields being discovered. Thus the decision was made to shut down operations in Iran. Although George Reynolds, the chief explorer in Iran, received a telegraph from London telling him to stop drilling, he continued exploring for oil until the order was confirmed by post (Kinzer 2003).

Before the letter from England reached Reynolds, large amounts of of oil was found in Masjid-i-Suleiman on 26 May 1908. With this discovery a new corporation was formed later that year called the Anglo-Persian Oil Company (APOC). In 1913, in exchange for secure and cheap oil supply from APOC, the British government, on the initiative of Winston Churchill, injected £2 million into the company and in doing so acquired a majority ownership (51 per cent of total shares). Thus in effect APOC controlled all oil operations in Iran and the interest of the British government and APOC became aligned. This partnership made sure that the British government became an important player in the Iranian oil industry, enhancing her sphere of influence in Iran.

During the first few years of APOC's operations a massive infrastructure of oil wells and pipelines were put in place. One of the largest oil refineries in the world (up until the first half of the twentieth century) was built in Abadan, which enabled APOC to become a major oil producer in the Persian Gulf region. The main impetus to demand for Iranian oil came when the British Admiralty, under Winston Churchill, decided to run the British naval fleets on oil instead of coal. This created an important demand for Iranian oil, which led to significant increases in oil production and exports especially during the First World War. Oil extraction, being merely 5,000 barrels per day in 1913, reached 33,000 barrels in 1920, and over 115,000 in 1929. In the early years and up until the mid-1920s the majority of the oil was sold at a discount to the Royal Navy, with whatever remained passed on to consumers in Britain and elsewhere in the world.

However, while oil production had increased by 23-fold between 1914 and 1929, the royalties to the Iranian government had increased less than five-fold. According to the D'Arcy concession these royalties were calculated as 16 per cent of net profits of the company. However, given the massive increase in oil production at the end of the 1920's and with it the soaring profits of APOC, the manner in which Iran's entitlement of net profits were calculated became questionable and Reza Shah raised concerns that APOC was falsifying its accounts (Kinzer 2003). Note that at no point before 1929 did the revenue from APOC exceed 19 per cent of the total Iranian government revenues (Ferrier 1982). Moreover, the share of government revenue from oil exports to the total oil export revenue by APOC was between 5.3 and 6.5 per cent over the years 1920–1929, see Table 1.1. This table

Table 1.1 Iranian royalties and taxation vs British taxation, 1914–1950

Years	Iranian royalties and taxation (£million)	British taxation (£million)	Ratio of Iranian government to total oil export revenues (%)
1914–1919	0.22	0.23	–
1920–1924	0.52	0.76	5.3
1925–1929	1.05	0.87	6.3
1930–1934	1.63	1.32	17.2
1935–1939	3.19	2.38	18.4
1940–1944	4.09	11.18	15.2
1945–1949	8.50	22.66	10.7
1950	16.03	51.40	8.1

Source: Royalties and taxation data is from Ferrier (1982) and Bamberg (1994), while government and total revenue data is from Esfahani and Pesaran (2009).

Note: The figures are averaged over the years considered.

also shows that the company's taxes to the British government was larger than the royalties paid to the Iranian government between 1914–1924, while the latter was marginally larger than the former between 1924 and 1929.

The employment generating effect of the oil industry was also very limited, and at its peak before nationalization in 1949 amounted to 78,162 Iranian nationals, most of whom were unskilled workers (see Table 14.1 in Bamberg 1994). This figure included both those directly employed by the Company as well as indirectly by contractors working on Company projects.

As already noted, the most important customer of APOC in the early years was the British government, which in July 1914 had requested that at least 6 million tons of fuel oil should be supplied to the Admiralty over a 20-year period, with this amount being larger in the event of a war. The Royal Navy received between 66 and 69 per cent of APOC's total refined oil during World War I, but even in 1919 and 1920 had over 53 per cent of its total fuel oil supplied by the company (Ferrier 1982). As set out in the D'Arcy concession the oil sold by APOC to the Royal Navy was at a discount and so the benefits of the British government from the Company was much larger than the amount of taxes reported in Table 1.1. Thus in the period from initial extraction up until 1929, the amount of revenues generated by oil production for the Iranian government was not significant and in most years amounted to less than 19 per cent of total Iranian government revenues.

Negotiations to revise the concession of 1901, due to the growing concerns about the way in which Iran's royalties were calculated, took place between the Iranian government and the company throughout 1928–1932, which culminated in Reza Shah cancelling the D'Arcy Concession in 1932. However, in 1933 Reza Shah signed a new agreement which extended the D'Arcy Concession, due to expire in 1961, up to the end of 1993. The new agreement resulted in a reduction of 80 per cent of the total area granted for exploration and extraction by the 1901 concession, although APOC would choose the 100,000 square miles that it would keep, see Bamberg (1994). But most importantly royalties were now based on actual volumes (tons of oil produced) rather than profits. While the agreement took effect from January 1933, the royalties of 1931 and 1932 were recalculated, with the 1931 payment being increased four-fold; from £306,383 (based on 16 per cent of net profits) to £1,339,132 (based on volume). For further details see Ferrier (1982).

Although, the change in calculation of Iran's royalties from oil production led to a large increase in Iranian oil income between 1930 and 1950, with oil production increasing from 126,000 to 648,000 barrels per day, British taxes throughout the period 1940–1950 were more than twice as much as the royalties that were paid to Iran by the Anglo-Iranian Oil Company (AIOC), which was the new name of APOC from 1935 onwards, as can be seen from Table 1.1.

After a series of disputes between the Iranian government and the AIOC during the 1940s, the Iranian oil industry was nationalized in 1951, through a mandate given by the Iranian parliament, Majles, to Prime Minister Mossadegh. The nationalization was followed by a dramatic fall in oil output and thus government revenues. During the years 1952 and 1953 only 28 thousand barrels per day were produced on average, which was around 4 per cent of the level of oil production which was achieved in 1950. Although this was partly due to the lack of technical skills as all British personnel had left the country, the main reason for the large slow down in production was the British government's embargo on Iranian oil and seizure of any oil tanker that tried to do business with the Iranian government.

One of the reasons for the nationalization was that Mossadegh and others felt that profits from the oil industry were not impacting the Iranian economy or the country's development due to the relative small per centage of the total oil revenues that the Iranian government actually received. In a speech to the United Nations Security Council on 15 October 1951, Mossadegh declared that "the petroleum industry has contributed nothing to well-being of the people or to the technological progress or industrial development of my country" (United Nations 1951).

The negotiations between the British and Iranian governments throughout 1951–53 did not result in any concrete progress, and eventually the British could see no way out other than to remove Mossadegh, and accordingly initiated and backed a successful coup against Mossadegh's government financed and organized by CIA in August 1953.[3] The end of the Mossadegh era meant that negotiations could open between the new pro-Western Iranian government of Prime Minister Fazlollah Zahedi and the British as well as the Americans. The negotiations resulted in the formation of the 1954 Consortium Agreement which gave the rights of extracting petroleum in the 100,000 square mile area covered by the 1933 Concession to a Consortium of eight European and American companies. Forty per cent of the shares of the Consortium was allocated to British Petroleum (BP), the name given to AIOC earlier, 14 per cent to Royal Dutch Shell, 6 per cent to Compagnie Française des Pétroles (CFP), with the remaining 40 per cent to be split equally between five American companies (Exxon, Gulf Oil, Mobil, Socony, and Standard Oil of California). Under the new agreement Iran would share the profits from the oil production with the Consortium members on a 50–50 basis, which was the agreement that most Middle Eastern countries had with foreign oil companies, but have no say in the administration of the Consortium, see Dean (2004) and NIOC (2011). In 1955 oil production had increased to 353,000 barrels per day and by 1959 reached the level of 951,000, which was 50 per cent more than the level of production in the pre-nationalization period.

On the external side, although oil exports formed a large part of total exports (51 per cent on average between 1936 and 1959, see Esfahani and Pesaran 2009), due to the royalty system in place, Iran's share of foreign exchange receipts from oil exports was relatively small, and non-oil exports continued to be the dominant factor in balancing Iran's external account.

1960–1978

As can be seen from Figure 1.1, oil production increased significantly from 1960 onwards compared to the earlier period. By 1961 over 1.2 million barrels of oil per day were being produced, which was twice as much as the pre-nationalization peak in 1950 (0.6 million). Oil production increased at a steady rate between 1960 and 1973 and peaked in 1974 at 6 million barrels per day before dropping slightly in the following years before the 1979 revolution.[4]

Figure 1.2 also shows the ratio of total oil export revenues to domestic output, which peaked at 23 per cent in 1950 just before nationalization. Despite this, due

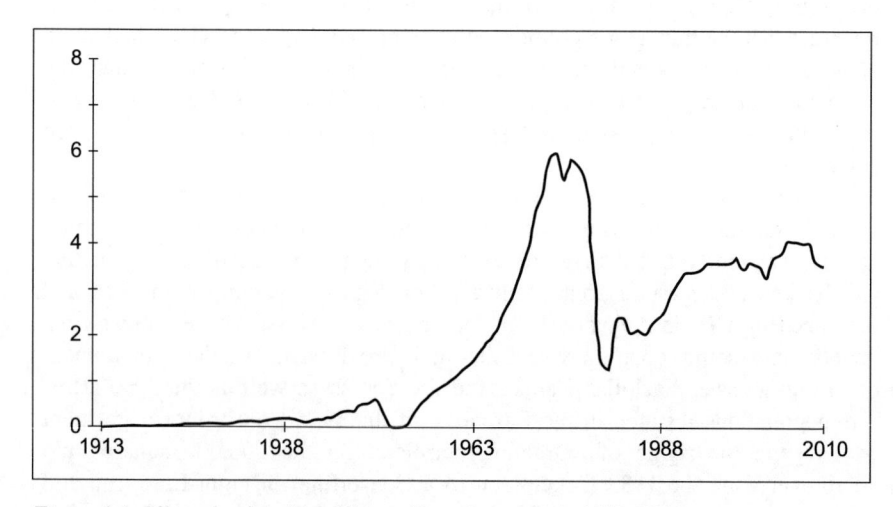

Figure 1.1 Oil production (in millions of barrels per day), 1913–2010.

Source: OPEC Annual Statistical Bulletin.

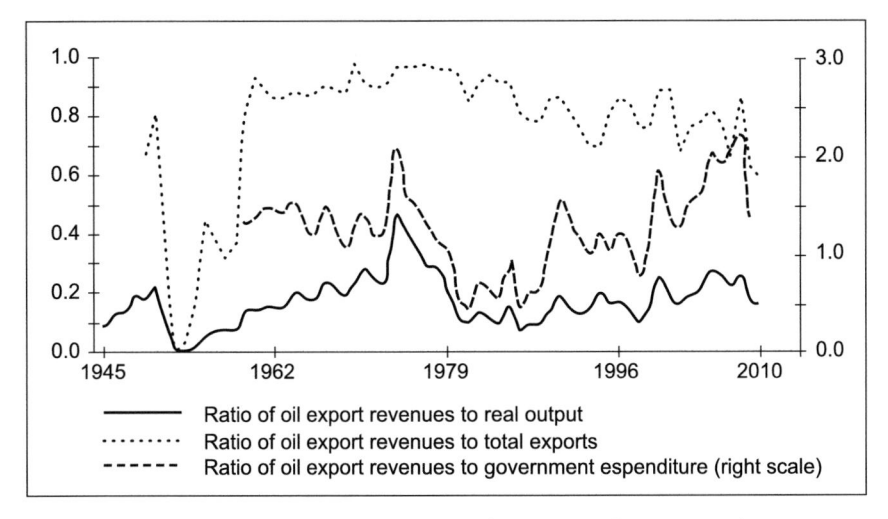

Figure 1.2 Ratios of oil export revenues to real output, total exports, and government expenditure, 1945–2010.

Source: IMF International Financial Statistics, OPEC Annual Statistical Bulletin, and Esfahani and Pesaran (2009).

to the unfavourable terms with the Anglo Iranian Oil Company, only 8.1 per cent of the total oil export revenues were actually received by the Iranian government in terms of taxes and royalties (Table 1.1). However, with the Consortium agreement of 1954, the Iranian government was entitled to 50 per cent of the total net profits from oil production, therefore, the significant increase in production during these two decades meant that government revenues from oil exports started to rise significantly and steadily. Consequently, the ratio of oil export revenues to GDP rose to 47 per cent by 1974. Thus, oil's role in the Iranian economy, although muted during 1908–1959, became gradually more and more important between 1960 and 1978.

Although significant increases in oil production had been achieved during the 1954–1975 period, this was not the only factor driving the Iranian oil export revenues and domestic output. Another important factor was oil prices. With the foundation of the Organization of the Petroleum Exporting Countries (OPEC) in 1960, oil prices which had been falling in real terms since 1920 started to stabilize (Figure 1.3).[5] Following the Yom Kippur War, and the decision by the Organisation of Arab Petroleum Exporting Countries (OAPEC), excluding Iraq, to introduce production cutbacks as well as an embargo against the United States and the Netherlands, international oil prices quadrupled in 1973–1974. Real oil prices then stabilized over the period 1975 to 1978.

Figure 1.4 shows a close positive relationship between real output and oil revenues. The relationship is particularly strong during the post 1960 period when oil revenues started to rise significantly and were sustained over a prolonged period. The quadrupling of oil prices in 1973–1974 presented Iran with a

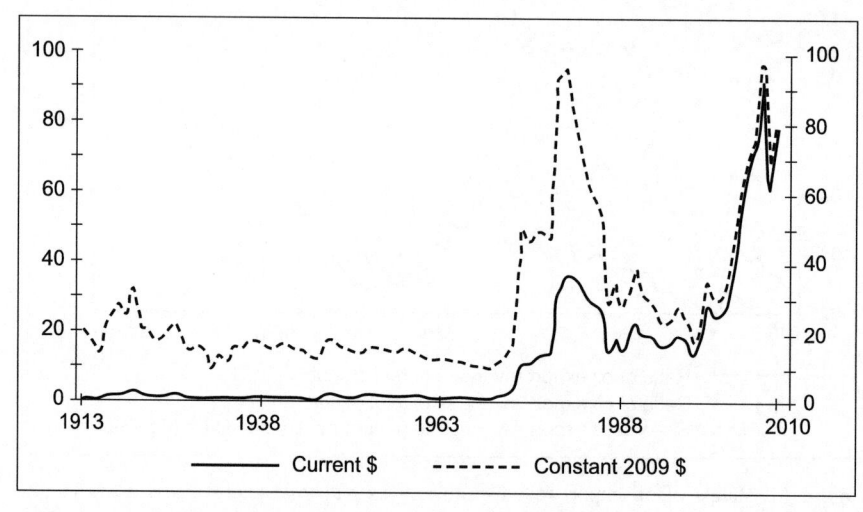

Figure 1.3 International price of oil per barrel, 1913–2010.

Source: British Petroleum Statistical Review of World Energy.

substantial, largely unexpected, increase in oil revenues. A prudent economic management of such large external funds would suggest a gradual and planned infusion of the new oil revenues into the Iranian economy. The remaining funds could have been invested abroad for future use and as a buffer against weak global economic conditions and lower oil prices. Such a policy was discussed in a critical meeting of technocrats and policy makers in Gajereh, but was flatly rejected by the Shah who insisted on spending almost all of the increased oil revenues domestically and over a relatively short period (Graham 1978). This resulted in an excessive expansion of aggregate demand, which could not be matched by increased supply, even from imports, due to limited port and road capacities and other infrastructure limitations and bottlenecks. As a result inflation started to rise rapidly, and heavy-handed tactics of the government by arrest and imprisonment of merchants and industrialists only resulted in political and economic alienation without any permanent success at curbing inflation (see, for example, Pesaran 1997). The rapid expansion of the economy also resulted in higher expectations which could not be fulfilled, and amplified the structural weaknesses of the regime and was one of the major factors behind the mass discontent that erupted in 1977–1978 which led to the February 1979 revolution and the downfall of the Pahlavi regime.

1979–2010

Upon seizing power, the Provisional Government of Mehdi Bazargan decided to reduce oil production from its height of 6 million barrels per day to around

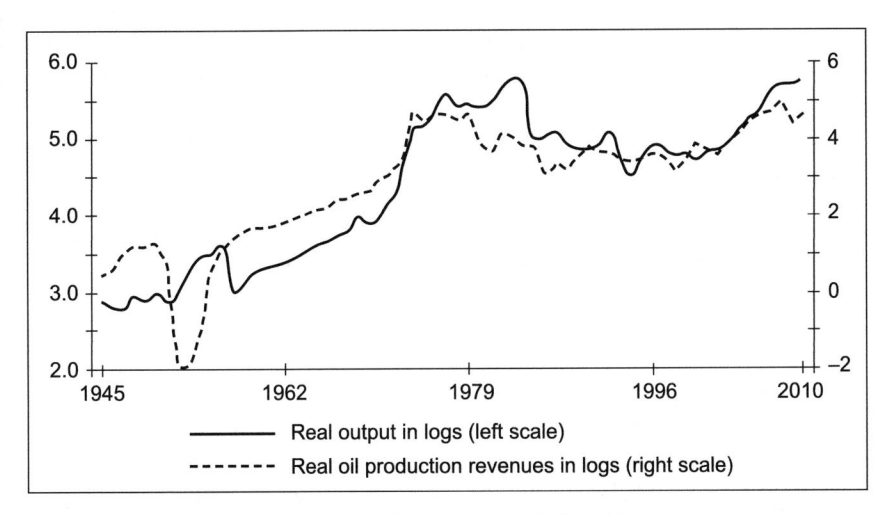

Figure 1.4 Real output and oil production revenues, 1948–2010.

Source: IMF International Financial Statistics and OPEC Annual Statistical Bulletin.

4 million. Although the revolutionary upheavals and the strikes by oil workers had halted oil production, it was a conscious decision by the Provisional Government to reduce the level of oil production to around 30 per cent below its average level over the 1971–1978 period (see Salehi-Isfahani (1996) and Figure 1.1).[6] This was the first time that an Iranian government had managed to control the level of her oil production, and the 1973 agreement between the Consortium and National Iranian Oil Company (NIOC), which bound Iran to production and sales at a discount to the Consortium, was cancelled in March 1979 (see Dean 2004).

During the pre-revolutionary period, the Shah's oil policy was heavily criticized, and in mass demonstrations people called for the conservation of the country's oil resources. The high levels of oil production were seen as responsible for waste, corruption and the relative decline of the agricultural sector (Hakimian 1988). It was argued that oil production and income needed to be reduced substantially if the agricultural and industrial sectors were to flourish. As it turned out, the invasion of Iran by Iraq in 1980 reduced oil production and refining capacity significantly. Technical difficulties and the start of the war with Iraq made the initial cut in production inspired by revolutionary ideals a permanent feature and production did not reach the post-revolution target of 4 million barrels per day until much later in 2003. The following eight years of war meant that Iran had to live with greatly reduced levels of oil production, by choice initially and by circumstances as the result of the war.

However, despite these production cutbacks oil revenues continued to form a large part of the country's foreign exchange receipts and government revenues. The ratio of oil exports to domestic output declined somewhat and fluctuated around 12 per cent between 1979 and 1988 before starting to rise slowly with the end of the Iran–Iraq war (Figure 1.2). The 1979 revolution, the eight-year Iran–Iraq war, and the US economic sanctions imposed on Iran, while reducing Iran's oil revenues also resulted in falling or at best stagnant real output, which has taken almost 30 years to return to its pre-revolution levels (Figure 1.4).[7]

Although agricultural production increased after the revolution, agricultural exports did not increase significantly. This was mainly due to the rapid population growth of the 1980s, which meant that most of the increased agricultural production was absorbed by the higher domestic demand for food. As a result, the role of oil exports and food imports in the Iranian economy remained as significant as it had been before the revolution.

Looking at Figure 1.5, we see that in nominal terms oil export revenues per capita, having dropped significantly after the revolution and during the eight years of war, has been increasing rapidly since 2003. Having peaked at $1,209 in 2008, it fell to around $795 in 2010. However, correcting for inflation we see that in real terms oil export revenues per capita peaked in 1974 at $2,558 (in 2009 US$), while in 2010 it had fallen to $715, or about 40 per cent lower than its peak before . the revolution (Figure 1.5). Therefore, although the total amount of export revenues has increased over time, this is not so after the effects of rising inflation is taken into account.

Figure 1.5 also shows the relative importance of oil in the Iranian economy since 1913. Taking into account the percentage of total oil export revenues that the Iranian government actually received in royalties and taxes (Table 1.1), oil export revenues per capita were not more than $25 before 1954 and below $85 after the Consortium agreement in 1954, which significantly increased Iran's take of profits from oil production. There is a clear divide between the period before and after 1960, and it is from 1960 onwards that oil started to play a significant role in the Iranian economy.

A further factor which had a major impact on Iran's oil export revenues was introduced in the early 1970s when oil prices were no longer administratively determined by the so-called 'Seven Sisters',[8] but instead were determined largely by international markets, and to some degree by OPEC until the mid-1980s. This in turn introduced a significant degree of volatility in prices, as compared to the remarkable stability of oil prices during the earlier periods, particularly in the 1960s (Figure 1.3).

To summarize, although oil has been produced in Iran for over 100 years, the importance of oil in the development of the Iranian economy had been relatively small up until the 1960s (Table 1.1 and Figure 1.5). The surge in oil prices in 1970s and the Shah's insistence on injecting almost all of the increased oil revenues into the economy further enhanced the country's dependence on oil income. This increased dependence coincided with a higher volatility of international oil prices. The effects of price volatility on oil revenues were further accentuated due to the volatile effects of revolution, war, and economic sanctions on oil production and exports. As a result the Iranian economy is

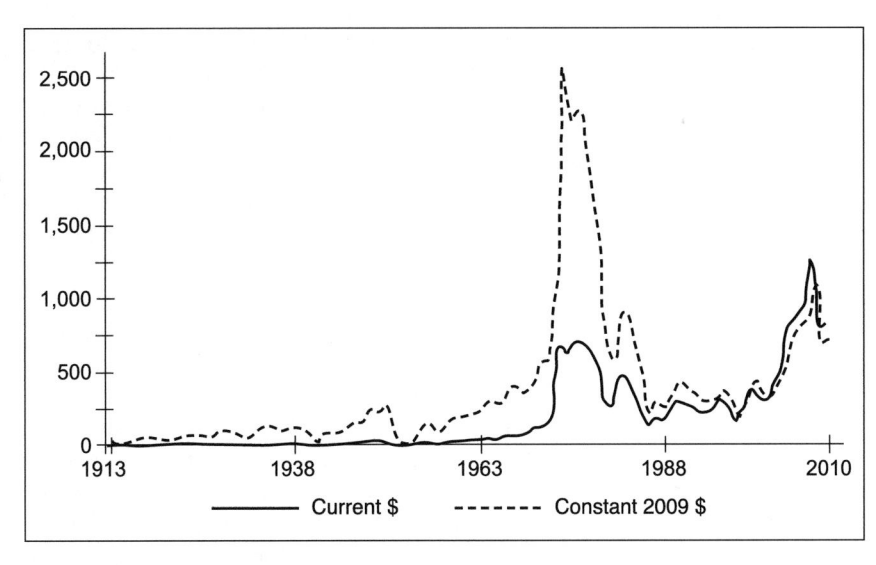

Figure 1.5 Per capita oil export revenues, 1913–2010.

Source: IMF International Financial Statistics and OPEC Annual Statistical Bulletin.

faced with the problem of how to deal with substantial but highly volatile oil revenues. In the rest of this chapter we argue that it is the volatility in oil export revenues and governments' inappropriate economic and political responses to these volatilities which is the curse and not the abundance of revenues from oil exports in itself.

Resource abundance and growth

Most papers in the growth literature do not include major oil exporting economies in their cross-country empirical analysis. The literature that specifically deals with resource abundant economies tends to focus on short-term effects of unexpected gains that flow from the resource discovery, which are viewed as 'intrinsically temporary' (van der Ploeg and Venables 2009). In this section we provide an overview of three prominent strands of the resource abundance and growth literature and examine their relevance to our understanding of the Iranian economy.

The Dutch disease

A number of early studies considered the macroeconomic effects of the resource discovery and focussed on the 'Dutch disease' phenomenon first experienced in Netherlands after the large, but short-lived, discovery of gas in 1959. The Dutch disease states that an exogenous unexpected increase in foreign exchange revenues from the resource discovery will result in a real exchange rate appreciation and a fall in output and employment of the non-resource traded goods sector, often manufacturing. Therefore, discovering natural resources is viewed as a curse for economic development (see, for example, Corden and Neary 1982, Krugman 1987, and Neary and van Wijnbergen 1986 among others). However, the Dutch disease by itself need not have adverse long-run implications for the economy as a whole. One would expect the economy to re-adjust once the revenues from the resource are diminished or vanish altogether, unless there are important non-convexities or imperfections in the economy. For example, if the manufacturing sector is subject to economies of scale or learning by doing, the loss of manufacturing capacity will be very costly to reverse.

Figure 1.6 shows the relationship between the evolution of real oil prices and the real exchange rate in Iran over the period 1945–2010. Note that since the exchange rate is measured in terms of the number of Rials per US$, a rise (fall) in the real exchange rate series indicates real depreciation (appreciation). The relationship between the two series is quite complicated. They tend to move in opposite direction in the short run, but not over the long run. There are also periods that the two series are basically flat. For example, over the period 1963–1973, when GDP per capita growth rate averaged 8.2 per cent per annum (Figure 1.4) coupled with low levels of inflation, the real exchange rate and oil prices did not change much. However, with the quadrupling of oil prices in 1973–74, while the Iranian oil revenues were rising in real terms (Figure 1.5), the real exchange rate also started to appreciate. This process continued until the start of the Iran–Iraq war in 1980 after which oil prices started to fall with the real exchange rate depreciating. Figure 1.6 also shows that the real exchange rate appreciated with the oil price boom in 2003 and the subsequent oil price increases.

In short, while the Dutch disease theory seems to hold in the short run, over the course of a given business cycle, the same cannot be said about the secular trends in the real oil prices and real exchange rates. Seen from the long-term perspective both series are trending upward over the whole period from 1945 to 2010. This is contrary to the prediction of the theory, which is more appropriate in the short run. The secular trend in the real exchange rate is determined by many factors beside the price of natural resources. For instance, political factors influence the way oil revenues are spent in the economy, whether the revenues are used for consumption or investment, and the management of the economy in general. In particular, policy responses to the volatile nature of oil prices seem to play an important role in this process.

The Dutch disease phenomenon is applicable to economies that have been subject to sudden unexpected income flows from resource discoveries that are temporary and are not expected to last that long. It is less relevant to economies such as Iran, where oil income has been, and is expected, to be an important feature of the economy for a long period to come. As we have seen, since 1960 oil has formed a large part of government finances and country's foreign exchange reserves. Furthermore, even after 100 years of exploration and production, the current estimated reserve-to-extraction ratio in Iran suggests a further 87 years of oil production. In addition, Iran has the second largest natural gas reserves after

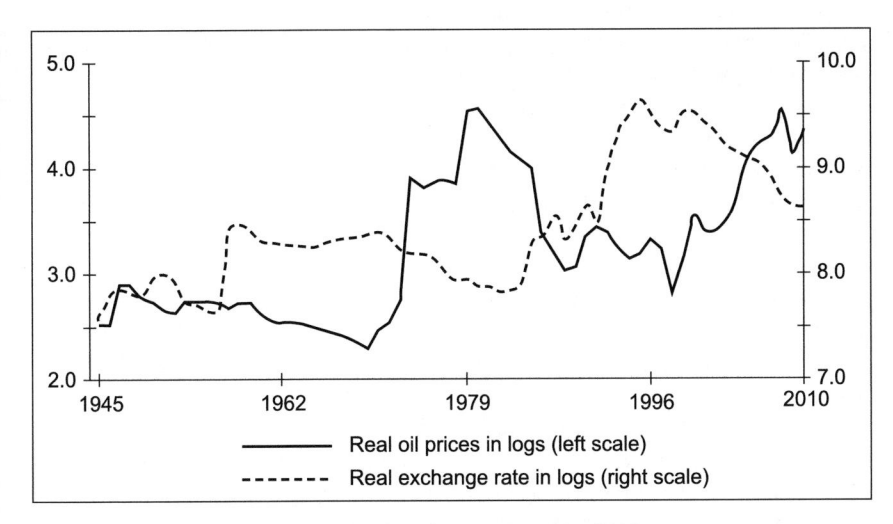

Figure 1.6 Real oil prices and the real exchange rate, 1945–2010.

Source: British Petroleum Statistical Review of World Energy and IMF International Financial Statistics.

Note: The real exchange rate measure used is the 'free market' rate. The real exchange rate is calculated as the nominal exchange rate in terms of the US$ deflated by the domestic consumer price index.

Russia, around 60 per cent of which is yet to be developed.[9] Although, it is clear that Iran's oil and gas reserves will be exhausted eventually, this is likely to take place over a relatively long period. In fact over the past two decades, even with low oil prices during 1990–2002, the ratio of Iran's oil export revenues to GDP has been on average 19 per cent (Figure 1.2). Of course, Iran is not unique in this regard. As Figure 1.7 shows, most other OPEC countries – such as Saudi Arabia, Venezuela, Nigeria, Algeria, the United Arab Emirates and Kuwait, and a few countries outside OPEC, such as Norway and Russia – have similar oil income GDP ratios that have remained relatively stable (and in some cases have even been rising, as in Norway). Therefore, there is little evidence to suggest that in these economies oil income will be diminishing any time soon.

The resource curse

According to the resource curse hypothesis, resource rich countries perform poorly when compared to countries which are not endowed with oil, natural gas, minerals and other non-renewable resources. Therefore, resource abundance is believed to be an important determinant of economic failure, which implies that oil abundance is a curse and not a blessing. Empirical support for the resource curse was originally provided by Sachs and Warner (1995) who showed the existence of a negative relationship between real GDP growth per capita and different measures of resource abundance, such as the ratio of resource exports to GDP. This finding is clearly paradoxical and has led to a growing theoretical and empirical literature.

However, the empirical evidence on the resource curse paradox is rather mixed. Most papers in the literature tend to follow Sachs and Warner's cross-sectional specification but try new measures for the resource dependence/abundance variable. See, for example, Rodriguez and Sachs (1999), Gylfason et al. (1999), and Bulte et al. (2005). The results could be quite sensitive to the measure of resource abundance employed. Sachs and Warner (1995), for instance, use the ratio of primary-product exports to GDP in the initial period as a measure of resource abundance. But as pointed out by Brunnschweiler and Bulte (2008), this ratio measures resource dependence rather than resource abundance. The latter should be introduced in the growth regressions as the stock or the flow of natural resources. In their study, Brunnschweiler and Bulte (2008) argue that the evidence in favour of the resource curse hypothesis is non-existent or at best weak, if the correct measure of resource abundance is used. They also show that while resource dependence, when instrumented in growth regressions, does not affect growth, resource abundance in fact positively affects economic growth.

There are also a number of other reasons why the econometric evidence on the negative effects of resource abundance on output growth might be questioned.

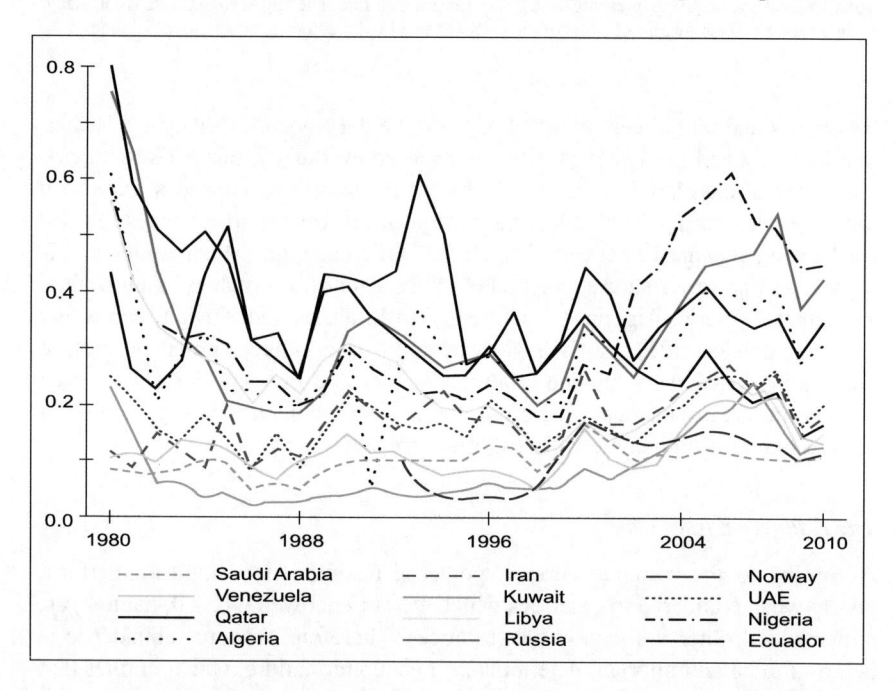

Figure 1.7 Ratio of oil export revenues to real output across oil exporters, 1980–2010.

Source: British Petroleum Statistical Review of World Energy, OPEC Annual Statistical Bulletin, and IMF International Financial Statistics.

First, the literature relies primarily on a cross-sectional approach to test the resource curse hypothesis, and as such does not fully take account of the time dimension of the data. Second, a cross-sectional growth regression augmented with the resource abundance variable could suffer from endogeneity and omitted variable problems, and this is perhaps the most important reason for being skeptical about the econometric studies suggesting a positive or negative association between resource abundance and growth. For example, Alexeev and Conrad (2009) show evidence against the resource curse hypothesis by considering a few additional regressors, such as exogenous geographical factors.

In addition, even when panel data techniques are used most studies make use of homogeneous panel data models, such as fixed and random effects estimators, the instrumental variable (IV) technique proposed by Anderson and Hsiao (1981) and Anderson and Hsiao (1982), and the generalized methods of moments (GMM) model of Arellano and Bond (1991), Arellano and Bover (1995), among others.[10] While homogeneous panel data models allow the intercepts to differ across countries all slope parameters are constrained to be the same. Therefore, a high degree of homogeneity is still imposed. As discussed in Pesaran and Smith (1995), the problem with these dynamic panel data techniques, when applied to testing growth effects, is that they can produce inconsistent and potentially very misleading estimates of the average values of the parameters, since growth regressions typically exhibit a substantial degree of cross-sectional heterogeneity.

In view of the above considerations Cavalcanti et al. (2011a) adopt the common correlated effects (CCE) estimator recently developed in Pesaran (2006) and estimate dynamic heterogeneous panel data models with interactive effects. The approach takes account of the institutional and geographical differences that exist across countries and unlike the standard FE estimator allows the coefficients of the growth regressions to differ across countries. The CCE estimator also takes account of error cross-sectional dependence (again ignored by the FE estimator) by augmenting the growth regressions with cross-sectional averages of the variables included in the regressions.[11] Such multi-factor processes have been used in the literature to model the effects of unobserved factors such as technological innovation, political and institutional developments that are difficult to measure, and factors that affect the degree of openness of economies. It is clearly important that such effects are also taken into account in estimation of growth regressions; otherwise the estimates of the effects of resource abundance on growth could be seriously biased.

Cavalcanti et al. (2011a) base their analysis on a panel of 53 countries (including Iran) over the period 1980–2006, and estimate the heterogeneous growth regressions using the CCE estimator. To check for the robustness of their results they consider three different proxies measuring resource abundance, namely the real value of oil production, the rent component of oil income, and oil reserves. They conclude that oil abundance is in fact a blessing and not a curse in the long run as well as in the short run, and challenge the consensus view that oil abundance affects economic growth negatively.[12]

The positive effect of resource abundance on development and growth is also supported by Arezki and van der Ploeg (2007), Cavalcanti et al. (2012), Esfahani et al. (2012b), Leong and Mohaddes (2011), and van der Ploeg and Poelhekke (2010). Therefore, using appropriate econometric techniques the recent empirical literature seems to provide evidence against the conventional resource curse literature, which argues for an unconditional negative relationship between resource income and growth.

Political economy considerations

Although the growth enhancing effect of oil income is now generally accepted, the volatility of oil income presents important policy challenges with political economy considerations that must be taken into account. As was noted earlier, Iran's revenues from oil exports have been even more volatile than international oil prices, due to revolution, war and economic sanctions. Such volatilities tend to affect economic growth negatively. To deal with the adverse effects of oil price volatility, some of the major oil exporters have set up oil stabilization or sovereign wealth funds. The success of such funds depends on the fund's political ownership (management and right of access), and the mechanisms governing the allocation of the proceeds from the fund to the government and other political bodies. In the case of Iran an Oil Stabilization Fund (OSF) was set up under Khatami's Presidency but was closed down by President Ahmadinejad in favour of a National Development Fund (NDF), which shifted the political power from the Parliament to the President.

Another important political economy consideration is rent-seeking activities that are primarily initiated due to the existence of large oil incomes. In the case of oil exporting countries the problem of rent seeking has been discussed by Mahdavi (1970), Amuzegar and Fekrat (1972), and Pesaran (1982). The accrual of large income from oil exports to the government also reduces government accountability, mainly because the government does not need to rely on taxation, tend to induce government intervention in the economy motivated more by short-term crises rather than long-term development perspectives, and encourages and sustains populists' policies longer than would have otherwise been possible. Finally, large oil revenues can promote dictatorship and lead to a system of dependent capitalism where the economic activities of the private sector are also dependent on active government support (Pesaran 1982). The state's dependence on oil revenues in turn makes it politically less accountable.

The more recent literature on resource abundance and economic growth focusses on some of these political economy considerations and argues that large windfalls from oil and other resources create incentives for rent-seeking activities that involve corruption (Mauro 1995 and Leite and Weidmann 1999), voracity (Lane and Tornell 1996 and Tornell and Lane 1999), and possibly civil conflicts (Collier and Hoeffler 2004). Some of these considerations have been recently formalized by Caselli and Cunningham (2009), with a recent survey provided in van der Ploeg and Venables (2009).

A number of recent empirical works have also focused on the role of institutions. Mehlum et al. (2006) and Béland and Tiagi (2009), using a cross-sectional approach, show that the impact of natural resources on growth and development depends primarily on institutions, while Boschini et al. (2007) illustrate that the type of natural resources possessed is also an important factor. These authors argue that controlling for institutional quality and including an interaction term between institutional quality and resource abundance a threshold effect arises. This suggests there are levels of institutional quality above which resource abundance becomes growth enhancing.

Political economy and institutional factors are clearly very important for a proper evaluation of the effects of oil income on the Iranian economy. However, an empirical investigation of these issues is complicated. It is difficult to obtain accurate measurements of rent-seeking activities and institutional quality, and most attempts made in the literature in this regard tend to use proxy measures that are highly correlated with oil revenues, thus making it impossible to separate the possible positive effects of oil income on growth from the negative effects of rent-seeking and poor institutional quality. An alternative approach that we follow in the rest of the chapter is to consider the overall macroeconomic effects of oil income and domestic inflation on real output in the long run. In a well-managed economy we do not expect inflation to have a significant impact on real output in the long run. Inflation tends to have a positive effect on real output in the short run (the Phillips curve effect), but not in the long run where output is determined by technological and endowment factors. By focussing on the long-run effects of inflation on real output we hope to provide some indirect evidence on the importance of political economy factors in the case of Iran.

Macro-econometric evidence

We begin with an investigation of the main macroeconomic trends of the Iranian economy using data on real output, consumption, oil export revenues and inflation. Using annual data over the period 1937–2010 we investigate the historical relationships that exist between these variables. We then briefly outline the growth model for major oil exporting economies developed in Esfahani et al. (2012), and discuss the results of a quarterly macro-econometric model for Iran estimated over the period 1979Q1-2006Q4. Interestingly enough, the econometric results are in line with the historical analysis that follows.

Macroeconomic trends, 1937–2010

Figure 1.8 depicts the growth rate of per capita real output, private consumption, and oil export revenues, from which we see that due to the revolution and the Iran–Iraq war both consumption and GDP have been quite volatile. However, in comparison with the oil revenue volatility experienced in Iran, these two variables seem relatively stable. Moreover, notice that as previously mentioned oil revenues are much more volatile than real output and consumption.

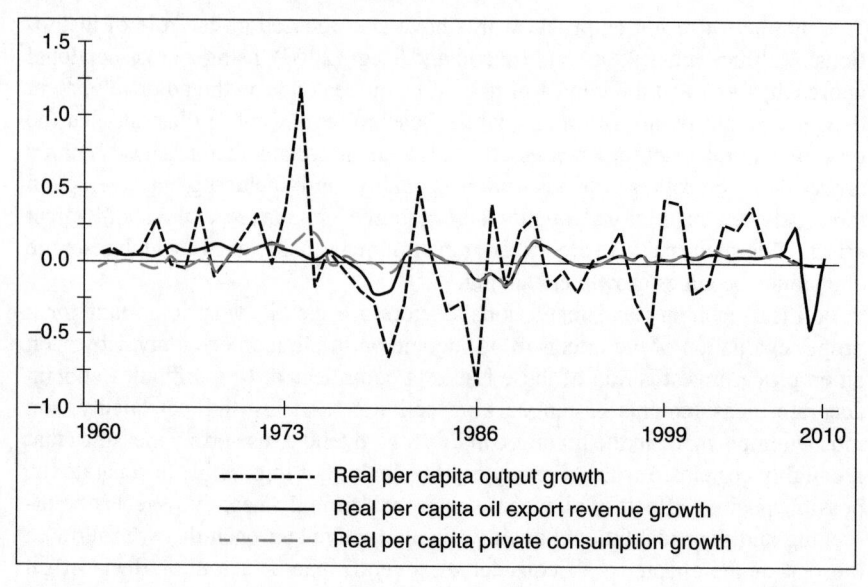

Figure 1.8 Growth rates of per capita real output, consumption, and oil export revenues, 1960–2010.

Source: Central Bank of Iran Economic Time Series Database, IMF International Financial Statistics, IMF World Economic Outlook, and OPEC Annual Statistical Bulletin.

Table 1.2 shows the growth rates of per capita real output and real oil export revenues over different sub-periods. We observe that since 1937 the growth rate of oil export revenues (denoted by g^o) has been higher than that of real output (g^y), with the two series being significantly positively correlated, with a correlation coefficient of around 40 per cent computed over the period 1960–2010 (see also Figure 1.4). Moreover, as to be expected, oil export revenues show a much higher degree of volatility than real output.

Table 1.2 Growth of real output and real oil export revenue (per capita), 1937–2010

Sample period	Real output per capita growth (%)	Real oil export revenues per capita growth (%)	Correlation
1937–2010	2.54	2.80	0.31
1960–2010	2.14	2.80	0.47
1960–1978	5.48	12.30	0.15
1979–2010	0.16	−2.84	0.53
1988–2010	2.20	3.63	0.33

Source: IMF World Economic Outlook, OPEC Annual Statistical Bulletin, and Esfahani and Pesaran (2009).

But it is important to bear in mind that the relationship between real output and oil exports is not stable and changes across the different sub-periods. For instance, over the period 1960–1978 real output per capita grew on average by 5.48 per cent per annum, as compared to oil revenues which showed a much higher annual average growth rate of around 12.3 per cent. These very high growth rates are to be contrasted with those of the post-revolutionary experience where output grew on average by 0.16 per cent per annum, as compared to the negative growth of oil revenues of around –2.84 per cent per annum over the period 1979–2010. The post-war picture is much more encouraging with output and real oil revenues rising on average by 2.2 and 3.63 per cent per annum, respectively. Despite these differences across the different sub-periods, the overall picture points to oil revenues being an important driver of the Iranian economy.

Consider now the relationship between GDP growth and inflation as depicted in Figure 1.9. It is clear that, in general, these two series tend to move in opposite directions. We also observe that over the whole period (1937–2010) inflation has been quite high at 12.69 per cent per annum, while output growth averaged around 4.96 per cent per annum (Table 1.3). Once again the high growth years of 1960–1978 proved to be an exception, where high output growth in fact coincided with a relatively low inflation. The average annual rate of inflation over this sub-period was less than half of the inflation rate experienced in all other sub-periods under consideration. More recent evidence also corroborate a negative relationship between inflation and output growth.[13]

The negative association between the two series is documented in Table 1.3. Over the full sample period the correlation coefficient between the two series amounted to –0.39, with the negative relationship between output growth and

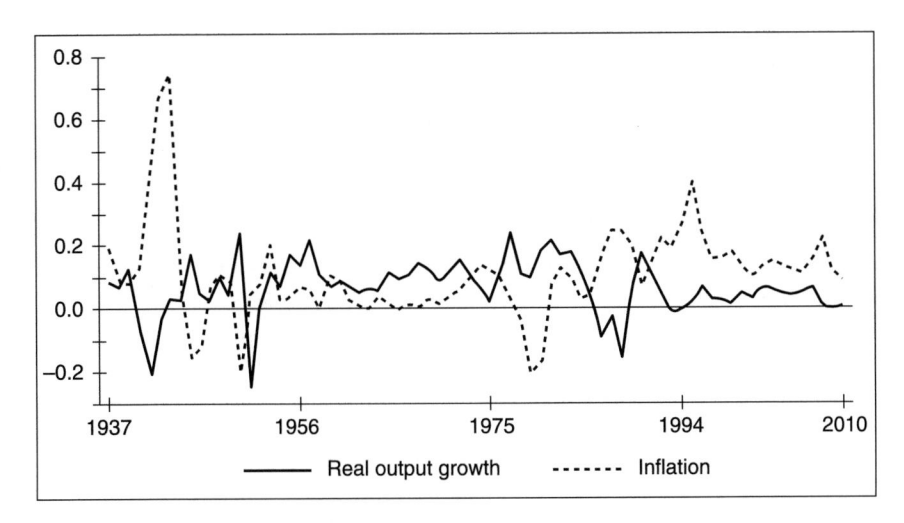

Figure 1.9 Real output growth and inflation, 1937–2010.

Source: IMF International Financial Statistics and IMF World Economic Outlook.

Table 1.3 Real output growth and inflation, 1937–2010

Sample period	Real output growth (%)	Inflation (%)	Correlation
1937–2010	4.96	12.69	−0.39
1960–2010	4.64	13.08	−0.39
1960–1978	8.37	6.18	−0.42
1979–2010	2.42	17.18	−0.14
1988–2010	3.82	17.65	−0.40

Source: IMF International Financial Statistics, IMF World Economic Outlook, and Esfahani and Pesaran (2009).

inflation being apparent in all sub-periods. This is a difficult result to explain using standard economic theory, which as noted earlier predicts no long-run relationship between output growth and inflation. The only theoretically justified relationship between output growth and inflation is for a positive (and not a negative) short-term relation, known as the Phillips curve. As already argued, we view the negative relationship between growth and inflation as an indication of rent-seeking activities, poor institutional arrangements for dealing with oil revenue volatility, and general economic mismanagement. Although it is beyond the scope of the present chapter to identify the relative contributions of these factors to the observed negative relationship between growth and inflation, we nevertheless consider our analysis as a first step towards this aim.

There is also the concern that the correlation analysis of the type offered above, namely a positive relationship between output growth and oil revenues and a negative relationship between output growth and inflation, might be spurious or could be due to other factors omitted from our discussion. Furthermore, it is unclear if such correlations are stable and/or statistically significant once other determinants of output growth such as technological innovation are also taken into account. In what follows we consider these issues using a simple quarterly econometric model developed for the Iranian economy by Esfahani et al. (2013).

A macro-econometric model for the Iranian economy

As outlined above, most macroeconomic analysis of oil revenues tend to take a short-term perspective. They usually focus on the effects of oil revenues on the real exchange rate (Dutch disease) and government budget expansion, thus failing to consider the effects of oil revenues on long-run growth. This approach makes sense for countries with a limited amount of oil reserves, but not for major oil exporting countries such as Iran, Iraq and Saudi Arabia for which oil income should be treated more as a part of the steady state growth outcome and not as a transient state.

To this end, Esfahani et al. (2012) develop a long-run output relation for a major oil exporting economy where the oil income to output ratio is expected to remain high over a prolonged period. The stochastic growth model developed in Binder and Pesaran (1999) is extended to allow for the possibility that a certain fraction of oil export revenues is invested in the domestic economy via the capital accumulation channel. The long-run output equation including oil exports is then given by:

$$y_t - \psi_1 y_t^* = \psi_2(e_t - p_t) + \psi_3 xo_t + c_y + \gamma_y t + \xi_{y,t} \tag{1}$$

where y_t (y_t^*) is the logarithm of real domestic (foreign) output, e_t is the log of the nominal exchange rate, p_t is the logarithm of the domestic Consumer Price Index (CPI), xo_t is oil export revenue in US\$, c_y is a fixed constant, and $\xi_{y,t}$ is a mean zero stationary process, which represents the error correction term of the long-run output equation. As discussed in Section 2.1, in Esfahani et al. (2012) the coefficient of the variables in equation [1] have further restrictions imposed on them based on economic theory, namely:

$$\psi_1 = \theta(1 - \psi_2), \ \psi_2 = \psi_3 = \alpha, \ \text{and} \ \gamma_y = (1 - \alpha)(n - \theta n^*) \tag{2}$$

where α is the share of capital in output, n (n^*) is the domestic (foreign) population growth rate, and θ measures the extent to which foreign technology is diffused and adapted successfully by the domestic economy in the long run. In this relationship, y_t^*, acts as a proxy for global technological progress. The diffusion of technology is at par with the rest of the world if $\theta = 1$, while a value of θ below unity suggests inefficiency that prevents the adoption of best practice techniques, possibly due to rent-seeking activities and general economic mismanagement. Note that the empirical literature which is mainly based on cross-section regressions (see above) most likely captures short-term deviations from the steady states and in view of the substantial heterogeneity that exists across countries can be quite misleading, particularly as far as the identification of θ is concerned, which most likely could differ across countries.

There is a need to distinguish between two cases where the growth of oil income, g^o, is less than the natural growth rate (the sum of the population growth, n, and the growth of technical progress, g) and when $g^o \geq g + n$. Under the former, the effects of oil income on the economy's steady growth rate will vanish eventually. In such a case, we have $\psi_1 = \theta$ and $\psi_2 = \psi_3 = 0$. For most of the resource abundant economies, where $g^o < g + n$, their steady state growth rates cannot exceed that of the rest of the world unless $\theta > 1$. However, when $g^o \geq g + n$, oil income enters the long-run output equation with a coefficient which is equal to the share of capital if it is further assumed that the underlying production technology can be represented as a Cobb-Douglas production function. In this case we have $\psi_2 = \psi_3 = \alpha$.

Esfahani et al. (2013) examine the empirical validity of the long-run output equation [1] for the Iranian economy by incorporating it into a vector autoregressive error correction model (VECX*) augmented with foreign output, y_t^*, treated as a weakly exogenous variable.[14] The foreign output variable is constructed as a weighted average of the log of real output of Iran's trading partners with the weights based on the relative size of their trade with Iran (exports plus imports). The domestic variables included in the model are real GDP, the rate of inflation computed using the consumer price index (CPI), the official and 'free' market exchange rates, and money and quasi money. All variables except for the inflation rate are log-transformed.

The Iranian VECX* model is estimated using quarterly observations over the period 1979Q1–2006Q4. The estimates support the existence of a long-run relation between domestic output, foreign output, and real oil exports. Therefore, as predicted by the theory, oil exports contribute to real income through capital accumulation. The estimates also confirm that Iran has experienced a similar rate of technological progress as its trading partners over the past three decades ($\theta = 1$) and that the share of capital (α) is about 0.26, which is in line with the estimates obtained in recent studies for oil exporting economics, see for instance Cavalcanti et al. (2011a).

However, the estimates also suggest that inflation has a statistically significant negative effect on real output even in the long-run, and establishes that the negative effect of inflation on output growth observed using the simple correlation techniques cannot be explained away by allowing for other factors such as money, exchange rates, and technology. The econometric results provide further evidence of the inherent inefficiencies in the Iranian economy that show up as high and sustained levels of inflation.

The above results seem to be reasonably robust regardless of how foreign output is constructed, what measure of the exchange rate is used, and whether a dummy variable for revolution and war (over the period 1979Q1–1988Q2) is included in the model. The historical analysis above and the econometric results in Esfahani et al. (2013) are surprisingly in line both when it comes to the growth enhancing effects of oil income and the growth dampening effects of high inflation.

Esfahani et al. (2013) illustrate the impact of oil export revenues on the Iranian economy, by considering the Generalized Impulse Response Functions of a unit shock (equal to one standard error) to oil exports. Figure 1.10 shows that the effects of the shock work themselves through the economy within two years. As such the Iranian economy adjust very quickly to shocks when compared to the response rates of other economies, especially the developed ones. This seems to be due to the limitations of Iran's financial markets that restrict expenditure smoothing options and thereby cause the economy to move up and down quickly as external and internal conditions change. The figures clearly show that a positive unit shock to oil exports significantly increases inflation, strengthens the real exchange rate $(e_t - p_t)$, increases real output significantly (by 3.2 per cent), but its effect on real money balances, while positive, is not statistically significant. The real exchange rate appreciation of around 7.6 per cent in the aftermath of the positive shock to oil exports can be viewed as supporting the Dutch disease, although here the rise in the real exchange rate is in fact accompanied with a rise in real output which does not sit comfortably with those that view the Dutch disease as a resource curse.

Esfahani et al. (2012) also test the empirical validity of the long-run theory on eight other major oil exporting economies, with a variety of development experiences and political systems, showing that the long-run output equation [1] applies equally to OPEC (Kuwait, Libya, Nigeria, Saudi Arabia, and Venezuela),

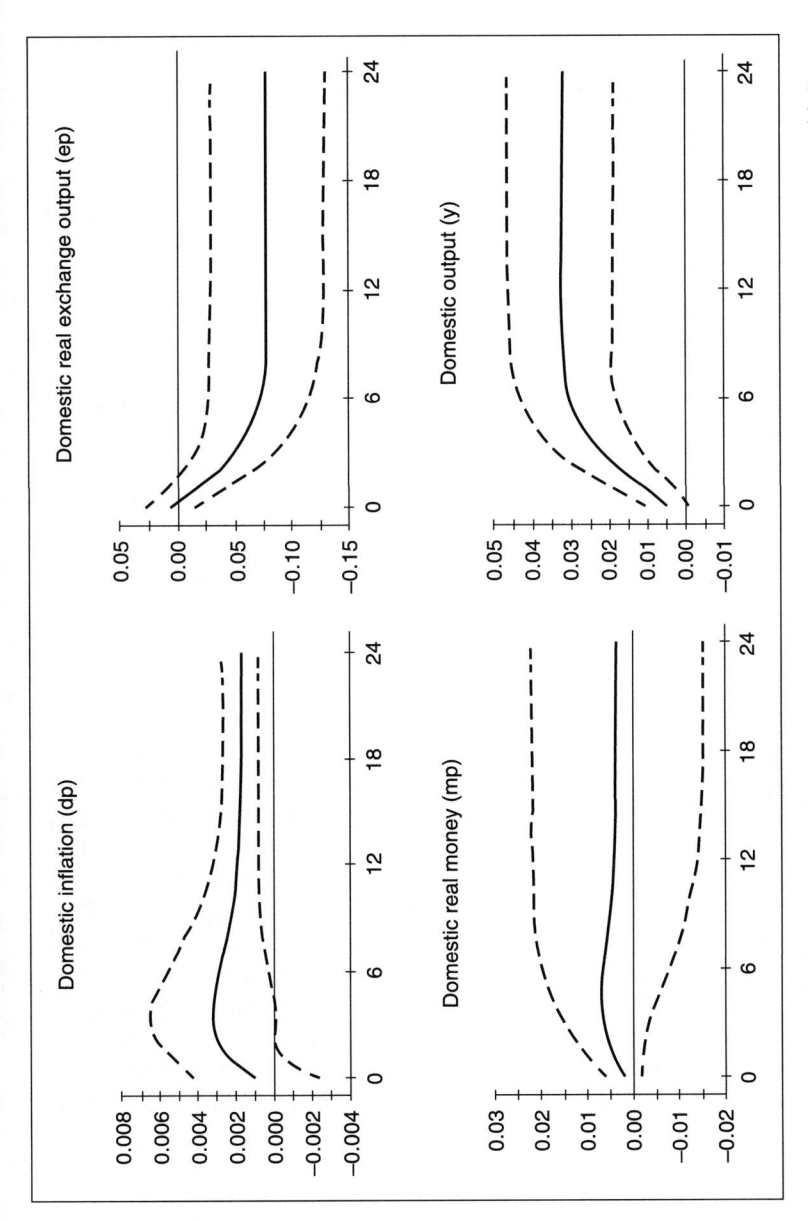

Figure 1.10 Generalized impulse responses of a positive one standard deviation shock to oil export revenues (with 95 per cent bootstrapped confidence bounds)

Source: Esfahani et al. (2013).

former OPEC (Indonesia), and OECD (Mexico and Norway) oil exporters. For most OPEC members, not surprisingly, the long-run estimates and short-run dynamics are very close to the ones obtained for Iran. Therefore, the results indicate that oil abundance by itself is not a curse.

Oil revenue volatility and economic performance

The above discussion and in particular the empirical analysis in Esfahani et al. (2013) strongly suggest that overall oil income has been a blessing for the growth and development of the Iranian economy. But the positive influence of oil income has often been counteracted by the adverse effects of excessive volatility of oil revenues and government's inappropriate responses to it. To investigate the impact of oil price volatility on the Iranian economy we follow the finance literature and use a measure of realized oil price volatility. See, for instance, Andersen et al. (2001), Andersen et al. (2003), Barndorff-Nielsen and Shephard (2002), and Barndorff-Nielsen and Shephard (2004). In the finance literature intra-daily data are generally used to compute daily realized volatilities for asset returns. Here we apply the same idea and calculate annual volatility using monthly changes in oil prices.[15] Our measure of realized oil price volatility for year t is then given by:

$$vol_t^o = \sqrt{\sum_{\tau=1}^{12}(g_{t,\tau}^o - \overline{g}_t^o)^2} \tag{3}$$

where $g_{t,\tau}^o = \Delta \ln(P_{t,\tau}^o)$, $\overline{g}_t^o = \frac{1}{12}\sum_{\tau=1}^{12} g_{t,\tau}^o$, and $g_{t,t}^o$ denotes the rate of change in oil prices ($P_{t,t}^o$) during month τ in year t. The same method is also used to calculate annual volatilities of oil production and oil revenues. The three series are plotted in Figure 1.11 from which we see that oil price volatility was rather small before 1970. This is not surprising as during this period oil prices were largely regulated by the major international oil companies. Substantial volatility was first experienced due to the first and second oil price shocks after which volatility continued to remain a major feature of the oil markets. Moreover, with the OPEC pricing system collapsing in 1985, crude oil prices were instead determined by international markets alone, which resulted in further price volatility.

However, the volatility of oil prices was not the only factor impacting the Iranian economy. The volatility of oil production and exports were also important features of the post 1970 period. In fact, as can be seen from our account of the theoretical growth model for major oil exporting economies, it is the volatility of export revenues that matters, and seen from this perspective it is the combined effects of price and quantity volatilities that should be considered. Figure 1.11 shows that although there is a strong co-movement between the volatilities of oil prices and production, there are also some important short-term deviations. For instance, production was more volatile between the first oil price shock and the end of the Iran–Iraq war, while oil prices have been more volatile since the late 1980s. This is also clearly illustrated in Table 1.4, which provides average

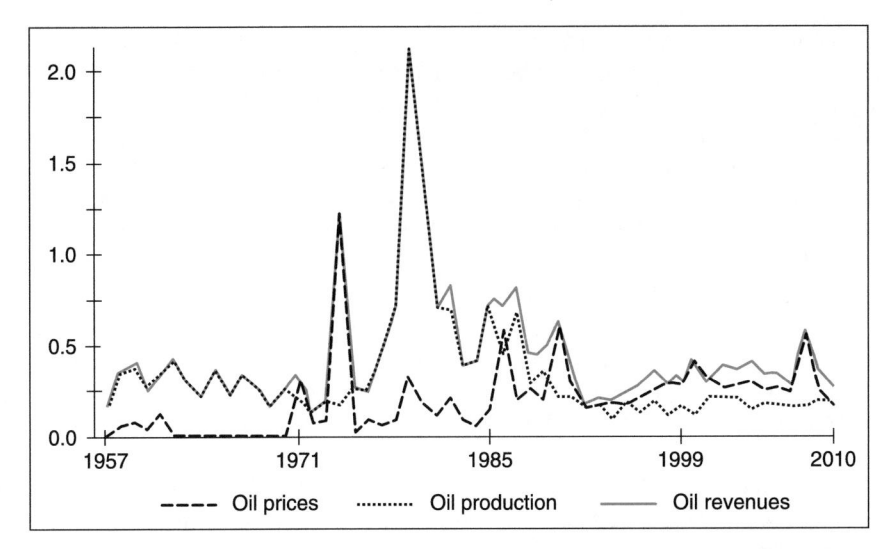

Figure 1.11 2010 Realized volatility of oil prices, production, and revenues, 1957–2010.

Source: IMF International Financial Statistics.

realized volatilities of the three series calculated over four sub-periods. In most economies oil price volatility and production/export revenue volatility are very similar. The reason for this is that production and exports usually remain reasonably steady over time, with some small year on year changes. However, due to the political developments in Iran since 1978 the Iranian oil industry has experienced several supply disruptions and restrictions. First, during the revolution production was halted due to strike by oil workers. Second, as noted earlier the post-revolutionary regime almost halved the rate of oil production with the aim of stimulating the agricultural sector. Finally, the Iran–Iraq war meant that exports during certain periods were not possible. Also, sanctions by the US, and more recently by the European Union, have further added to the volatility of Iran's oil exports, and hence oil revenues.[16]

Table 1.4 Realized volatility of oil prices, production, and revenues, 1960–2010

Sample period	Oil price volatility (%)	Oil production volatility (%)	Oil revenue volatility (%)
1960–2010	20.6	34.8	45.3
1960–1978	11.3	29.3	35.5
1979–2010	26.1	38.0	51.1
1988–2010	27.9	18.8	35.3

Source: IMF International Financial Statistics.

Figure 1.11 and Table 1.4 both show that, starting from 1973, Iran's oil revenues have been extremely volatile, and much more volatile than the volatility of international oil prices.[17] Quantitatively, over the period 1960–2010 the volatility of Iran's oil revenues was around 45.3 per cent per annum, as compared to the oil price volatility of 20.6 per cent per annum over the same period, see Table 1.4. This volatility differential although higher during the revolution and the war period (1979–1988), has declined significantly since 1988. Over the period 1988–2010, volatility of Iran's oil revenues was around 35.3 per cent per annum as compared to the volatility of oil prices of 27.9 per cent per annum.

Although oil revenue volatility has dropped since 1988, it still remains well above 35 per cent. This is to be compared with the volatility in private consumption which was below 7 per cent between 1960 and 2007 and dropped even lower post 1988 averaging 3.6 per cent.[18] Therefore, oil revenue volatility is around ten times that of consumption volatility.

Comparing the results in Table 1.2 and Table 1.4, we notice that while there is a positive correlation between the growth rates of real GDP and oil export revenues, it is also the case that the sub-periods with higher growth coincide with those of lower oil revenue volatility. To examine whether oil revenue volatility is a curse for Iran we plot annual observations on real output per capita growth against oil revenue volatility for the period 1957–2010. Figure 1.12 shows a clear negative relationship between the two variables, with a correlation of –0.62. We also observe that there is a positive relationship between output and oil revenue growth, also evident in Figure 1.4 and Table 1.2. The existence of a negative relationship between commodity price volatility and growth has also been documented in Leong and Mohaddes (2011) and Cavalcanti et al. (2012). Using a panel of 62 primary commodity abundant countries (including Iran), these papers argue that it is the commodity price volatility, rather than resource abundance as such, that drives the "resource curse" paradox.

Therefore, while abundance of oil in itself is growth enhancing there are two main problems with this oil income for the Iranian economy: one is the volatility of oil revenues, and the second is that it accrues to the government. Because revenues are highly volatile their management needs appropriate institutions and political arrangements so that the domestic expenditures from oil revenues become less volatile. The fact that oil revenues accrue to the government tends to make the government less immediately accountable for their policies and actions, and increases incentives for rent-seeking activities, as discussed above.

However, even if oil income did not accrue to the government, or the government was politically accountable (as is the case in Norway), excessive revenue volatility might still be a problem. Therefore, while democracy and accountability are both important, it is also crucial to have a system in place that deals with adverse effects of excess oil revenue volatility. Moreover, as already noted, in the case of Iran the unexpected changes in oil revenues tend to work themselves through the economy rather rapidly. See, for instance, Figure 1.10 that shows how quickly the effects of an oil export revenue shock dies out. This is mainly due to the relative under-development of money and capital markets in Iran,

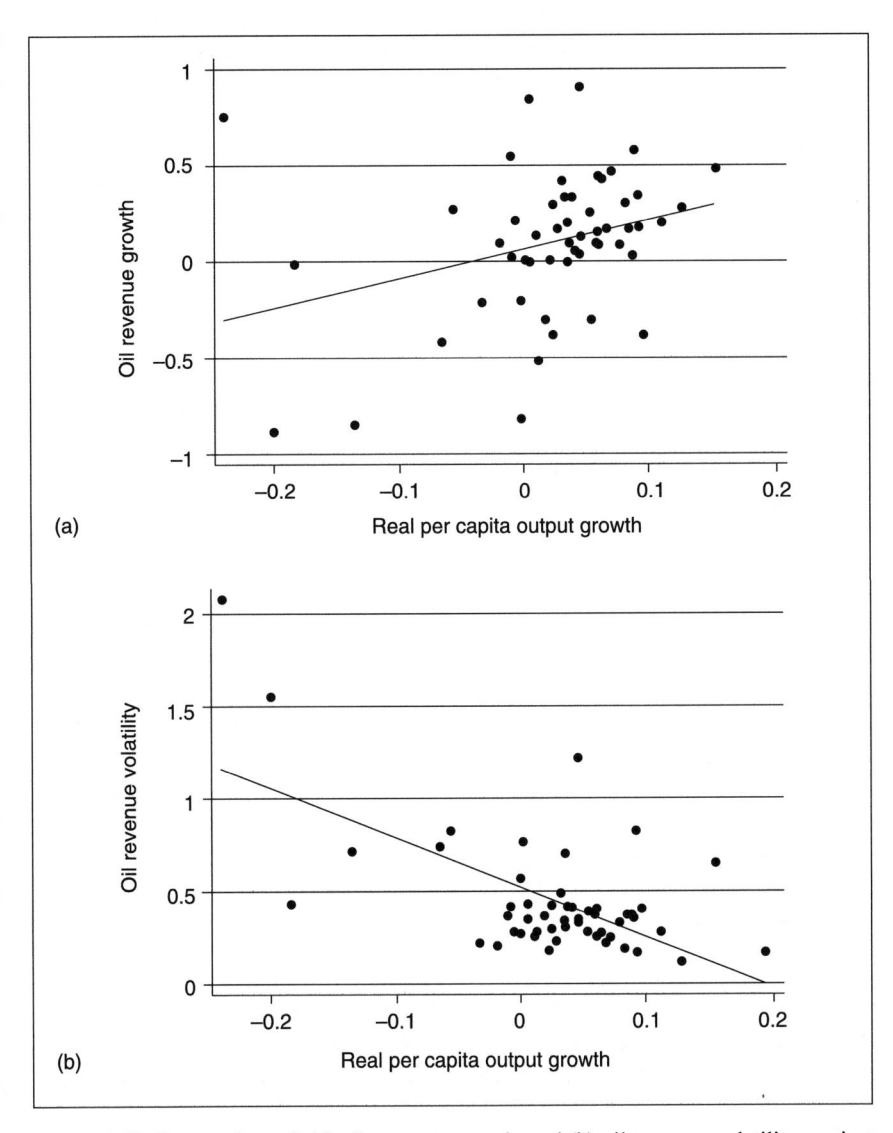

Figure 1.12 Scatter plots of: (a) oil revenue growth; and (b) oil revenue volatility, against real per capita output growth, 1957–2010.

Source: IMF International Financial Statistics.

and the country's relative isolation from the world economy and the financial community. Because of the lack of shock absorbers, oil revenue volatility has an even bigger impact on the Iranian economy in the short term, which makes having a policy of how to govern the country in terms of dealing with this volatility even more important.

The establishment of the OSF in Iran, which was approved by the Iranian parliament in 2000, was an important step towards managing the volatility curse with the aim of insulating the economy from fluctuations in oil prices. However, the adoption of populist policies since the start of the Ahmadinejad presidency in 2005 resulted in the fund being used during good times when oil prices were rising, and was thus rendered ineffective as an instrument of stabilization when oil prices started to collapse in 2009. The OSF was replaced by the NDF in 2011, but it is not clear whether the NDF is going to be any more effective. Therefore, good institutions and accountable governments are a prerequisite to creating a mechanism of short-term management of oil revenue volatility through stabilization funds. However, there needs to be further checks and balances on how oil incomes are spent and how the OSF is managed.

Finally, it is important to note that the lack of an appropriate mechanism for the management of oil revenue volatility can also result in excessive exchange rate volatility, as witnessed in Iran particularly since the revolution. We have seen periods of relative stability in the rate of the Rial to the US$ punctuated with large devaluations of the Rial, generally reflecting the differential levels of inflation in Iran relative to the rest of the world. We have also seen that high inflation and excess oil revenue volatility both affect output growth negatively, which harms the competitiveness of the Iranian economy domestically (in the case of imports) and abroad (in the case of non-oil exports). But such losses in competitiveness do not show up in the rate of the Rial to the US$ immediately, and their effects work gradually and are often triggered by some exogenous shock, such as major domestic political developments, military events, or the announcement of new sanctions. The establishment of an effective oil revenue stabilization fund can therefore also play a crucial role in the stabilization of the Rial, which is a worthy objective in its own right.

Concluding remarks

The historical data presented in this chapter show that in terms of maintaining and sustaining GDP growth, oil income has been a blessing. But it has also been a curse in inducing excess inflation, exchange rate volatility and macroeconomic inefficiencies, with adverse political and institutional implications. The econometric model of the Iranian economy, as developed in Esfahani et al. (2013), supports these results and quantifies the positive effects of oil income on growth in the long run. However, it also points to certain inefficiencies in the demand management of the economy that manifest themselves as a significantly negative effect of inflation on real output. The estimates also suggest a rather rapid response of the economy to shocks, which could be due to the relatively underdeveloped nature of the money and capital markets in Iran. Such markets tend to act as shock absorbers in developed economies during normal conditions although, as we have seen recently, they can also act as shock magnifiers during crisis periods.

We also illustrated the adverse effects of oil revenue volatility on growth in

Iran and showed that not only oil price volatility, but also volatility in production and exports has remained high over the past 50 years. The question is whether we can avoid some of the undesirable consequences of oil revenue volatility. Norway's experience suggests that it might be possible within a democratic political system with good institutions and an accountable government. The Norwegian Government Pension Fund, which aims to manage petroleum revenues in the long term is an example of how a stabilization and sovereign wealth fund can help offset not only the volatility of oil revenues but also help to smooth out government expenditures.

Appropriate policy responses are needed to deal with the large swings in oil revenues that Iran has been facing, particularly over the past three decades. In this regard it is crucial that large swings in government expenditures be avoided, and government finances and private credit expansion be set at levels that are conducive to relatively low rates of inflation. Once inflation is brought under control and it is seen by the public as a credible outcome, we would expect greater private investment, as well as a more stable currency market with reduced possibilities for rent-seeking activities.

Notes

1 Faculty of Economics and Girton College, University of Cambridge, UK.
2 Department of Economics, University of Southern California, USA, and Trinity College, Cambridge, UK.
3 For an extensive discussion of the coup see Elm (1992), Gasiorowski (1987), Kinzer (2003), and Pesaran (2011).
4 See Pesaran (1985) for a discussion of macroeconomic trends in Iran between 1954 and 1979.
5 For an early history of OPEC see Rouhani (1979), and for an extensive survey of different models emphasizing the oil market as being non-competitive and the role of OPEC as a price maker during this period see Crémer and Salehi-Isfahani (1991).
6 See also Karshenas and Hakimian (2005), Karshenas and Hakimian (2007) and Pesaran (2000) for a discussion of economic trends and macroeconomic policies in post-revolutionary Iran.
7 Karshenas and Hakimian (2005) also show that the technological gap between Iran and the rest of the world (Korea, Malaysia, and Turkey) has widened since 1979.
8 Anglo-Iranian Oil (British Petroleum), Gulf Oil, Royal Dutch Shell, Standard Oil of California (Socal), Standard Oil of New Jersey (Esso), Standard Oil of New York (Socony), and Texaco.
9 See, for example, Amuzegar (2008) and British Petroleum Statistical Review of World Energy.
10 For a comprehensive survey of the econometric methods employed in the growth literature, and some of their shortcomings, see Durlauf et al. (2005) and Durlauf et al. (2009).
11 Different forms of cross-section dependence are discussed and formally defined in Pesaran and Tosetti (2011).
12 See also Cavalcanti et al. (2011b).
13 See also the following articles in Farsi by M. H. Pesaran arguing that controlling the high inflation rate must be one of the most important objectives for the Iranian economy: "Inflation: The Most Important Issue for the Iranian Economy" in *Jam-e Jam* (May 20, 2012), and "One Needs to Find the Underlying Causes of Exchange Rate Volatility" in *Donya-e Eqtesad* (July 2, 2012).

14 See Esfahani et al. (2013) for a review of earlier work on macroeconomic models for Iran.
15 When available, weekly or daily observations can be used to construct more accurate annual realized volatility measures. But for the present analysis we do not expect the results to be much affected if instead of monthly data we used weekly or daily observations.
16 See also Pesaran (2012) for a discussion on the economic impact of the most recent sanctions, as well as the article in Farsi by M. H. Pesaran: "Economic Sanctions and the 'Market Economy'" in *Donya-e Eqtesad* (November 17, 2012).
17 Figure 1.11 also shows that, except for the first oil shock in 1974, the realized volatilities of oil revenues and production are very similar over the period 1957–1985. This is partly due to the fact that oil prices did not vary much before 1973, and even though oil price volatility started to increase after the first oil price shock, the volatility of oil revenues was much more affected by production rather than price volatility.
18 As monthly data is not available for consumption, we calculated the annualized consumption volatility using quarterly observations.

References

Alexeev, M. and R. Conrad (2009). The Elusive Curse of Oil. *The Review of Economics and Statistics 91*(3), 586–598.

Amuzegar, J. (2008). Iran's Oil as a Blessing and a Curse. *The Brown Journal of World Affairs 15*, 46–61.

Amuzegar, J. and M. A. Fekrat (1972). *Iran: Economic Development under Dualistic Conditions.* University of Chicago Press, Chicago. IL.

Andersen, T. G., T. Bollerslev, F. X. Diebold, and P. Labys (2001). The Distribution of Realized Exchange Rate Volatility. *Journal of the American Statistical Association 96*, 42–55.

Andersen, T. G., T. Bollerslev, F. X. Diebold, and P. Labys (2003). Modeling and Forecasting Realized Volatility. *Econometrica 71*(2), 579–625.

Anderson, T. W. and C. Hsiao (1981). Estimation of Dynamic Models with Error Components. *Journal of the American Statistical Association 76*(375), 598–606.

Anderson, T. W. and C. Hsiao (1982). Formulation and Estimation of Dynamic Models Using Panel Data. *Journal of Econometrics 18*(1), 47–82.

Arellano, M. and S. Bond (1991). Some Tests of Specification for Panel Data: Monte Carlo Evidence and an Application to Employment Equations. *The Review of Economic Studies 58*(2), 277–297.

Arellano, M. and O. Bover (1995). Another Look at the Instrumental Variable Estimation of Error-components Models. *Journal of Econometrics 68*(1), 29–51.

Arezki, R. and F. van der Ploeg (2007). Can the Natural Resource Curse be Turned into a Blessing? The Role of Trade Policies and Institutions. *CEPR Discussion Paper 6225.*

Bamberg, J. (1994). *The History of the British Petroleum Company, Volume 2: The Anglo-Iranian Years 1928–1954.* Cambridge University Press, Cambridge.

Barndorff-Nielsen, O. E. and N. Shephard (2002). Estimating Quadratic Variation Using Realized Variance. *Journal of Applied Econometrics 17*(5), 457–477.

Barndorff-Nielsen, O. E. and N. Shephard (2004). Econometric Analysis of Realized Covariation: High Frequency Based Covariance, Regression, and Correlation in Financial Economics. *Econometrica 72*(3), 885–925.

Binder, M. and M. Pesaran (1999). Stochastic Growth Models and Their Econometric Implications. *Journal of Economic Growth 4*, 139–183.

Boschini, A., J. Pettersson, and J. Roine (2007). Resource Curse or Not: A Question of Appropriability. *Scandinavian Journal of Economics 109*(3), 593–617.

Brunnschweiler, C. N. and E. H. Bulte (2008). The Resource Curse Revisited and Revised: A Tale of Paradoxes and Red Herrings. *Journal of Environmental Economics and Management 55*(3), 248–264.

Bulte, E. H., R. Damania, and R. T. Deacon (2005). Resource Intensity, Institutions, and Development. *World Development 33*(7), 1029–1044.

Béland, L.-P. and R. Tiagi (2009). Economic Freedom and the "Resource Curse": An Empirical Analysis. *Studies in Mining Policy, Fraser Institute.*

Caselli, F. and T. Cunningham (2009). Leader Behaviour and the Natural Resource Curse. *Oxford Economic Papers 61*(4), 628–650.

Cavalcanti, T. V. d. V., K. Mohaddes, and M. Raissi (2011a). Growth, Development and Natural Resources: New Evidence Using a Heterogeneous Panel Analysis. *The Quarterly Review of Economics and Finance 51*(4), 305–318.

Cavalcanti, T. V. d. V., K. Mohaddes, and M. Raissi (2011b). Does Oil Abundance Harm Growth? *Applied Economics Letters 18*(12), 1181–1184.

Cavalcanti, T. V. d. V., K. Mohaddes, and M. Raissi (2012). Commodity Price Volatility and the Sources of Growth. *IMF Working Paper WP/12/12.*

Collier, P. and A. Hoeffler (2004). Greed and Grievance in Civil War. *Oxford Economic Papers 56*, 563–595.

Corden, W. M. and J. P. Neary (1982). Booming Sector and De-Industrialisation in a Small Open Economy. *The Economic Journal 92*(368), 825–848.

Crémer, J. and D. Salehi-Isfahani (1991). *Models of the Oil Market.* Harwood Academic Publisher.

Dean, L. E. (2004). *Regional Studies of the World: The Middle East and North Africa 2004, Volume 50.* Europa Publications, London.

Durlauf, S. N., P. A. Johnson, and J. R. Temple (2005). Chapter 8 Growth Econometrics. P. Aghion and S. N. Durlaug, *Handbook of Economic Growth, Vol. 1*, pp. 555–677. Elsevier, Amsterdam.

Durlauf, S. N., P. A. Johnson, and J. R. W. Temple (2009). The Methods of Growth Econometrics. *Palgrave Handbook of Econometrics, Volume 2.* Palgrave Macmillan, London.

Elm, M. (1992). Oil, Power, and Principle: Iran's Oil Nationalization and Its Aftermath. Syracuse University Press, Syracuse, NY.

Esfahani, H. S., K. Mohaddes, and M. H. Pesaran (2012). An Empirical Growth Model for Major Oil Exporters. *Journal of Applied Econometrics, forthcoming.*

Esfahani, H. S., K. Mohaddes, and M. H. Pesaran (2013). Oil Exports and the Iranian Economy. *The Quarterly Review of Economics and Finance*, 53(3), 221–3.

Esfahani, H. S. and M. H. Pesaran (2009). The Iranian Economy in the Twentieth Century: A Global Perspective. *Iranian Studies 42*, 177–211.

Ferrier, R. W. (1982). *The History of the British Petroleum Company, Volume 1: The Developing Years 1901–1932.* Cambridge University Press, Cambridge.

Gasiorowski, M. J. (1987). The 1953 Coup d'état in Iran. *International Journal of Middle East Studies 19*(3), 261–286.

Graham, R. (1978). *Iran: Illusion of Power.* Croom Helm, London.

Gylfason, T., T. T. Herbertsson, and G. Zoega (1999). A Mixed Blessing. *Macroeconomic Dynamics 3*(2), 204–225.

Hakimian, H. (1988). The Impact of the 1970s' Oil Boom on Iranian Agriculture. *Journal of Peasant Studies 15*(2), 218–237.

Karshenas, M. and H. Hakimian (2005). Oil, Economic Diversification and the Democratic Process in Iran. *Iranian Studies 38*(1), 67–90.

Karshenas, M. and H. Hakimian (2007). Managing Oil Resources and Economic Diversification in Iran. In H. Katouzian and S. Hossein (eds), *Iran in the 21st Century: Politics, Economics and Confrontation.* Routledge, London.

Kinzer, S. (2003). *All the Shah's Men: An American Coup and the Roots of Middle East Terror.* John Wiley & Sons, New Jersey.

Krugman, P. (1987). The Narrow Moving Band, the Dutch Disease, and the Competitive Consequences of Mrs. Thatcher: Notes on Trade in the Presence of Dynamic Scale Economies. *Journal of Development Economics 27*(1–2), 41–55.

Lane, P. R. and A. Tornell (1996). Power, Growth, and the Voracity Effect. *Journal of Economic Growth 1*, 213–241.

Leite, C. and M. Weidmann (1999). Does Mother Nature Corrupt? Natural Resources, Corruption and Economic Growth. *IMF Working Paper WP/99/85.*

Leong, W. and K. Mohaddes (2011). Institutions and the Volatility Curse. *Cambridge Working Papers in Economics CWPE 1145.*

Mahdavi, H. (1970). The Patterns and Problems of Economic Development in Rentier States: The Case of Iran. In M. Cook (ed.), *Studies in the Economic History of the Middle East.* Oxford University Press, London.

Mauro, P. (1995). Corruption and Growth. *The Quarterly Journal of Economics 110*(3), 681–712.

Mehlum, H., K. Moene, and R. Torvik (2006). Institutions and the Resource Curse. *The Economic Journal 116*, 1–20.

Neary, J. P. and S. J. G. van Wijnbergen (1986). *Natural Resources and the Macroeconomy.* MIT Press, Cambridge, MA.

NIOC (2011). The National Iranian Oil Company. *Website Accessed: 15 April 2011.*

Pesaran, E. (2011). *Iran's Struggle for Economic Independence: Reform and Counter-Reform in the Post-Revolutionary Era.* Routledge, London.

Pesaran, E. (2012). Challenges Facing the Iranian Economy. In R. Parsi (ed.), *Iran: A Revolutionary Republic in Transition.* European Union Institute for Security Studies, Paris.

Pesaran, M. H. (1982). The System of Dependent Capitalism in Pre- and Post-Revolutionary Iran. *International Journal of Middle East Studies 14*(4), 501–522.

Pesaran, M. H. (1985). Economic Development and Revolutionary Upheavals in Iran. In H. Afshar (ed.), *Iran: A Revolution in Turmoil.* Macmillan, London.

Pesaran, M. H. (1997). The Iranian Economy During the Pahlavi Era. In E. Yarshater (ed.), *Encyclopaedia Iranica*, Volume VIII Fascicle 2, Economy V-Education XX, pp. 143–156. Mazda Publishers, Costa Mesa, CA.

Pesaran, M. H. (2000). Economic Trends and Macroeconomic Policies in Post-Revolutionary Iran. In P. Alizadeh (Ed.), *The Economy of Iran: Dilemmas of an Islamic State.* I.B. Tauris, London.

Pesaran, M. H. (2006). Estimation and Inference in Large Heterogeneous Panels with a Multifactor Error Structure. *Econometrica 74*(4), 967–1012.

Pesaran, M. H. and R. Smith (1995). Estimating Long-run Relationships from Dynamic Heterogeneous Panels. *Journal of Econometrics 68*(1), 79–113.

Pesaran, M. H. and E. Tosetti (2011). Large Panels with Common Factors and Spatial Correlations. *Journal of Econometrics 161*(2), 182–202.

Rodriguez, F. and J. D. Sachs (1999). Why Do Resource-Abundant Economies Grow More Slowly? *Journal of Economic Growth 4*, 277–303.

Rouhani, F. (1979). *A History of O.P.E.C.* Praeger, New York.

Sachs, J. D. and A. M. Warner (1995). Natural Resource Abundance and Economic Growth. *National Bureau of Economic Research Working Paper 5398.*

Salehi-Isfahani, D. (1996). The Oil Sector after the Revolution. In S. Rahnema and S. Behdad (Eds.), *Iran after the Revolution: Crisis of an Islamic State*, pp. 150–173. I.B. Tauris, London.

Tornell, A. and P. R. Lane (1999). The Voracity Effect. *The American Economic Review 89*(1), 22–46.

United Nations, (1951). Security Council Official Records. *Document S/PV.560*, October 15.

van der Ploeg, F. and S. Poelhekke (2010). The Pungent Smell of "Red Herrings": Subsoil Assets, Rents, Volatility and the Resource Curse. *Journal of Environmental Economics and Management 60*(1), 44–55.

van der Ploeg, F. and T. Venables (2009). Symposium on Resource Rich Economies: Introduction. *Oxford Economic Papers 61*(4), 625–627.

2 Institutional change, policy challenges and macroeconomic performance, 1979–2004

Introduction

Since the Revolution in 1979, Iran has witnessed important socio-economic and institutional changes and has been affected by significant economic and political upheavals. The macroeconomic scene, in particular, has experienced a number of major shocks, including oil booms and busts, war, trade sanctions, and internal political strife – all affecting prospects of accumulation and growth.

Despite Iran's considerable human and natural resource riches, the economic record of the post-revolutionary period is lacklustre, with many Iranians experiencing setbacks to their living standards by regional and international standards. It is widely recognized that, in fact, Iran's ability to live off her oil rents has pushed back and delayed the agenda for economic reforms, to the point of obstructing the largely overdue modernization of her ailing economy to date.[1]

This chapter examines the post-revolutionary's macroeconomic policies and performance in a comparative context appraising it against Iran's past trends and future potential. The chapter argues that two sets of factors have conditioned Iran's performance and are likely to continue to taint her prospects for sustainable growth into the future. These are: limited economic diversification and continued dependence on the oil sector on the one hand, and the institutional setting in which post-revolutionary economic policies have been formulated and implemented for much of the last three decades on the other.

The structure of this chapter is as follows. First, we chart Iran's growth and development path, highlighting political economy changes before and after 1979, and explore their implications for the model of growth and development pursued. Second, we examine a broad overview of Iran's comparative economic performance over the last few decades in both regional and historical contexts. Next, we turn to a discussion of policy challenges and responses in three sub-periods after 1979: (a): 1979–88 (the heyday of revolutionary populism and the war with Iraq); (b) 1989–93 (the years of reconstruction and reform); and (c) 1994–2004 (the decade of austerity and reform). It will be demonstrated how recurrent cycles of populism and pragmatism have characterized these two and a half decades. After this, we examine Iran's principal characteristics as an oil economy, and the way the agenda for economic policy and reform has been affected by the institutional setting in place in this period.

The final section offers a summary and some concluding remarks regarding Iran's economic track record and its future challenges.

Charting Iran's growth and development path

Iran's recent past presents a rare – arguably a 'laboratory' like – case for the study of growth and development. In the span of nearly three decades after the 1979 Revolution, Iran has witnessed sweeping institutional changes and has been affected by significant economic and political upheavals. At the macroeconomic level, in particular, she has experienced a number of shocks, ranging from oil booms and busts, to war (with Iraq), trade sanctions, and internal political strife – all affecting long-term accumulation and growth. These changes offer us unique insights into, and rich rewards for, a case study of growth and development in the context of fast-changing economic and socio-political environments.

Two particular features of this case stand out with some distinction: the fact that Iran is a large, resource-rich country, and the character of the emergent post-revolutionary institutions which infuse, atypically, religion with politics. These features add to the complexity and challenge confronting any study of Iran's recent past. Yet they also render it potentially more interesting from the point of view of their wider implications for a study of growth and development.

The 1979 Revolution overthrew one of the most stable and enduring monarchies in the Middle East and North Africa (MENA) region, backed by a large and modern army. This momentous event of great international significance was also notable in at least two respects. First, the revolutionary course was driven by one of the broadest and largest mass-based movements of the twentieth century and harboured with it high expectations of change for the supporting masses. Second, by installing the world's arguably single theocracy in modern times, it has created an unfamiliar and unorthodox institutional and political setting, which continues to challenge conventional thinking to date.

Prior to the Revolution, Iran was led by a variant of what may be described as a 'developmental state' (Alizadeh, 2000: 17–18). The state had substantial autonomy from social groups and pursued policies that were conducive to the development of the private sector.[2] Moreover, as with other military dictators, the Shah had a strong commitment to growth, which he saw as the principal way to lift the country out of a century of poverty and underdevelopment. To achieve this, he implemented a wide-ranging programme of social and economic reforms from above in the 1960s, and pursued an active import-substitution industrialization policy to accelerate capital accumulation in the 1960s and 1970s (Karshenas, 1990). Steadily growing oil incomes and a sizeable domestic market offered Iran an opportunity to emerge as a semi-industrialized country by the 1970s. The advent of the oil boom in this decade, in particular, fostered this vision as it now seemed feasible to use the underground wealth to elevate Iran to a regional economic and military power.

Two obstacles, however, interfered with this course of development. First, was the weak, if not missing, domestic political legitimacy given the Shah's strong dependence on Western powers.[3] Second, and no less important, was the uneven and highly differentiating impact of economic growth in these years, which heightened social tensions, especially in urban areas (Hakimian, 1988: 19).[4] These tensions were further fuelled by the 1970s' oil boom, leading to much social and economic dislocation (Graham, 1978; Hakimian, 1990). When dissent and social discontent finally erupted, the fact that all meaningful political channels had already been eliminated did not prove a tactical advantage for the regime. On the contrary, it helped channel all opposition into an effective mass movement focused against the Shah.

In this context, the role of the mosques as the only organization with nation-wide grassroots activity became crucial. It enabled the Shiite clergy to forge a broad, cross-class coalition, which embraced the bazaar, the modern middle classes, the intelligentsia, the industrial workforce, the urban poor and other groups and social strata. The broad base from which this alliance drew from shattered the state's relative autonomy from social groups and, as we shall see, has been at the base of the post-revolutionary state's popular constituency with which it has to contend.

Two further features of the Iranian Revolution have continued to play important roles in shaping the institutional landscape in this period: the twin promises of bringing about 'social justice' and achieving 'economic independence'. Both were strong ideals of the revolution, and have made an imprint on both the vision and practice of economic policy ever since (Pesaran, 2011).

The strong anti-imperialist, anti-Western stance and rhetoric of the Revolution reflected a rejection of the *ancien regime*'s dependency on external powers in general, and the United States in particular. Powerful aspirations were thus in force from the start to turn Iran into an 'independent' economy. These were indeed behind Iran's pursuit of an isolationist development path since 1979, shunting the globalization trends that have swept the developing countries in recent decades.

Moreover, despite the religious form and leadership of the Revolution, which has overshadowed its democratic and anti-dictatorial aspirations, the populist element in this process has been strong and lasting – particularly in the economic domain (Abrahamian, 1993; Behdad, 1996).[5]

As with Latin American populism, the Iranian Revolution too was built around a broad coalition of the middle classes led by a strong and charismatic leadership (see Dornbusch and Edwards, 1991 on populism in Latin America). It had popular and egalitarian aspirations based on promises of fraternity, equality and social justice – in direct contrast to the previous era's focus on growth and development. While respecting private property, it had strong connotations of class conflict between the *mostazafin* (the downtrodden) and the *mostakberin* (the oppressors) and promised to emancipate the former from all injustices of the monarchist era. This involved pledges to build a society 'free from want and hunger, slums, drugs and inequality, and nepotism and corruption' (Abrahamian, 1993: 32).

As Acemoglu and Robinson (2006) have demonstrated, the transition from dictatorship to democracy is not necessarily a linear process with an assured outcome. In the Iranian example, after nearly three decades, this contradictory process seems to have resulted in a *hybrid* political form, which combines aspects of both democracy and non-democracy.

On the one hand, Iran was unique in offering universal suffrage after the Revolution, starting at the early age of 15.[6] Moreover, participation rates in most elections tend to be high especially by the standards of established democracies.[7] Yet, these 'popular' elections operate on the basis of a highly limited franchise and are subject to vigorous, and controversial, vetting of candidates by the Guardian Council.[8] This system thus combines elements of 'democracy' on the 'demand' side (offering opportunities for expressions of 'popular' choice) with 'non-democracy' entailing restrictions on the 'supply' side (which limits the pool of candidates and political parties).[9] Given the contradictory nature of the system, which, for lack of a better term, we may describe as a *'participatory non-democracy'*, it is not surprising that it often confounds both critics and supporters alike.

At an abstract level, Iran's quest for democracy, and the upheavals leading to the Revolution in 1979, too, may be viewed as strategic behaviour involving 'conflictual social choices' between two broad opponent groups (Acemoglu and Robinson, 2006): citizens (a broad coalition of different classes and social groups), and the elite (the Shah and the Royal Court backed by higher echelons of the military, and external powers). Yet, in the Iranian case, both the process and outcome of this confrontation have been distinct in a number of ways.

First, rational choice and optimal behaviour would imply knowledge and information that was clearly absent in this context. There were no known blueprints for the promised type of (Islamic) Republic and much of what was on offer by way of the new social and economic order had to hinge on broad perceptions, if not promises and hopes. For this reason, an element of ambiguity has permeated developments in Iran in the post-revolutionary period with far-reaching consequences, particularly in the economic policy area (we shall come back to this below).

Second, Iran's quest for democratization did not arise in the classic conditions of economic and political crises.[10] On the contrary, it followed the prosperity associated with the oil-boom period of the 1970s, implying that desire for revolutionary change may have had more to do with growing inequality and perceptions of (relative) poverty in these years than with actual impoverishment and hunger.

As we shall see below, oil revenues have continued to exert an undue influence over Iran's growth and economic performance as well as shaping popular expectations over the distribution of political space and economic resources in the post-1979 period.

In the next section, we examine the growth record in the post-revolutionary period before coming back to examine the economic policies and challenges in the period under study.

An overview of growth

Overall, Iran's economy recorded an annual average real growth rate of 4.6 per cent over the four and a half decades between 1960 and 2005. While this aggregate long-term growth rate is above the comparable rate for the MENA region as a whole (3.8 per cent per annum), it is below the rate for the wider group of Lower Middle Income Countries (LMCs), of which Iran is part (estimated at 5.3 per cent per annum).[11]

This record should, however, be qualified in at least three important ways. First, it masks gross variations over time (especially after the late 1970s). Second, it needs to be studied in a comparative context to take account of Iran's relative performance vis-a-vis her peers. And last, but not least, allowing for population growth (especially after the 1980s), would depict a different picture.

In general, evidence suggests that Iran's growth performance deteriorated after the late 1970s. This is true both in a comparative light as well as compared to the period over time (see Hakimian and Karshenas, 2000, and Karshenas and Hakimian, 2005).

Comparison with a high performing economy such as South Korea underlines the sharp trend reversal in Iran's growth performance (Figure 2.1). Between 1955 and 1975, Iran's per capita income outstripped that of Korea. The situation was, however, reversed after the mid-1970s when Iran's growth began to falter. South Korea has continued to improve its per capita GDP ever since with a wide gap separating the two countries as a consequence.

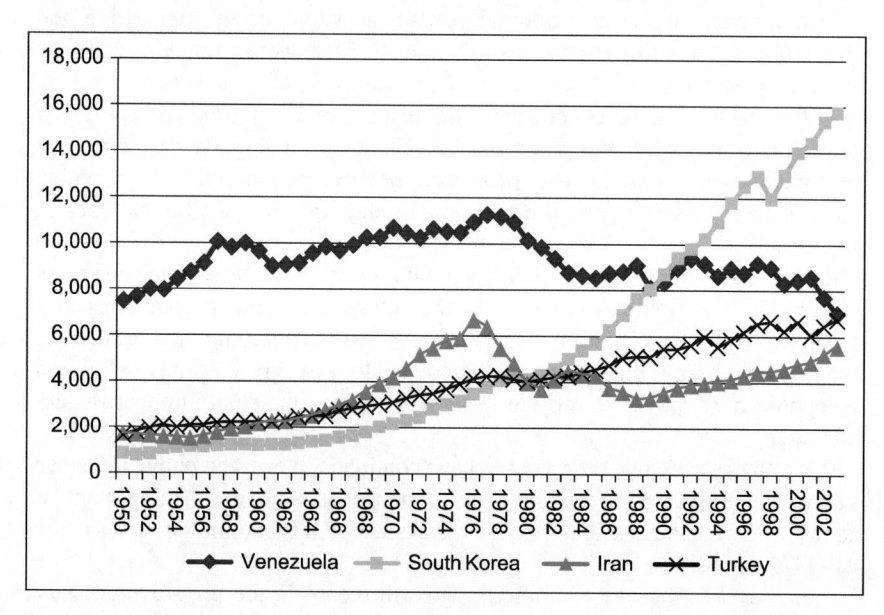

Figure 2.1 Per Capita GDP Trends in Iran, Korea, Turkey and Venezuela, 1950–2003
Source: Maddison (2010).

Turkey offers an interesting contrast. Starting from similar per capita income levels in the early 1960s, she has followed a more steady growth path, overtaking Iran, especially after the collapse of growth in the 1980s. It is true that much of the catching-up by Turkey took place during Iran's war with Iraq in the 1980s (from which Turkey and other neighbouring countries benefited economically). However, sustained economic growth would not have been possible without far-reaching economic reforms introduced after the early 1980s and resulting in a higher efficiency of investment and greater economic diversification, especially rising manufacturing exports (Karshenas and Hakimian, 2005: 71).

An examination of the Venezuelan experience shows that some of the difficulties Iran encountered in the 1980s were in fact shared by other oil economies. Of further interest, is that whereas Venezuela's growth and hence its GDP per capita has continually regressed, Iran's performance recovered after the 1990s – albeit gradually, indicating a degree of convergence with Venezuela.

Iran's story is equally interesting in comparison with other LMCs and oil economies. Figures 2.2 and 2.3 show a 'league table' of rankings for the growth performance of LMCs and oil economies, respectively. Figure 2.2 shows that Iran was a top performer in the 1960s – judged by annual real growth rates, and then sank below the median position in the 1970s before plunging to the bottom of the table in the harsh 1980s decade. After that, Iran has improved its relative performance, again both the in GDP and GDP per capita bases, among the LMC group of countries, moving to the top three deciles in the 1990s and after 2000.

Figure 2.3 offers a useful comparison against the oil economies. Here too a similar 'U-shaped' trajectory is observed, whereby Iran's relative performance

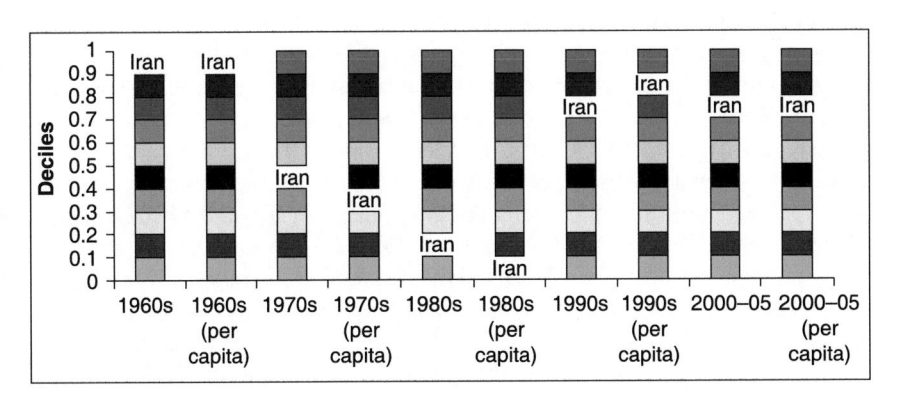

Figure 2.2 Iran's GDP and GDP per capita Growth Ranking among Lower Middle Income Countries, 1960–2005

Source: calculated from World Bank, development indicators.

Note: World Bank classification as of July 2006. Lower Middle Income Countries (LMCs) comprise 58 countries including eastern block countries and former Soviet republics for which data refer to the period after the early 1990s. The number of countries embraced by the classification is therefore variable between different decades and should be treated with caution.

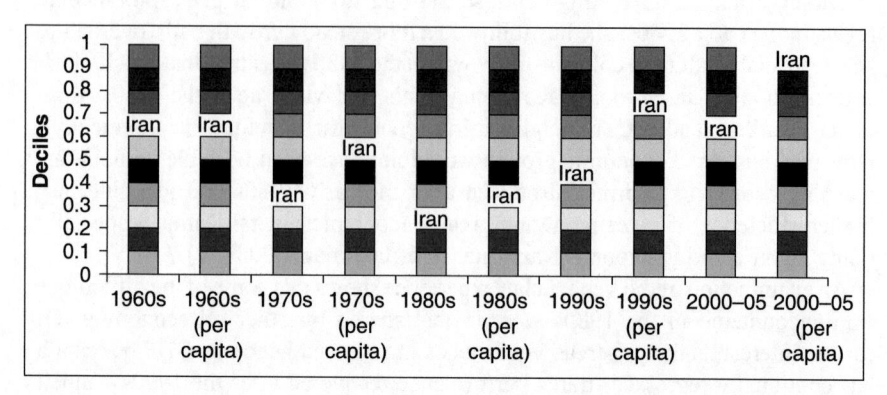

Figure 2.3 Iran's GDP and GDP per capita Growth Ranking among Oil Economies, 1960–2005

Source: Calculated from World Bank, development indicators.

Note: Oil economies included are: Algeria, Bahrain, Indonesia, Iran, Kuwait, Libya, Nigeria, Oman, Saudi Arabia, UAE, Venezuela and Yemen. Qatar is excluded due to data limitations. The number of countries embraced by the classification here is variable between different decades reflecting data limitations, and should hence be treated with caution.

suffered in the 1980s before recovering later, but with a less severe 'trough', indicating that the 1980s' oil market turbulence affected other oil exporters, too. Indeed, Iran did relatively better on a *per capita* basis against the oil economies as opposed to its general GDP growth rankings. This happened despite sharp sways in Iran's demographic behaviour after the 1970s (Hakimian, 2006). That is to say that Iran's population growth has outperformed other oil-producing nations including, perhaps somewhat surprisingly, during the 1980s, when she experienced a notable fertility surge resulting in one of the fastest growing population rates in the world (reaching almost 4 per cent in the 1980s; see below).[12]

Figure 2.4 depicts Iran's GDP in real terms since 1959 (in constant 1997–8 prices). Three general phases are readily evident from this long-term trajectory of Iran's real income and its evolution over time: the rapid rise in the decade and a half prior to the Revolution (1960s and the first half of the 1970s); the collapse and contraction period of the 1980s; and the resumption of growth after the early 1990s. This rather clear-cut and well-differentiated pattern of two GDP growth phases, punctuated by one (albeit long) collapse period, may lead one to conclude that Iran has been a high performer during most of the last four and a half decades and is now back on its 'sustainable growth track'. A more detailed examination of Iran's *growth* performance disaggregated into the relevant sub-periods, however, suggests otherwise.

Figure 2.5 depicts the GDP growth performance in Iran since 1960 and Table 2.1 provides more detailed information on various sub-periods since then. It can be seen that growth has specially suffered setbacks and endured heightened volatility for much of the period since the late 1970s. While real GDP

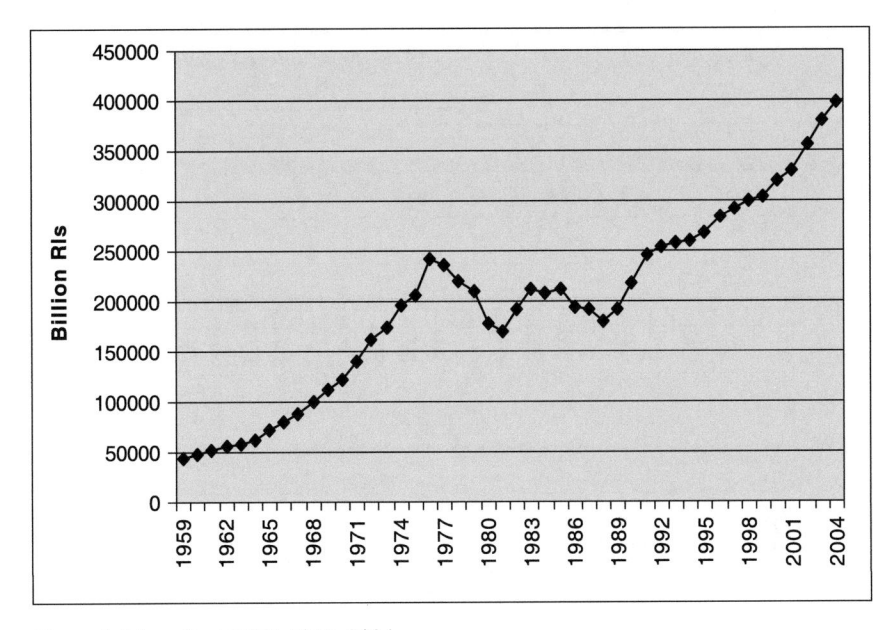

Figure 2.4 Iran Real GDP: 1959–2004

Source: Central Bank of Iran.

growth has averaged 5.3 per cent per annum for the four and a half decades after 1960, there has been a gross discrepancy between the growth performances before and after the Revolution. Prior to 1979, Iran's economy grew 9 per cent per annum in real terms or more than three and a half times faster on average than after 1979 (real GDP growth averaged 2.5 per cent per annum during 1979–2004; see Table 2.1). While growth averaged 10.6 per cent per annum in the period 1960–72, the fastest growth rates ever attained were during the heyday of the oil boom in the 1970s, with growth hitting an all time high of about 17 per cent in 1972 and 1976.

As stated above, the Iranian economy suffered most in the 1980s following the revolutionary upheavals of the late 1970s and a long and destructive war with Iraq: the economy contracted by 1.3 per cent per annum in real terms for most of the 1980s. Even excluding this difficult phase from the growth picture, it is clear that Iran's growth has under-performed compared to the period before the Revolution: the growth rate for the post-war period (1989–2004) has been 5.1 per cent, or just over half the rate of the Shah's years.

The most significant episode of growth in recent years occurred during a brief period of post-war reconstruction and economic reform when growth nearly matched the pre-revolutionary record (averaging 7.5 per cent per annum during 1989–93 compared to 8–9 per cent per annum in the 1960s and 1970s). This period, however, abruptly ended amidst the debt crisis of the mid-1990s (see below). More recently, growth rose again during the Third Plan years

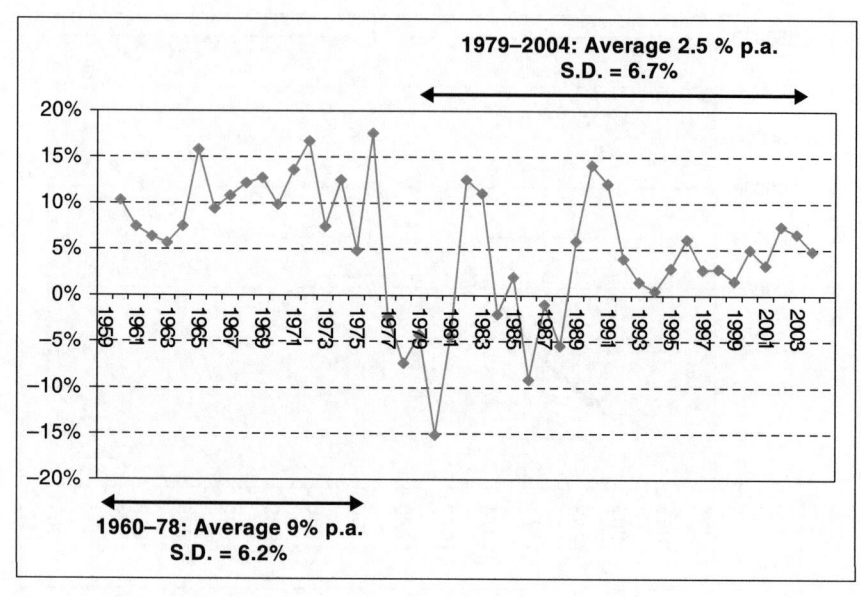

Figure 2.5 Iran's Growth Rate (1960–2004)

Source: Central Bank of Iran.

(2000–4), helped – as we shall see – by another period of buoyancy in international oil prices.

As Table 2.1 shows, Iran's post-revolutionary economic growth can be more specifically studied in three sub-periods:

1. **The 1979–88 period**: this period covered the early years of the Revolution, a long war (with Iraq) and a general trend of economic populism in Iran. We may think of these years as the 'ideological' period during which the new regime was consolidating its control over the economy.
2. **The 1989–93 period**: these years saw a major drive at economic reconstruction and reform under the auspices of the First Five-Year Development Plan, after the end of war with Iraq. This period signified the onset of a new 'pragmatist' phase in the Islamic Republic.
3. **The 1994–2004 decade**: this period faced initially the twin challenges of managing an external debt crisis at the beginning of the Second Development Plan (1994–9) and restoring equilibrium in Iran's external accounts. Having emerged through this crisis, the task was then to resume macroeconomic reforms and achieve greater macro stability during the Third Plan (2000–4). The road from crisis to reform in this long decade was paved with much uncertainty over the direction of economic policy, in general, and one in which Iran's political economy scene was rocked by intense political strife and factional politics.

Table 2.1 Overview of Iran's growth by sub-periods (1960–2004)

Average annual real GDP growth rate (%)[a]

	Mean	STD	
Before the Revolution			
1960–72	10.6	3.5	Before the oil-boom years
1973–77	8.0	7.6	The 1970s' oil-boom years
1960–78	**9.0**	**6.2**	**The Shah's years**
After the Revolution			
1980–88	–1.3	8.9	War years
1989–93	7.5	5.4	First Plan
1994–99	2.8	1.9	Second Plan
2000–2004	5.4	1.7	Third Plan
1989–2004	5.1	3.7	Post-war years
1979–2004	**2.5**	**6.7**	**All Islamic Republic Years**
1960–2004	**5.3**	**5.3**	**Entire period**

Source: Central Bank of Iran.

Note: [a] At constant 1997–98 prices.

We now offer a broad discussion of the nature of challenges and policy responses in each of these sub-periods before coming back to examine the structural features of, and institutional impediments to, growth in Iran in the following section.

Policy challenges and responses

Populism and war (1979–88)

This period was characterized by the ideological fervour of the early revolutionary period and the destructive effects of war with Iraq (1980–88). The most prominent populist themes throughout the 1980s embraced such issues as the Islamization of the economy, emphasis on social redistribution and attaining economic independence and self-sufficiency (Behdad, 1996; Mazarei, 1996; Pesaran, 2011). However, there was a tension between the new administrations' religious idealism and the requisite economic management by government, which lacked coherence and clarity. The result was intense debates and political scrutiny by different forces and factions in the society and within the government. While war provided a pretext for tactical patching up of some of these differences, many ambiguities persisted and, as we shall see, have continued to mar policy-making in the coming years (for instance, the role of interest in banking, attitudes to foreign direct investment, and more generally the boundaries between the state and the private sector).

In the immediate aftermath of the Revolution a considerable portion of the large-scale modern industry as well as the entire banking and insurance system was nationalized. These nationalizations were to some extent forced on the government as in many cases the owners and managers of these factories had left the country and some enterprises were on the verge of collapse.

With the advent of war in 1980, the debates about the role of the private sector and markets took a new turn as the government introduced an intricate system of rationing and direct subsidies for a large number of commodities. Government controls in other economic spheres also increased significantly. Foreign exchange shortages, which became particularly acute from the mid-1980s, led to a policy of import compression and strict foreign exchange controls and rationing.[13] The shortfall in oil revenues precipitated by the collapse of the international oil prices in the mid-1980s coincided with increasing demand on government resources leading to budget deficits and heightening inflationary pressures in these years.

The government's role in this period expanded significantly leading to the state's direct intervention in many aspects of Iran's economy. These included the operation of foreign exchange controls, maintenance of a system of elaborate and multiple exchange rates system, control of interest rates and bank credits as well as direct price controls in a large number of markets. By the end of the war, an extensive network of controls had emerged embracing some 300 products that were subject to official price controls (Hakimian and Karshenas, 2000).

Despite the government's concerted efforts to keep the economy afloat and to avert the worst consequences for the populace, the Iranian economy suffered major setbacks in this period. The resource base continued to shrink as there was a massive diversion of resources for military purposes to sustain the ongoing war effort; the country continued to suffer a significant international brain drain; and physical and human destruction went on on a large scale.

Particularly severe was the contraction of the oil sector, which had taken the brunt of the war with Iraq. The destruction of oil production facilities and lack of investment had severely affected Iran's oil production, which collapsed from 5.8 million barrels a day in the 1970s to about 1.4 million early on in the war (1981). The oil sector's share of GDP plummeted from a peak of about 25 per cent in the mid-1970s to merely five per cent in 1981 (World Bank, 2003: Chapter 1: 3).

Another development of lasting significance was a major surge in Iran's population growth during the first decade after the Revolution. Reaching an average annual growth rate of almost four per cent in the mid-1980s, Iran's population was by now one of the fastest growing in the world (see Figure 2.6).[14] In the intercensal period 1976–86, Iran's population had expanded by nearly 50 per cent to embrace a total of just under 50 million people, a net total addition of about 16 million on a population base of just below 34 million in 1976 (the last census before the Revolution). Measured by child–woman ratio (CWR), fertility rose 17 per cent during this period (reaching almost 860 children per thousand women of reproductive age – up from 732 a decade earlier; Hakimian, 2006).

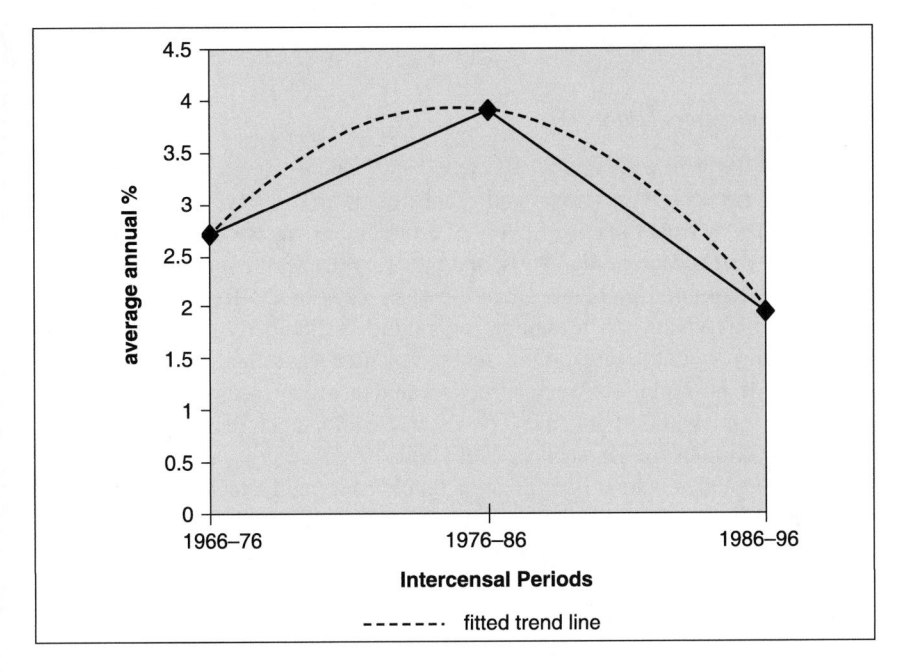

Figure 2.6 Iran – Population Growth Rate (1966–96)

Source: based on census data by the Statistical Centre of Iran.

Soon after the Revolution, the government introduced strong pronatalist measures, initiating what proved to be a reversal of Iran's earlier demographic transition. Steps taken included shutting down family planning clinics, promoting early marriage, lowering the legal age of marriage (to nine for girls and 14 for men), and discouraging birth control. These were further reinforced by new 'Islamization' trends which shaped and re-defined the regulatory and socio-economic environments, affecting the role of women. In general, these redefined their position in the economy and encouraged their retreat into the family and domestic domains. It was in this context that the baby boom of the 1980s was officially hailed as an important indicator of 'success'. However, as we shall see below, by the late 1980s concerns over rapid population growth, and its growing burdens on the economy, led to one of the most notable population policy, and in due course, demographic trend reversals of modern times (Hakimian, 2006).

A dramatic collapse in international oil prices in 1986 compounded these pressures raising the war burden for the government to unsustainable levels by the latter part of the 1980s. The economy shrank more than five per cent in real terms in the three-year period 1986–8 and the government budget was approximately 50 per cent in deficit by the last year of war. By 1988, Iran's real per capita GDP had shrunk back to levels attained in the mid-1960s (see Figure 2.1).

It was against such austere and harsh economic backgrounds that the eight-year war with Iraq came to an end.

The pragmatic years (1989–93)

The end of the war with Iraq in the late 1980s opened up a new window of opportunity for economic reform and reconstruction. The impetus for this new drive came partly from the long process of economic exhaustion Iran had suffered during the harsh decade of the 1980s, and partly by the accumulation of long and deep-rooted economic problems since the early days of the Revolution. It was against a background of mounting economic difficulties, shrinking living standards and a contracting public sector resource base that the government embarked on an ambitious reconstruction and economic reform programme within the framework of its first Five-Year Development Plan in the period 1989–93 (Hakimian and Karshenas, 2000; Nili, 1997).

The plan aimed at market liberalization by dismantling the intricate network of price and quantity controls that had evolved over the war years, a gradual liberalization of foreign trade, including the removal of quantitative restrictions on imports and exports, and the unification of the exchange rate system.

This was the first significant step, in principle at least, towards promoting the private sector and a general reduction in the state's hitherto dominant position in the economy. In practice, however, the implementation of the plan ran into problems as reforms were accompanied by an overly ambitious fiscal and monetary expansion leading to serious macroeconomic imbalances. Despite much emphasis on the private sector and the need to reduce the extent and scope of state intervention in the economy, the record in practice was very different. In the end, the implementation and commitment to reforms were scaled back to make space for the public sector-led reconstruction efforts. The outcome of the First Plan reflected some of these tensions and inconsistencies in kick-starting the economy.

There was some early success, no doubt. For instance, the GDP growth rate shot up to 12–14 per cent per annum in 1990 and 1991, which was particularly impressive coming after the contraction and decline of the war years (see Figure 2.5). However, success was short-lived and proved unsustainable. Economic activity slowed down noticeably in the last two years of the plan when GDP growth dropped back to single figures (four per cent in 1992 and a mere 1.5 per cent in 1993). The slow-down in growth was also accompanied by inflationary build-up, with the consumer price index jumping by about 23 per cent in 1993 and liquidity expansion (growth of M2) exceeding 34 per cent in the same year.

The plan's implementation was, however, additionally marred by an external debt crisis, which broke out in the latter part of the period causing severe imbalances in the external accounts. Austerity measures adopted in 1994 to deal with the crisis signalled the end of the rapid growth phase. By 1994, the economy was virtually at a standstill and the reforms were gradually scaled back and reversed. Thus was the case of the newly unified exchange rate system which was thwarted in late 1993 less than a year after it had been introduced (Farzin, 1995). Matters were further complicated in these years by declining oil revenues after 1992 (falling from $18 billion in 1990 to about $14 billion in 1993 and 1994).

Despite the First Plan's mixed fortunes and the government's subsequent wavering commitment to reforms, the Plan was a watershed in the development of Iran's post-war economy. First, it played a major part in dismantling the country's largely centrally-administered economy in the late 1980s. Second, it initiated – albeit slowly – the beginnings of the economic adjustment and reform agenda with its ramifications continuing to the present.

The first plan's successes emanated partially from the energizing effect of the reform measures themselves, which proved to be particularly important after years of central control and state administration of the economy. Although few far-reaching measures were adopted to address the problem of weak productive efficiency in the economy (such as in the ailing industrial sector), the reforms did, by virtue of their focus on allocative efficiency, take important, if somewhat modest, steps to address some of the gross distortions that had crept into the Iranian economy during the earlier populist years.

Another impetus came from the *'peace dividend'* itself. For the first time in about a decade, resources did not have to be diverted for maintaining an expensive war effort and could be used to foster construction instead.

The boom was also fuelled by improving oil revenues. In the early years of the Plan, government spending was boosted by a doubling of oil revenues: foreign exchange revenues from oil sales rose from $9.7 billion in 1988 to about $18 billion in 1991, accounting for some 60 per cent of all government revenues (up from 39 per cent in 1988).[15] Oil export revenues averaged about $14.5 billion for the entire plan period of 1989–3 (Table 2.2). There were other contributory factors too.

First, the baby boom of the early 1980s had moderated substantially by now, although the lasting effects of the population momentum continued to pose a serious burden for the economy. Reflecting mounting concerns over population growth, the earlier pronatalist policies were swiftly and decisively reversed by the late 1980s. A hallmark of this period was the introduction of an active population control programme, which marked a significant U-turn in official thinking and policy after 1988. At the heart of this policy was a supply-side approach in which the Ministry of Health and Medical Education (MOHME) set up an extensive Primary Health Network (PHC) made up of the so-called Health Houses in rural areas to distribute and promote contraceptives. Later on, demand-side factors too were introduced which offered incentives to limit family size. For instance, starting in the early 1990s, official child benefits were limited to three children per household only.

Such was the extent of the population policy reversal – and arguably its success – that by the early 1990s Iran had managed to resume her stalled demographic transition with a vengeance and was now established at the forefront of demographic transition in the MENA region (Hakimian, 2006).

As we saw, Figure 2.6 showed that over three decades, the population growth rate first rose sharply and then fell back (suggesting a 'hump' shape). As mentioned before, the average annual population growth rate climbed to nearly four per cent in the intercensal period 1976–86, followed by a steep fall in the 1990s. The fall was especially pronounced in the second half of the 1986–96 period, with the annualized growth rate dropping to just 1.47 per cent in the five-year period 1991–6.

Figure 2.7 sheds more light on Iran's experience of 'fertility boom and bust' in the span of the three decades between the mid-1960s and mid-1990s. It shows annual percentage changes in the number of young Iranian children below the age of five between 1967 and 1996. This too confirms a rapid surge in fertility in the 1980s followed by a steep decline in the 1990s. It can be seen that a moderately declining trend of the early 1970s was suddenly reversed in 1978, when the annual growth rate of the number of young Iranians jumped to six per cent (it had been less than two per cent in much of the previous decade, before the Revolution). Thereafter, the population growth tempo stayed high until 1986 when a sudden and sharp fall put an end to the booming number of the young. Evidence of baby bust is particularly manifest in the sharp falls in the growth rates recorded in 1986 and 1987, but also sustained thereafter. As we have seen, dramatically reversing the baby boom of less than a decade earlier, the growth rate of this cohort of population has continued to fall sharply, edging close to minus six per cent per annum since 1992.

Another important factor in these years is Iran's changing interaction with the rest of the world. It was in the First Plan years that external savings began to supplement domestic resources. After years of pursuing isolationist policies and relative insulation from the international economy, now foreign capital (mostly bank loans) began to flow into Iran soon after the reconstruction programme got

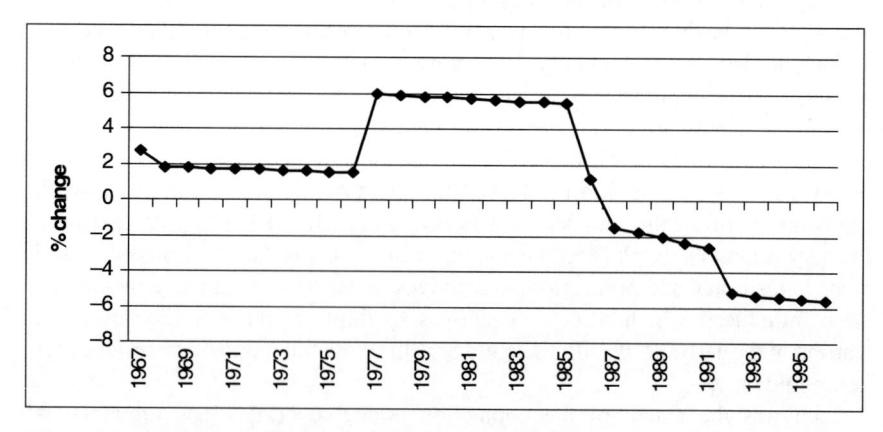

Figure 2.7 Annual % Change in Iran's Population of Children Aged 0–4 (1967–96)

Source: Hakimian (2006) based on census data by the Statistical Centre of Iran

under way. While foreign competition for lending to Iran was keen, the Iranian appetite for foreign loans to finance its post-war reconstruction drive was also significant. By 1992, however, it was already clear that short-term (mostly trade-related) debt had accumulated in an unsustainable manner and the country was in the throes of a big debt crisis. Although neither the volume ($23 billion in 1993) nor the relative size of external debt (reaching one-third of GDP at its peak in 1993) should have been of direct concern, its composition was and led to a full-blown external crisis. It was principally made up of short-term trade finance (debts of less than one-year's maturity averaged 80 per cent of the total during the entire First Plan period). Most importantly, the onset of the debt crisis revealed serious gaps in Iran's macroeconomic policy management and exposed the absence of cohesion in communication, monitoring and coordination of policy-making during this period of increasing exposure to the international economy (Farzin, 1995; Hakimian and Karshenas, 2000: 51–7).

Above all, perhaps, the debt crisis also exposed the high economic cost of Iran's isolationist stance. The inability of the country to raise long-term credit on international markets meant that much of the debt consisted of suppliers' credit, suggesting that short-term finance had been used on a large scale for medium- and long-term investment projects with longer gestation periods.

The government's abortive attempt at unification of the exchange rate system in March 1993 too was another example of failing reforms in these years. The timing and the manner of the unification attempt was indicative of implementation weaknesses rooted in administrative inconsistency and lack of cohesion and coordination that ultimately marred the results of the reforms (Farzin, 1995).

From crisis to reform (1994–2004)

The decade after the mid-1990s was characterized by a gradual – and non-linear – move towards restoring macroeconomic stability and introduction of limited reforms. First, the economy contracted sharply during the implementation of the Second Five-Year Plan (1994–9). In this phase, as mentioned above, much of the First Plan reforms were either aborted or reversed in response to the international debt crisis of 1993–4. Second, and after the introduction of the Third Plan (2000–4), Iran's economy witnessed the return of relative stability and the resumption of gradual reforms. These two phases were separated by a period of policy ambiguity and wavering, punctuated by a major collapse in the international price of oil in the late 1990s.

The austerity measures which had been introduced in 1994 to deal with the debt and balance of payments crises were swift, decisive and ultimately highly successful in restoring external equilibrium.[16] However, they retarded growth and their short-term impact was particularly harsh.[17] Consequently, real GDP growth plummeted to 0.5 per cent per annum in 1994, falling below the population growth rate (of 1.5 per cent) for the first time after the end of war. Overall, growth averaged just under three per cent in the five years to 1999, against the plan's

Table 2.2 Selective comparative economic indicators for the first, second and third plan years (1989–2004)   (Average annual figures)

	First plan (1989–93)	Second plan (1994–9)	Third plan (2000–04)
Real GDP growth (%)	7.5	2.8	5.4
Non-oil GDP (%)	7.2	3.7	5.8
Fixed Investment (% GDP 1997 prices)	29.4	26.7	33.6
Real private consumption (% change)	7.8	2.8	7.3
Inflation (urban CPI)	18.8	27.2	14.1
Liquidity (M2)	25.2	26.3	28.9
Oil Exports Revenues (million US$)	15,451	15,245	26,153.4
Non-Oil Exports Revenues (million US$)	2,348	3,540.7	5,645.8
Imports (fob, million US$)	19,905.8	13,703.7	24,290.2
Current Account Balance (million US$)	–4,006.2	3,368.0	5,401.8

Source: Central Bank of Iran.

Note: All figures refer to realized or actual outcomes during the three plans.

projected target of 5.1 per cent, and well below half that achieved during the First Plan (7.5 per cent; see Table 2.2).

These years also witnessed persistent inflationary pressures signalling the return of stagflation, which had adversely affected Iran for much of the 1980s. Inflation reached a peak of nearly 50 per cent in 1995, and its period average was about 30 per cent, well above the period average for the First Plan (itself a double digit at about 19 per cent).

The final years of the Second Plan saw renewed hopes for breaking out of the economic doldrums of the 1990s as a new reformist administration, led by Mr Khatami, took office. Despite its strong political mandate, however, two factors militated against the adoption of a decisive approach to economic reforms: the difficult combination of internal and external macroeconomic conditions it faced from the outset, and the high popular expectations that came with the wide electoral support base it enjoyed. The latter, in particular, led to an initial fuzzy period during which strong but vague populist overtures were punctuated by occasional bouts of pragmatist policies and overtones.[18]

It was not until the introduction of the Third Plan (2000–4), when the direction of government policy became clearer. Although the plan recognized the need for certain structural reforms (in areas such as trade, public finances, exchange rate and divestiture of public enterprises), its main focus was, however, to resume growth and macroeconomic stability. By this time, external conditions had also improved and the Plan's implementation was aided by the recovery of international oil prices after 1999–2000.

Table 2.2 shows comparative indicators of this plan against the previous two. It can be seen that a realized annual growth rate of 5.4 per cent was almost double that achieved in the Second Plan period (2.8 per cent). In addition, the Third Plan managed to dent the stagflationary trap of the previous period by resuscitating aggregate demand whilst moderating persistent inflationary pressures. Both total investment and private consumption expenditures rose again, and inflation rate was almost halved (falling to a period average of 14.1 per cent against 27.2 per cent previously).

Significantly, however, and after a long decade grappling with austerity and policy ambiguity, the Third Plan saw the early stages of a number of important structural reforms in the Iranian economy. One of the earliest reforms involved the setting up of an Oil Stabilization Fund (OSF), which aimed to cushion the impact of fluctuations in oil prices on government expenditure. This reform had been necessitated by endemic fluctuations in government oil income in the past, and especially the oil price collapse of the late 1990s, which had reinforced the need to reduce the dependency of public finances on oil revenues.

The setting up of the OSF was accompanied by further budgetary reforms in 2002 to make transparent the exchange rate subsidies, and from 2003 also the energy subsidy, which amounted to ten per cent of GDP. Until 2002, most government subsidies were provided implicitly through the subsidized exchange rate. These covered a wide range of essential household commodities (such as wheat, rice, oil, sugar, milk, and cheese) as well as imports of medical equipment and pharmaceuticals, fertilizers and debt service payments on publicly-guaranteed debt. Although the government had gradually tried to reduce explicit subsidies on food, they still amounted to substantial sums and constituted about 4 per cent of GDP in 2003–4.

In March 2002, following far more favourable external circumstance than the last unification in the early 1990s, the exchange rate was unified, leading to the elimination of most foreign exchange restrictions for current account purposes. This unification enabled the government to make food and energy subsidies explicit in its budget.

A spate of other reforms too were introduced during these years. Regarding the external accounts, for instance, steps were taken to liberalize trade: the tariff structure was rationalized and non-tariff barriers were replaced with tariffs during 2000–4. Most export restrictions were eliminated too and a new legal framework for the promotion of foreign direct investment (FDI) was approved in 2002 after a long and drawn-out judicial process.

A number of financial reforms were introduced to encourage savings, too. For instance, more flexibility was allowed in setting the rates of return for both deposits and lending and several private banks were licensed to operate. 'Participation papers' ('oragh-e mosharekat' or saving bonds) were introduced to finance government projects in a non-inflationary way and to mop up excess liquidity from the market. Iran also adopted a number of important fiscal reforms in these years, including the tax reforms of 2002–3, which reduced both personal and corporate tax rates (the latter were reduced from a high of 68 per cent to a single rate of 25 per cent).

Although taking a few modest steps in the direction of reform, the Third Plan's main success was in restoring macroeconomic balance and regenerating growth.

It was far less successful in achieving its more strategic goals in areas such as reducing unemployment, encouraging foreign investment, achieving large-scale privatization and reducing reliance on oil exports.

Overall, therefore, the success of this Plan came against a background of increased openness to international trade and widening economic reforms, but it also benefited from improved oil prices and sustained fiscal stimulus. Despite these, by the end of the plan in 2004, official unemployment was still as high as 11.2 per cent (against 13.4 per cent at the start); foreign investment was largely absent from the Iranian economy and the reform of ailing State-Owned Enterprises (SOEs) had hardly begun.

Structural constraints and institutional impediments to growth

The above discussion of policy challenges and responses in Iran since 1979 has highlighted a number of structural and institutional features that have affected the performance of the Iranian economy since the Revolution. First and foremost, although Iran has a longer history of industrial development and capital accumulation compared to most other MENA countries, its economic structure still continues to be dominated by oil. As we shall see below, reliance on oil has arguably increased during the period under consideration and continues to influence resource allocation at a macroeconomic level.

Second, prospects for growth are also constrained in Iran by the institutional setting in which government policies have been formulated and implemented in these decades. We now turn to a discussion of both structural and institutional issues below.

Oil dependency

The importance of oil in Iran's economy is clearly reflected in the dominance of oil exports in both the balance of payments and the government's fiscal revenues. Despite the varied internal and external conditions facing the first three Plans discussed above (1989–2004), the share of oil exports in total exports has been consistently high at about 80–5 per cent. Only during oil price crashes (such as in 1998) did this share drop (still no less than about 75 per cent). Similarly, oil revenues have amounted to more than half all government revenues in this period.

Although non-oil exports have risen in recent years (by 250 per cent between the First and Third Plans), there are as yet few signs of real economic diversification away from the oil sector. This is in sharp contrast to the experience of other countries in the MENA region. For instance, Turkey and Tunisia have managed to raise their shares of manufactured exports in total exports to as high as three-quarters. Egypt and Morocco too have much higher comparable shares (over one-third) in contrast to Iran's only nine per cent in the late 1990s.

A lack of sufficient diversification and continued high oil dependency are indeed at the heart of Iran's long-term economic problems. Figure 2.8 underscores the interlinked cycles of oil exports income and real GDP in Iran suggesting a close fit between the two.

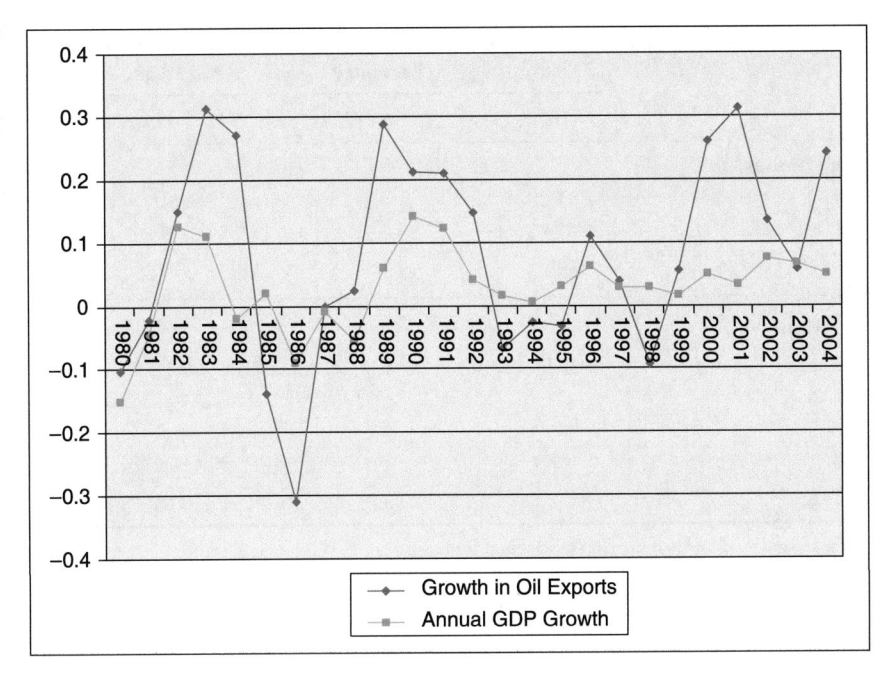

Figure 2.8 Cycles of Economic Growth and Oil Exports Income in Iran: 1980–2004

Source: based on data from the Central Bank of Iran.

Note: oil exports are measured in current US$, three-year moving averages.

This is further supported by a more detailed examination of the nature of economic cycles in Iran and their correlation with the oil boom and bust periods. Table 2.3 shows a strong relationship between changes in Iran's oil exports earnings and her real GDP growth rates during both boom and bust phases since the late 1970s. It can be seen that there is a very strong association between these two variables, both on the up and down phases of the growth cycle. For instance, the strongest relative recovery in economic activity after the Revolution (during the two-year period 1982–3) was helped by a strong recovery in oil revenues (exceeding 51 per cent on an average annual basis). Similar growth revivals occurred during 1989–91 (the initial stages of the First Plan), 1996, and again in 2000–4 (during the Third Plan). In these instances, too, it is clear that buoyant oil revenues have aided recovery.

Strong negative associations too can be observed on the downswing, when contracting oil incomes have been closely associated with declining economic activity. Prominent examples of these are:

1. the early days of the Revolution and the outbreak of war (1978–81);
2. the OPEC crisis of the mid-1980s (1984–6);
3. the last year of war with Iraq (1988);

Table 2.3 Boom and bust cycles (% change in GDP & Oil revenues)

	% change GDP	% change Non-oil GDP	% change Oil revenues
Boom phases:			
1982–3	11.8	8.2	51.2
1989–91	10.7	10.2	21.0
1996	6.1	7.1	27.6
2000–04	5.5	5.8	18.8
Bust phases:			
1978–81	–7.8	–0.9	–9.9
1984–6	–3.1	–1.7	–31.1
1988	–5.5	–7.8	–10.1
1994	0.5	1.8	1.9
1997–8	2.8	3.6	–27.8

Source: based on data from the Central Bank of Iran.

4.   the austerity package associated with the debt crisis (1994); and finally,
5.   the oil price slump of 1997–8 and the subsequent recession in 1998.

There is thus little doubt that there has been a strong long-term relationship between oil export revenues and economic growth in both pre- and post-revolutionary periods. However, and perhaps contrary to most expectations, evidence also suggests that oil dependency has increased during the years of the Islamic Republic. Table 2.4 puts oil dependency in a broader perspective, showing simple and partial correlation coefficients calculated for annual percentage changes in oil exports income and real GDP over sub-periods since the early 1960s. Remarkably, oil dependency appears to have risen during the post-revolutionary periods. In fact the correlation coefficient for the period after 1979 is twice that for the period before (+0.62 against +0.31). Although the peak – meaning the strongest positive correlation – was achieved in the heyday of the 1970s' oil boom (with a coefficient of +0.77), most sub-periods after 1979 have exhibited a higher coefficient than the long-term trend coefficient of +0.53 for the entire period (1961–2004).

It is perhaps ironic that oil dependency has increased overall during the relatively more insular periods after 1979 despite more emphasis being placed on achieving self-sufficiency and economic independence, as discussed above. The root cause of this phenomenon is lack of economic diversification and weaknesses in the competitiveness of the non-oil sector in Iran, which cannot be remedied without deep-rooted policy reforms.

The one notable exception in recent years is the Third Plan period (2000–4) when, on the contrary and for the first time, a strong negative correlation (–0.88) can be perceived. As discussed in the last section, this is the period during which

Table 2.4 Real annual GDP and oil income growth rates: correlation coefficients, by sub-periods, 1961–2004

	Correlation coefficient	
Before the Revolution		
1973–7	+0.77	The 1970s' oil-boom years
1961–78	**+0.31**	**The Shah's years**
After the Revolution		
1980–8	+0.64	War years
1989–93	+0.61	First Plan
1994–9	+0.50	Second Plan
2000–04	−0.88	Third Plan
1979–2004	**+0.62**	**All IR Years**
1961–2004	**+0.53**	**Entire period**

Source: calculated from data from Central Bank of Iran.

Note: oil exports are measured in current US$, three year moving averages.

an Oil Stabilization Fund was set up to soften the impact of oil price fluctuations on government revenue. It would thus appear that setting up the OSF did contribute, at least in this short period, to a partial de-linking of Iran's growth and oil exports earnings for the first time.

Policy ambiguity and its impact on growth

The foregoing discussion has focused on structural weaknesses in Iran's economy as manifested in a persistent and increased state of oil dependency. This feature has been exacerbated by inadequate, ambivalent or contradictory policy responses during the different sub-periods after 1979 (which were examined above). Despite its renowned mineral riches, therefore, Iran has continued to exhibit severe economic fragility characterized by an uncertain investment climate, fragile public finances and an inward-orientated economy for much of the last two and a half decades discussed here.

The root cause of these weaknesses can be perceived at two inter-related levels, both of which impinge on the institutional setting in which economic development has taken place in the period under study. These are: the post-revolutionary legal framework and policy formulation and implementation. These are discussed below.

The legal framework

There is little doubt that both the public discourse and the conduct of economic policy in Iran have been heavily shaped and influenced by the legal framework that has emerged after the Revolution. Iran's constitution is in fact different from Western constitutions in its direct interest in economic issues and the attention it pays to defining economic aspects of the post-revolutionary society (Abrahamian, 1993: 33–6).[19] Although respecting private property, the notion of ownership embedded in the constitution has, for instance, set the boundaries between the private and public sectors and has constrained in the main the former's role in the economy.

Most prominently, perhaps, Article 44 assigns ownership of all large-scale and 'mother industries' to the state sector consigning, by contrast, the private sector a role that is to 'supplement' the economic activities of 'the state and cooperative sectors'. This vision was formulated in the 1970s when state ownership of industries was widely acceptable and popular. Despite much public debate in the 1980s and 1990s, only in 2004 was this clause revisited to take account of Iran's present fiscal realities as well as the economic performance of the loss-making State-owned Enterprises (SOEs). Meanwhile, the continued ambivalence towards the private sector tainted discussions of reforms in general, and privatization, in particular.

Such ambivalence is also reflected towards foreign ownership and involvement in the Iranian economy. Deep-rooted in Iran's economic history and going back to the popular backlashes against the exploitative concessions granted by the monarchs in the late nineteenth century, the Iranian legislature has, ever since the Constitutional Revolution in the early twentieth century, felt obliged to keep a watchful eye on the extent of foreign involvement in Iran. This is evident from the current constitution which goes into some detail to spell out the limits to foreign involvement; several of its provisions either severely curtail, or directly ban, foreign ownership or interference in any sphere of the economy.

For instance, Article 81 prohibits the establishment of foreign companies or organizations in most key sectors of commerce, industry, agriculture, mining and services. Article 82 forbids the employment of 'foreign experts except in cases of necessity' and only then subject to parliamentary approval. Likewise, Article 83 prohibits the transfer of property to foreigners without such approval. And last, but not least, Article 153 prohibits the conclusion of agreements that would result in foreign control of natural resources, economic resources, military affairs, culture, as well as 'other aspects of the national life.'[20]

Law-making has also been complicated by the legislative process, which requires all approved parliamentary bills to be vetted by another clerical body – The Guardian Council – for their compliance with Islamic principles. Since this body can (and frequently does) reject legislation approved by the parliament, a third high-level body – The Expediency Council – was created to adjudicate between them. The result, as we shall see below (in the context of legislation for the protection and promotion of foreign investment), is a complex labyrinth of decision-making amenable to intense internal strife and factional politics with predictably adverse consequences for economic growth.

Policy formulation and implementation

As we have seen, official policy in Iran has evolved in an ambiguous and contradictory manner punctuated by recurrent cycles of populism and reform. For most of the time after 1979, Iran was ideologically set on an isolationist path which stressed self-sufficiency and shunned foreign investment. Partial attempts under the First Plan to encourage greater international integration ran into deep problems. For instance, the unification of the exchange rate system in 1993 failed due to bad timing, poor design and weak implementation. Moreover, the international debt crisis, unleashed by the imports spree after the war, led to greater austerity for much of the 1990s. Both these events helped set the clock back in terms of redefining Iran's role and place in the international market place. Following several years of hesitancy and wavering, the Third Plan finally seemed to begin to address some of the pressing reforms. By 2000, attention was being given – albeit in a modest way – to increasing the role of the private sector, reducing obstacles to foreign and domestic invest-ment, initiating privatization, supporting export-led growth and developing the non-oil sectors.

The outcome, as we have seen, was encouraging, at least judged by short-term macroeconomic indicators. Realized growth rate almost doubled over the previous plan period (Table 2.2). External accounts improved significantly aided partly by favourable oil prices after 2000. The current account, trade balance and external debt obligations all stabilized and foreign exchange reserves strengthened substantially (IMF, 2003 and 2004). Of more long-term significance, perhaps, non-oil exports, which had dipped after 1997, climbed back, achieving on average 14 per cent year-on-year growth in the period 2000–4. Inflation moderated at about 15 per cent. However, unemployment continued to be stubbornly high at a double digit figure of over 11 per cent.

Such short-term improvements should not mask the environment of institutional ambiguity which continued to adversely affect economic performance, inhibiting Iran from achieving its greater economic potential (see comparative growth data presented above). Indeed, some of the toughest structural changes that could transform the competitiveness of the economy were postponed both in domestic and external economic spheres.

This has led some observers to characterize Iran's failure to achieve structural transformations since 1980 as a state of 'structural trap'. This is defined as the situation 'in which political and economic obstacles avert the reallocation of capital from low productivity firms and sectors to high productivity ones' (Alizadeh, 2003). Accordingly, Iran's economy remains dominated by inefficient, subsidized and loss-making SOEs, as well as by unregulated and opaque parastatal organizations ('*bonyads*' or religious foundations), which operate as conglomerates receiving substantial implicit and explicit government subsidies. Ironically, perhaps, these foundations also highlight one of the most notable contradictions of Iran's post-revolutionary populism: despite the veneer of religious probity, they have enabled a new elite to emerge, which accumulates wealth through opaque and unaccountable means.

But policy outcomes depend only partially on the choice of policies adopted. Policy implementation too has an important bearing on economic performance, and in both these respects (policy choice and implementation) Iran's experience has been marred by the institutional setting after the Revolution. Key in this context has been the emergent legal framework discussed above, and intensified political strife in recent years.

During the Third Plan, for instance, fractured internal politics and factionalism spilled over into several key areas, leading at times to gridlock in decision-making. Perhaps most notable was the struggles over the Foreign Investment Law, which became the cause of intense wrangling between the (reformist) legislature backing a major overhaul of the anachronistic 1955 Law and the conservative Guardian Council, which opposed it in many ways. The law was finally approved in 2002, following intense debates impinging on fundamental aspects of Iran's place in the global economic system.[21] Unsurprisingly, despite this important step for stimulating foreign investment, persistent uncertainty continued to mar foreign investment flows and Iran's ability to attract FDI remained notably weak: average annual FDI inflows amounted to $326 million only in the period 2000–4, less than three per cent of all FDI inflows into the MENA region at large. This is in sharp contrast with Turkey, for instance, which has a similar population size but succeeded in attracting six-fold the volume of FDI of Iran ($2 billion) in the same period.

In other key areas, too, the adoption and implementation of reforms were impeded by the institutional setting in which they were introduced. For instance, the divestiture of SOEs was a major objective of the Third Plan. Although the required legislative and regulatory environments were put in place during the plan years, the actual pace of privatization proved to be very slow. Given that SOEs are politicized institutions in which both workers and managers strive to prolong subsidies and perpetuate their redistributive function (Alizadeh, 2003), privatization remained largely limited to the sales of government equity shares to private investors and *bonyads*, with the majority control still retained by the government.

Another area of reform with modest outcomes was the setting up of the Oil Stabilization Fund (OSF) in 2000 (see above). This was ostensibly to allow the government to manage its finances more independently of fluctuations in oil prices. This was clearly a step in the right direction as in practice favourable oil prices have allowed the government to divert its excess revenues from the oil windfalls for purposes other than short-term budgetary needs (such as drawing down foreign debt). The OSF fund is nevertheless different from long-term development funds (such as in Kuwait), which are set up explicitly as a source of savings 'for future generations'.

Withdrawals from the OSF are unsurprisingly controversial, if not politically charged, in Iran. This can come about in two ways: indirectly, by the projected oil prices built into the budget (oil allocations to the OSF are a residual saving after budgetary allocations have been made); and more directly through withdrawals for 'special purposes'. Given that this requires parliamentary approval, such negotiations can become effectively a source of factional fighting between the executive and the legislative branches of the government.[22]

Summary and conclusions

Nearly three decades after the Revolution, the structural features of the Iranian economy remained remarkably unchanged: a state of severe oil-dependency continued; the general investment climate was weak and beset by uncertainty; public finances were fragile; and the economy continued to be inward-looking and unsure of its position in the wider international economy.

During this period, the economy leapfrogged through cycles of populism and pragmatism, with macroeconomic performance reflecting inevitably some of the internal tensions as well as external dislocations experienced due to isolationism and the vicissitudes of the international oil markets.

Internationally, Iranians witnessed considerable retrogression in their living standards measured in GDP per capita terms and compared with other countries with similar or even lower initial conditions at the end of the 1970s. The domestic economic setting too was marked by an uneven, and generally disappointing, set of economic fundamentals over the three sub-periods studied in this chapter. The chapter has highlighted Iran's macroeconomic challenges, the broad policies adopted by the government in response to different external and internal conditions and the general economic track record since the fall of the Shah to the last year of Mr Khatami's Presidency (2004).

We have seen that debates over the nature and direction of economic policy in Iran intensified – rather than subsided – in those years. We have also seen how, during three ostensibly different phases, Iranian policy makers confronted specific challenges in each period: from external war to reconstruction and reform; from foreign debt and currency crises to austerity and consolidation of the economy during peace time, followed by the modest structural reforms introduced under the Third Plan (2000–4). After the demise of the reformists in 2005, there has been a resurgence of populism, a period which is addressed in the following chapter.

While differences have been substantial and this chapter has highlighted many, they should not mask the constancy of the challenge faced by the Islamic Republic since its inception: the need for achieving clarity and consistency over the very direction of economic policy and the system that has been shaping up in Iran since 1979. It is clear that persistent cycles of slow growth and high inflation in the Iranian economy cannot be resolved without contemplating more fundamental institutional changes and a reform of the system of governance.

But whether and when these challenges can be successfully met will depend only partially on the design and adoption of appropriate economic policies, important though these are. The experience of economic reforms in Iran, both under the First and the Third Plans (when there were bouts of growth), points strongly to the need for an equally far-reaching and comprehensive package of political and institutional reforms. Delaying these reforms can only add to the eventual costs and pains of future adjustments.

Notes

* An earlier version of this chapter was published as a working paper for the *Commission on Growth and Development* (see Hakimian, 2008). I am grateful to the Commission for permission to include it in this volume. I am also grateful to the Commission's Chairman, Mike Spence, and others in particular, Gary Becker, Mustapha Nabli, Homi Kharas, and Anton Dobronogov for their comments and suggestions on earlier drafts. The views expressed here as well as any errors or omissions are my sole responsibility and not of any other individuals' or institutions'.

1 For a broad discussion and analysis of Iran's economy in this period, see: Hakimian and Karshenas (2000), Pesaran (2000), Behdad (2000), Mazarei (1996), Hakimian (1999), and Salehi Esfahani (2002).

2 Its industrial drive was, however, oriented towards the domestic markets unlike in Korea and Japan where it was export driven (Alizadeh, 2000: 18).

3 The Shah was restored to power in 1953 through a CIA-engineered coup that overthrew Iran's elected Prime Minister – Mr Mossadegh – following his nationalization of the oil industry (Kinzer, 2003 and Abrahamian, 2013 provide an account of this well-known external interference in Iran's affairs).

4 Accordingly, 'as wealth poured into some urban sectors, . . . its transparent lack in others . . . visibly heightened growing social contrasts and a deepening image of social stratification.' (Hakimian, 1988: 29)

5 According to Abrahamian (1993), characterizations of the Islamic regime as 'fanatical' and 'fundamentalist' have contributed to such obfuscation of its populist characteristics.

6 In Cuba, Nicaragua and Brazil, the minimum voting age is 16. Elsewhere, it is almost universally 18. In 2007, minimum voting age was raised back to 18 in Iran.

7 The turnout in Iran's presidential election in 2005 was 63 per cent (first round) and 60 per cent (second round). In the 1997 and 2001 elections, these were 80 per cent and 66 per cent, respectively.

8 This body consists of six clergymen appointed by the Supreme Leader and six laymen selected by the head of the judiciary chief. The latter are subject to parliamentary approval.

9 The Iranian Constitution permits the establishment of political parties and professional syndicates as long as 'they conform to the Islamic basis of the Republic'. In the 2005 presidential elections, about one thousand candidates were disqualified by the Guardian Council, only eight were approved of whom seven stood for elections. Similarly, of the 814 candidates who declared their intention to run in the 2001 presidential election, only ten were approved by this body.

10 Acemoglu and Robison predict that pressure for democratization is more likely to arise in a situation of economic and political crisis. Relevant examples are: harvest failure, economic depressions, international financial or debt crises, and wars (2006: 30–31 and 65).

11 World Bank Development Indicators data (2006). The latter figure (5.3 per cent) for the LMCs should, however, be treated with caution as: (a) it refers to an ex-post country classification consisting of 58 countries deemed to fall in this category as of July 2006; and (b) it embraces a heterogeneous and diverse set of countries (for the former Soviet Republics, for instance, data stretches back to the early 1990s only).

12 For a discussion and overview of the phenomenon commonly referred to as the Middle Eastern 'demographic puzzle', see Omran and Roudi (1993).

13 See Lautenschlager (1986); Behdad (1988); Pesaran (1992); and Karshenas and Pesaran (1995) for a discussion of the foreign exchange regime in Iran in these years.

14 For a more in-depth discussion of Iran's population issues after the revolution, see Aghajanian (1991) and Hakimian (2000 and 2006).

15 The rise in oil revenues was partly due to price increases in the wake of Iraq's invasion of Kuwait and partly due to the expansion of output. Crude oil exports increased by 43 per cent between 1988 and 1990, and by another 28 per cent between 1990 and 1993, as production and export facilities damaged during the war were gradually restored.

16 This was done primarily through a strict import compression regime. Imports were slashed by one-third in 1994 alone, and overall the Second Plan's average annual imports bill was about a third lower than that for the First Plan ($13.7 billion against $19.9 billion; Table 2.2). Total foreign debt was thus successfully re-negotiated and by the end of 1997 slashed down to about half its peak in 1993.

17 Import compression, in particular, exacerbated macro inefficiency as it worsened the problem of low capacity utilization in industrial units by restricting their access to imported intermediate products and capital goods, in turn, accentuating the low growth cycle.

18 This was, for instance, evident in the period 1997–9, when ideals of social justice and 'sustainable development' were stressed alongside those of economic and managerial efficiency (see Hakimian, 2006, for details).

19 The constitution, for instance, 'promises to make Iran fully independent, pay off external loans, cancel foreign concessions, nationalize foreign companies . . . balance the government budget and encourage "home ownership" ' (Abrahamian, 1993: 36).

20 See details of '*Constitution of the Islamic Republic of Iran*, 24 October 1979'; and its amendment on 28 July 1989, http://www.servat.unibe.ch/icl/ir00000_.html (accessed on 27 July 2012)

21 At the heart of these were: the definition of 'foreign investor' (and whether it included Iranian expatriates); ownership of immovable property by foreigners; the ratio of foreign ownership, as well as areas permissible for foreign investment (Hakimian, 2003; Pesaran, 2011).

22 According to the IMF data, about 70 per cent of the average annual oil revenues accrued to the OSF account was withdrawn for further government financing during the period 2002–6.

References

Abrahamian, E., *Khomeinism: Essays on the Islamic Republic*. Berkeley: University of California Press, 1993.

Abrahamian, E., *The Coup – 1953, The CIA, and Roots of Modern U.S.-Iranian Relations*, New York: The New Press, 2013.

Acemoglu D. and Robinson J. A., *Economic Origins of Democracy and Dictatorship*, Cambridge and New York: Cambridge University Press, 2006.

Aghajanian, A., 'Population change in Iran, 1976–86: a stalled demographic transition?', *Population and Development Review*, 17: 703–15, 1991.

Alizadeh, P. ed., *The Economy of Iran: Dilemmas of an Islamic State,* London: I.B. Tauris, 2000.

Alizadeh, P., 'Iran's quandary: economic reforms and the "structural trap"', *The Brown Journal of World Affairs*, ix. 2003.

Behdad, S., 'Foreign exchange gap, structural constraints, and the political economy of exchange rate determination in Iran', *International Journal of Middle East Studies*, 20 (1): 121, 1988.

Behdad S., 'The post-revolutionary economic crisis' in Rahnema S. and Behdad, S., eds, *Iran after the Revolution: Crisis of an Islamic State*, London: I.B. Tauris, 1996.

The Central Bank of Iran (Bank Markazi Iran), *Annual Report and Balance Sheet*, and *Economic Trends*, various issues, Tehran.

Dornbusch, R. and Edwards, S., *The Macroeconomics of Populism in Latin America*, Chicago and London: The University of Chicago Press, 1991.

Esfahani, S. H., *The political economy of growth in Iran, 1963–2002*, mimeo, Urbana: University of Illinois, 2002.

Farzin, Y.H., 'Foreign exchange reform in Iran: badly designed, badly managed', *World Development*, 23: 987–1001, 1995.

Graham, R., *Iran: The Illusion of Power*, London: Croom Helm, 1978.

Hakimian, H. 'Industrialisation and the standard of living of the working class in Iran', 1960–79, *Development and Change*, 19 (1): 3–32, 1988.

Hakimian, H., *Labour Transfer and Economic Development: Case Studies from Iran*, Harvester Wheatsheaf: Hemel Hempstead (UK) and Lynne Rienner: Boulder, CO, USA, 1990.

Hakimian, H., 'Population dynamics in post-revolutionary Iran: a re-examination of evidence', in Alizadeh ed., 2000.

Hakimian, H., 'The economy and foreign investment in Iran', Tokyo: The Japanese Institute of Middle Eastern Studies (JIME), *mimeo*, April, 2003.

Hakimian, H., 'From demographic transition to fertility boom and bust: Iran in the 1980s and 1990s', *Development and Change*, 37 (3): 571–97, 2006.

Hakimian, H., 'Institutional change, policy challenges and macroeconomic performance: case study of Iran (1979–2004)'; Washington: The International Bank for Reconstruction and Development/ The World Bank on behalf of the Commission on Growth and Development, Working Paper No. 26, 2008.

Hakimian H. and M. Karshenas, 'Dilemmas and prospects for economic reform and reconstruction in Iran', in Alizadeh, ed., 2000.

International Monetary Fund, 'Islamic Republic of Iran: 2003 Article IV Consultations', IMF Country Report, No 03/279, September, Washington DC, 2003.

International Monetary Fund, 'Islamic Republic of Iran—Selected Issues', Country Report No. 04/308, August, Washington DC, 2004.

Karshenas, M., *Oil, State and Industrialization in Iran*, Cambridge and New York: Cambridge University Press, 1990.

Karshenas, M. and Hakimian, H., 'Oil, economic diversification and the democratic process in Iran', *Iranian Studies*, 38 (1): 67–90, 2005.

Karshenas, M. and Pesaran, M.H., 'Economic reform and reconstruction of the Iranian economy', *Middle East Journal*, 49: 89–111, 1995.

Kinzer, S., *All The Shah's Men: An American Coup and the Roots of Middle East Terror*, Hoboken, N.J.: John Wiley & Sons, Inc, 2003.

Lautenschlager, W., 'The effects of an over-valued exchange rate on the Iranian economy, 1979–1984', *International Journal of Middle East Studies*, 18: 31–52, 1986.

Maddison, A., Statistics on World Population, GDP and Per Capita GDP, 1–2008 AD., 2010, http://www.ggdc.net/MADDISON/oriindex.htm (accessed 27 July 2012).

Mazarei, A., 'The Iranian economy under the Islamic republic: institutional change and macroeconomic performance (1979–1990)', *Cambridge Journal of Economics*, 20: 289–314, 1996.

Nili, M., '*Tahlil-e Amal-Kard-e Siasathay-e Ta'dil-e Eqtesadi* (An Applied Analysis of the Economic Liberalization Policy)' in Nili, M. ed., *Eqtesad-e Iran (The Iranian Economy)*, Tehran: Institute for Research in Planning and Development: 357–444, 1997.

Omran, A.R. and Roudi, F., 'The Middle East population puzzle', *Population Bulletin*, 48 (1): 1–40, 1993.

Pesaran, E., *Iran's Struggle for Economic Independence: Reform and Counter-Reform in the Post-Revolutionary Period,* London and New York: Routledge, 2011.

Pesaran, M. H., 'The Iranian foreign exchange policy and the black market for dollars', *International Journal of Middle East Studies,* 24: 101–25, 1992.

Rahnema, S. and Behdad, S., eds, *Iran after the Revolution: Crisis of an Islamic State,* London: I.B. Tauris, 1996.

The Statistical Centre of Iran, census publications for 1966, 1976, 1986 and 1996, Tehran.

UNCTAD, Foreign Direct Investment (FDI) online data.

World Bank, *World Development Indicators.* CD ROM, Washington, DC.

World Bank, 'Iran: medium term framework for transition – converting oil wealth to development', Report No. 25848-IRN, A Country Economic Memorandum, Social and Economic Development Group, Washington, April, 2003.

3 The political economy of petro populism and reform, 1997–2011

Parvin Alizadeh

Introduction

This chapter examines Iran's divergent economic performance during the cycle of reform and populism in the period 1997 to 2011. In the first phase of this period, which corresponds to Mr Khatami's Presidency (1997–2005), Iran witnessed a sustained drive for economic reform. This, however, gave way to strong populist policies and tendencies after 2005, when Mr Ahmadi-Nejad took office. This study provides a broad analysis of comparative economic performance over these two sub-periods (1997–2005 and 2005–11), although our emphasis will be on the more recent or populist sub-period.

It is argued that the conceptual framework of 'petro populism' and 'mature' rentier state are intertwined in this period in Iran. The availability of external rent from the sale of oil enables the state to pursue redistributive policies as an important policy device to ensure the domestic legitimacy of the state or to create popular support for a particular faction of political elite against other factions. However, in spite of their redistributive objectives in favour of the poor, populist policies are inflationary and erode the purchasing power of the lower income groups. The Iranian experience with populist policies over the period 2005–11, which benefited from an unprecedented growth of oil income, is a clear example of the failure of populist policies to improve growth and prosperity. By contrast, higher rates of economic growth and lower rates of inflation characterized the period of reform over the period 1997–2005. Ironically, evidence suggests that the cycle of reform in Iran was more conducive to poverty reduction than that of populism.

In addressing economic performance in the context of political institutions of the state in these sub-periods, the chapter shows that the polycentric structure of governance and political institutions in post-revolutionary Iran is characterized partly by elected and partly by unelected bodies. Unelected bodies have veto power over elected institutions and are by and large extremely conservative in their interpretation of Islamic law. Moreover, the power and influence of unelected institutions have been rising continuously since the Revolution and particularly since 2005. This structure of governance has not been conducive to the creation of a vibrant private sector. Instead conservative political institutions have continuously undermined the institution of private property in favour of the organization of economic activity by parastatal organizations and the prolongation of government control. Hence, not surprisingly, large-scale privatization over the period of populist policies has not witnessed the creation of a strong private sector.

The unintended consequence of these policies has been prolonged inflation and low efficiency of investment in the economy with severe implications for long-term growth and prosperity of the population.

The structure of the chapter is as follows. I shall first present an analytical discussion of populist policies, petro populism and the rentier state in developing countries. The next section examines comparative economic performance over the period 1997–2011 with an emphasis on the populist period. This is followed by a political economy analysis of the Iranian state and its institutions. The last section offers some concluding thoughts.

Petro populism and the rentier state

Economic populism is broadly defined as strongly expansionist macroeconomic policies that focus on growth and redistribution and understate the risks of inflation and deficit finance (Dornbusch and Edwards, 1990; Sachs, 1989; Dornbusch and Edwards, 1991). A number of empirical studies show that expansionary policies in their early phase are fully vindicated, leading to high growth of output and real wages. However, strong expansion in demand for domestic goods leads to inflationary pressures while real wages keep up. Expansionary policies lead, after the early phase, to the worsening of the budget deficit resulting from pervasive subsidies to maintain high wages. This process soon leads to unsustainable budget deficit and hyperinflation. The government tries to stabilize the economy by cutting subsidies and by real depreciation. Ultimately real wages fall massively and government loses credibility over its economic policies. Populist policies are usually followed by IMF type stabilization policies and prolonged austerity measures, including massive wage cuts and rising unemployment, to restore internal and external balance. The unwelcome outcomes of populist policies are in contrast to their original objectives of raising the income of the lower social classes. Populist policies are known to fail and their failure is at significant cost to the very social groups who were supposed to be favoured (Dornbusch and Edwards, 1990).

Empirical studies of economic populism, which are mainly based on the experience of Latin American countries, point to the presence of high income inequality as an important precondition for implementation of expansionary macroeconomic policies. High income inequality contributes to intense political pressures to raise the incomes of lower income groups (Sachs, 1989).

Populist policies are usually preceded by the cycle of economic reforms and the implementation of austerity measures. Expansionary policies, for instance, might be a reaction to the slow pace of economic growth induced by the previous economic reforms.

More recent empirical studies, however, indicate that politicians in economies rich in natural resources use their resource revenues to secure or to generate political support. The concept of petro populism has been used to describe populist policies in oil-based economies (Parenti, 2005; Looney, 2007; Foroohar, 2009; Matsen *et al.*, 2012; and Acemoglu *et al.*, 2011). In this context, petro populism is closely intertwined with what can be labelled here as the second strand of the rentier state, which can be distinguished from the first strand associated with the social autonomy of the state.[1] Gray (2011) describes this second strand as a 'late rentier state'.

The conceptual frameworks of the rentier state were first established by Mahdavi (1970) in his influential work to describe the structural characteristics of the Iranian economy in the pre-revolutionary phase (Mahdavi, 1970; Karshenas and Moshaver, 2011). Rentier states receive a substantial amount of external rent, either from the sale of oil/minerals or rental paid by foreign governments and individuals for shipping passage and similar transactions on a regular basis. The rent is paid in foreign currency and provides the government with an independent source of income. This income 'enables the governments of the oil producing countries to embark on large public expenditure programmes without resorting to taxation' (Mahdavi, 1970: 432). The earlier studies of states in rich natural resource-based economies labelled here as the first strand of the rentier state emphasized the autonomy of the state from the society in countries where the external rent provided a substantial share of government revenue and foreign exchange (Mahdavi, 1970; Beblawi, 1987). These studies were concerned with the formation and evolution of the state in a relatively early phase of economic development in oil-exporting Middle Eastern countries.

In these studies the influence of the citizen over the state is assumed to be minimal provided the state allocates a minimum amount of wealth to domestic economy similar to what the economy in a wealthy rentier state would produce. This is well articulated by Gray in his reference to the earlier literature:

> the state also need not concern itself with domestic bases of support or legitimacy either: the population in effect is 'bought off', with democratic input sacrificed by society in exchange for a share of the rental wealth accruing to the state from abroad. Those who do not accept this 'rentier bargain' are subdued by the strong repressive apparatus affordable to the rentier state.
>
> (Gray, 2011: 6)

However with the development and evolution of the rentier state over time, alongside industrialization, growing urbanization, population growth and above all the threat of political descent and the Revolution – manifested in the popular Iranian Revolution of 1979 – a more nuanced approach to rentierism has evolved. As Kamrava (2011) has pointed out, regardless of the financial might of the rentier state there exists a mutual dependence between the state and its social beneficiaries:

> Even in cases where rent-reliant states enjoy tremendous wealth, rentier arrangements tend to place both the states and their social beneficiaries in positions of mutual dependence on one another, curbing the autonomy of both.
>
> (Kamrava, 2011: 6)

Hence rentierism also inhibits the autonomy of the state. In this context, petro populism and rentierism are closely interlocked. Redistributive policies are important in ensuring the domestic legitimacy of the state or in creating popular political support for a particular faction of the political elite in competition with other factions. Indeed there is a growing literature based on 'game theory rhetoric' showing how 'signalling' of populist policies attractive to the left of the median voters in resource rich economies may generate political competition with undesirable outcomes (Acemoglu *et al.*, 2011; Matsen, 2012).

Does this imply that countries endowed with natural resources are doomed to suffering from the 'natural resource curse'? Two accounts of this curse, namely operating through the 'Dutch Disease' and 'corruption' channels, have received considerable attention in the literature and are not our main focus here.[2] Nevertheless there are growing empirical studies that point to the diversity of experiences in countries endowed with natural resources. It is known that several resource-rich economies, such as Botswana, Canada, Australia and Norway, have been managing their resources more successfully in contrast to many other resource-based economies that have performed poorly despite their vast natural wealth (Van der Ploeg, 2011).

The diversity of experiences across countries endowed with natural resources has highlighted the very importance of governance, broadly defined as the form of the exercise of authority including the process through which political institutions are selected, held accountable and monitored (Kaufmann *et al.*, 2000). Fast-growing empirical studies of governance and institutions influenced by the work of North (1990) highlight the importance of political institutions. There has now emerged a general consensus that political institutions through which authority is exercised shape economic institutions which in turn are the main explanatory factors for the diversity of growth experiences across countries and over time (Knack and Keefer, 1995; Hall and Jones, 1999; Acemoglu *et al.*, 2004; Rodrik *et al.*, 2004). There is ample evidence that the disparities in per capita income across countries, even taking into account differences in physical and human capital, lie to a large extent in institutional differences across countries (Helpman, 2008).

From this perspective the institutions of private property and the rule of law have been considered as important determinants of economic growth (North and Weingast, 1989). The well-known historical reference is the impact of the Glorious Revolution in strengthening the institution of private property in England in 1688.

This reinforced the power of the parliament vis-a-vis the King, who used to have unrestricted power of expropriation of private property. The familiar contemporary example is the case of the Chinese economy after Deng Xiaoping's reforms after 1979. These reforms transformed China from an economy in which private property and market forces had minimal roles in managing economic activity to one in which these forces dominate the functioning of the economy (Tisdell, 2009).

Petro populism and reforms

Recurrent sequences of populism and reform have dominated government policies of the Islamic Republic since the Revolution in 1979 (see Hakimian in Chapter 2). Earlier waves of populism and reform over the period 1979–97 have been fully explored in several studies including those by Mazarei (1996), Behdad (2000), Pesaran (2000) Karshenas and Hakimian (2000) and Hakimian (Chapter 2 of this book). This phase is thus not the focus of our concern here, so only a brief discussion is offered below for clarification purposes.

This study is concerned with the second wave of reform and populism over the period 1997–2011. Broadly speaking, the period is divided into two sub-periods of 1997–2005 and 2006–11. The former corresponds to a period of reforms while the latter has witnessed a reinvigoration of populist policies fuelled and financed by a sharp increase in the price of oil. The expansionary macroeconomic policies of this period are in sharp contrast to the reformist policies of the earlier period. This section provides a broad comparative analysis, depicting contrasts in policy and macroeconomic performance between these two sub-periods. This section also includes a discussion of privatization over the 2006–11 period.

Before turning to an in-depth discussion of the second wave, a brief reference to the earlier cycle of populism and reforms over the period 1979–1997 is presented below.

The populist Revolution of 1979 and the war with Iraq (1980–8) strengthened the role of the state in the Iranian economy (Mazarei, 1996; Pesaran, 2000; Karshenas and Hakimian, 2000). There was large-scale nationalization of Iran's key modern industries and finance in 1980. This combined with the emergencies of an eight-year-long war, including the rationing of basic commodities and the introduction of a multiple exchange rate system, led to the development of a highly inflated, high cost, inefficient and financially unsustainable public sector. State-Owned Enterprises (SOEs) that were highly dependent on subsidies became a burden on government resources. Revolution and war also gave rise to the emergence of parastatal or quasi-public organizations, most notably Bonyads (charitable foundations) and the Islamic Revolutionary Guards Corp (IRGC).The former's function was to safeguard the redistribution of income to the poor and families of martyrs while the latter was to defend and protect the Revolution. Both had accumulated political credentials during the long years of war.[3] In addition to disruption caused by the Revolution and war, external shocks – including trade sanctions by the United States and the volatile and dwindling international crude oil prices in the mid-1980s – led to a sharp reduction in the growth of output, investment and GNP per capita, while stagflation prevailed (Pesaran, 2000). In order to rebuild the shattered economy after the war the reformist government of Mr Rafsanjani (1989–97) tried to introduce structural adjustment policies including deregulation of the labour market, unification of the exchange rate, privatization of SOEs and wage and price liberalization. The broad objective was to transform the redistributive, populist state of the 1980s into a rational state capitalism (Ehsani, 2009).[4] Rafsanjani's administration succeeded in reviving and activating the technocracy and bureaucracy of the pre-revolutionary period that had been sidelined after the Revolution. Though the technocracy revived the tradition of mapping out the economy in the form of five-year development plans, these reforms did not succeed due to lack of popular support from lower social strata, the state's ambiguity concerning the definition and boundaries of private property and Iran's isolationist stance in the international financial market (Behdad 2000; Pesaran, 2000; Karshenas and Moshaver, 2011; see also below on privatization).

Economic policies: the return of reforms and populism (1997–2011)

The second wave includes the reform period of 1997–2005 followed by the populist policies of 2006–11.

The most vigorous market-oriented reforms in the post-revolutionary period were implemented over the period 1997–2005. This period corresponds to the administration of President Khatami who won the election for two terms with the support of youth, women, intellectuals and the business community. His administration advocated political reforms including freedom of expression, rule of Law, dialogues of civilizations, and civil society, as well as market-oriented reforms including the encouragement of private and foreign investment. Although Khatami's main concern was political liberalization, his political reforms faced severe challenges and setback from the conservative factions of the political elite who blocked his political reforms. Nevertheless his administration instituted a host of market reforms, particularly during 2000–2005, which included exchange rate unification, the setting up of an Oil Stabilization Fund (OSF), trade reform, ratification of the law on foreign investment, tax reforms, and the licensing of four private banks. Pivotal to these reforms were exchange rate unification in 2002 and the OSF in 2000. Both reforms had a significant potential impact on improving the 'transparency' and 'accountability' of the state.

Multiple exchange rates (MER), introduced in 1980 to accommodate growing foreign exchange shortages during the war with Iraq, were at the heart of government's implicit subsidies to SOEs and revolutionary foundations for more than two decades. MER enabled the government to allocate foreign exchange resources in accordance with its political priorities (Farzin, 1996; Alizadeh, 2003). Imports were subject to different exchange rates depending on the type of imports and their users. By the mid-1980s, seven rates were in operation. Though the number of exchange rates was reduced to three by 2000, the official rate was three to four times below the market rates.

> The MER provided implicit foreign exchange subsidies to those groups who had privileged access to the official and preferential exchange rates. Importers of essential goods, public enterprises, and *Bonyads* (state-related foundations) were the main beneficiaries of MER.
>
> (Alizadeh, 2005: 120)

Exchange rate unification increased the fiscal transparency of the government budget and paved the way for reform in the subsidy system. Nevertheless, for the policy to succeed, the government assumed the entire cost of the exchange rate difference. The previously implicit foreign exchange subsidies associated with imports of basic consumer goods and capital goods were made explicit in the 2002–03 budget. On the downside, however, exchange rate unification imposed substantial fiscal costs, around three to six per cent of GDP (IMF, 2002a; IMF, 2002b).

Another important reform that intended to improve the financial accountability of the state was the establishment of the OSF in 2000. OSF was intended to protect the economy against the financial impact of oil price fluctuations. That is to safeguard 'fiscal discipline through decoupling public spending from oil price volatility so that planned levels of annual government expenditures would be maintained regardless of the behaviour of world oil prices' (Amuzegar, 2005).

This period also witnessed the licensing of four private investment institutions and banks although the scale of privatization and the contribution of the private sector remained limited.

This set of reforms – originally formulated by the World Bank and the IMF in the early 1980s – is considered the first generation of structural adjustment reforms (FGSAR). Reforms were focused on greater trade and exchange rate liberalization, more openness to foreign capital, and an overall shift toward the use of market mechanisms (Alizadeh, 2003). A logical sequence to these policies would have been the removal of explicit subsidies, trade liberalization, and promotion of private investment and also invigoration of political and social institutions to improve public accountability, transparency and efficiency of the governance structure.

Instead Mr Ahmadi-Nejad, who came to office in August 2005, won the presidential election on a platform of increased social services with the oft-cited campaign slogan of 'taking the oil money to people's table'. This slogan combined with Mr Ahmadi-Nejad's emphasis on the centrality of 'piety and simplicity' by the President and members of his cabinet were part and parcel of the political mobilization strategy and recurrent rhetoric to inspire the lower social strata of the population.[5] Mr Ahmadi-Nejad's economic populism combined with his conservative political agenda won the outright support of a coalition of conservative political forces and institutions that included parastatal organizations, the traditional clergy, lower economic classes and the supreme leader.

Farzanegan (2009), in his study of the populist macroeconomic policies of this period, has argued that the precondition for Mr Ahmadi-Nejad's first election victory was the rise in inequality during the previous administration. He refers to data by the Central Bank of Iran indicating a rise in the Gini coefficient for urban areas from 0.396 in 1998 to 0.415 in 2003. By contrast, Salehi-Isfahani, using household survey data measuring trends in poverty and income inequality in the post-revolutionary period, has argued that 'the evidence undermines the conventional wisdom that blames rising inequality for the populist backlash in the 2005 election' (Salehi-Isfahani, 2009: 23). He argues that although poverty has been reduced significantly in the post-revolutionary period inequality has been resilient to policy change. His data does not support the growth of inequality arising from the implementation of reforms during 1997–2005. 'Unlike poverty, inequality has been relatively constant in the post-revolutionary period, after its initial decline immediately after the Revolution. The Gini index of inequality in 2005 was about the same as it was in the early 1970s' (Salehi-Isfahani, 2009: 24). Isfahani further maintains that:

> estimates of the trends in poverty and inequality based on extensive survey data . . . question the importance of poverty and inequality as underlying factors in the rise of populism in Iran. . . . After increasing sharply during the war with Iraq, poverty has declined fairly continuously and is now considerably lower than it was before the Revolution. Furthermore, the sharpest reduction in poverty took place during the period of pro-market reforms under the Rafsanjani and Khatami administrations, thus undermining the thesis that resurgent populism in Iran is a reaction to these reforms.
>
> (Salehi-Isfahani, 2009: 24)

Nevertheless there is no doubt that Mr Ahmadi-Nejad's first term election campaign struck a chord with the lower income groups. However, what enabled the newly elected government to implement expansionary policies was the rapid growth of oil income (Figure 3.1). Annual oil income was in the range of 17 to 36.3 billion dollars during 1999–2005, increased to 62 billion dollars in 2006–7 and later on to 86.6 billion dollars by 2008–9. This was an unprecedented growth of the oil income arising not from the growth in the volume of the oil exports (that in turns requires high level of investment in the oil industry) but rather from the sharp increase in the price of oil (Figure 3.2).

The main transmission mechanisms for the implementation of expansionary populist policies were through the reduction of interest rate below the rate of inflation and provision of cheap credit to low income groups and religious organizations.[6] The stated intention for the implementation of populist policies was to facilitate entrepreneurial activities and self-employment as well as to improve the wellbeing of the poor through subsidization of marriage's expenditures for low income population.

The forced reduction of interest rates below the rate of inflation faced opposition from two governors of the Central Bank who later resigned (Forohhar, 2009).

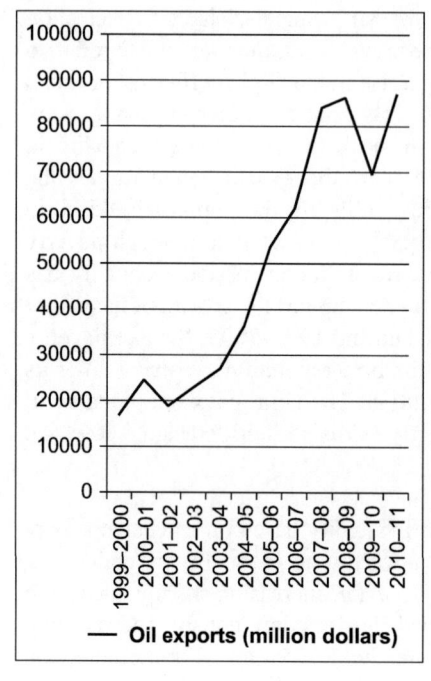

Figure 3.1 Oil Exports (Million Dollars)

Source: Bank Markazi Iran.

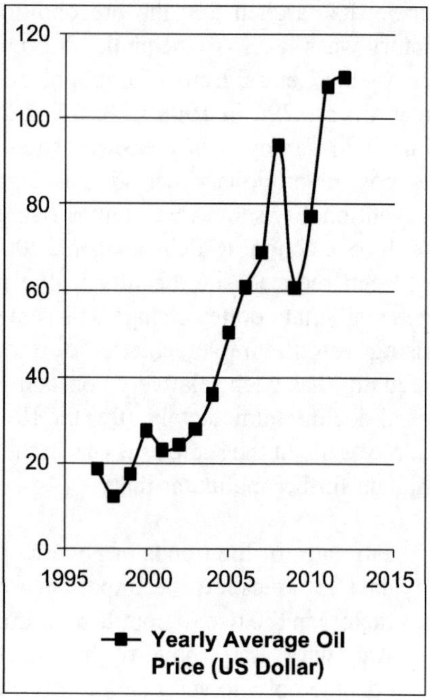

Figure 3.2 OPEC Oil Price (US Dollars/ Barrel)

Source: OPEC.

Furthermore by early 2006, one of the private banks faced severe financial difficulties as the imposed low rate of interest reduced banks' income. This bank floated a very significant section of its share in the Tehran Stock Exchange that was bought as a block by another SOE. In other words, the forced reduction of interest rates undermined the viability of the privatized bank that was then forced to sell a significant block of its shares to the government.

The populist policies were not welcomed by the Management and Planning Organization of Iran (MPO) either, a relatively independent public organization that had been fully responsible for preparing the country's budget and its medium and long-term development plans and policies since 1948. In 2007, MPO was dissolved after a direct order from the President. Subsequently, Mr Ahmadi-Nejad established a new budget planning body that was directly under his control.

Reform of subsidies was postponed until December 2010 when the Iranian Parliament passed the bill known as '*subsidy reform*' in response to the severe budget deficit that was crippling the government (IMF, 2011). The prolongation of subsidies was also accompanied by a substantial increase in energy subsidy as domestic prices were not adjusted to reflect rapid growth in international prices after 2005. Consequently, domestic energy consumption and energy intensity in

Iran increased sharply turning Iran into one of the most energy-intensive economies in the world (IMF, 2011).

Despite the unprecedented rise of oil income, the government faced a budget deficit arising from its over commitment to spending. Hence as early as 2007 it resorted to drawing from the Oil Stabilization Fund to finance its budget deficit.[7] Thus, the OSF, designed to moderate the impact of the oil price decline on the government's budget, became a major balancing influence on the government's budget during the booming oil prices and oil income.

The government, which had overwhelming support from conservative political institutions, including the conservative-dominated Parliament, implemented a raft of populist policies without difficulty, at least before the eruption of the economic crisis in 2010.

Another important component of populist policies was mass privatization known as the 'Justice Shares'. This is discussed later on.

An overview of economic performance (1997–2011)

A comparative analysis of macroeconomic performance over these two periods (1997–2005 and 2006–11) is not without pitfalls particularly since the sanctions against Iran have increased in intensity and scope since 2006 in response to its uranium enrichment programme. As Chapter 7 in this book shows, these restrictive economic measures have not been confined to the United States but have also included sanctions by the United Nations, the European Union as well as a raft of bilateral sanctions against Iran in recent years. Although the impact of these measures has been somewhat tempered by the emergence of Asia as a major trading partner for Iran, there is little doubt that the imposition of sanctions on the financial sector and trade embargo on Iranian oil exports have contributed to the deepening economic crisis since 2011.

A broad macroeconomic analysis of the two periods, based on data from the Central Bank of Iran is presented in Table 3.1. The growth figure for the period 2006–11 should be viewed with a significant degree of scepticism. As was mentioned earlier the management and operations of the Central Bank and the MPO were undermined significantly under the populist government of Mr Ahmadi-Nejad. These organizations, that were responsible for consolidation and presentation of national statistics, were reorganized to validate and support official government policy by depicting good economic performance and inflated growth figures. The prime objective has been to show the resilience of the economy in spite of the intensification of sanctions since 2006. It is worth mentioning that, in addition to significant delays in the public release of data by these organizations, the data from the Central Bank are often at odds with those from the Statistical Centre of Iran that operated under the auspices of the MPO.

However even allowing for or disregarding the possibly inflated nature of growth data for the second period, Table 3.1 indicates a higher growth rate of the economy and a better macroeconomic performance over the first period. Average annual growth of the GDP over the period 1997–2005 was 4.9 per cent compared

Table 3.1 Overall Economic Indicators

	1997–05	2000–05	2006–2011
Agriculture, hunting, forestry and fishing	3.1	2.1	5.1
Industries and Mines	8.8	10.1	6.9
Mining	7.4	9.6	8.7
Manufacturing	10.3	11.1	7.1
Electricity, Gas and Water Supply	7.1	7.4	5.5
Construction	5.3	7.4	6.7
Services	5.1	5.3	4.6
Gross Domestic Product	4.9	5.4	4.6
Consumer price Index	17.06	18.1	20.08
Gross fixed capital formation as % of GDP	31.7	33.3	38.5
Share of Machinary in GFCF	57.7	58.2	58
Share of Construction in GFCF	43.3	41.8	42

Source: Bank Markazi Iran.

with 4.6 per cent in the later period. The higher growth rate of the first period was also accompanied by lower rates of inflation even though the rate of inflation was quite high in the first period. The consumer price index (CPI) increased to 20.08 in the latter period compared with 17.1 per cent in the earlier one. Table 3.1 also includes data for the period 2000–5 that corresponds to the actual implementation of reforms in the first period. As was mentioned previously, the reformist administration over the earlier years of 1997–2000 was focusing on political reforms. Economic reforms were implemented over 2000–5. The average growth of GDP over this period was 5.4 per cent and considerably above the 4.6 per cent growth rate for 2006–11.

Another noticeable contrast between the two periods is the substantial growth differential of the manufacturing sector, declining from 10.3 per cent annual growth rate in the first period and 11.1 over 2000–5 to 7.1 per cent in the second. In contrast, construction industry grew faster over the second period although the fast growth of construction had started and was evident over the period 2000–05. The declining growth of the manufacturing is an indication of the contraction of the semi-tradable sector. Given that the Iranian manufacturing sector is still highly protected it is more of a sem-tradable nature than tradable. Manufacturing is estimated to have the highest level of productivity and forward and backward linkages compared with other sectors, such as agriculture, construction and services.[8]

It is worth noting that the lower growth of the economy over period the 2006–11 was accompanied by a much higher rate of capital formation. Gross fixed capital formation to GDP ratio increased to 38.5 per cent in the second period compared with 31.7 per cent over the earlier phase. This in turn indicates higher investment inefficiencies in the latter period. Other studies, including those by Karshenas and Moshaver (2011) and the World Bank (2011), have indicated a low level of productivity and investment efficiency in the Iranian economy in the post-revolutionary period. In a study of investment efficiency in MENA, the World Bank (2011) has shown that:

> Libya, Iran and Algeria stand out as developing oil exporters with least efficient investments in 2000s. MENA oil importers and GCC (Gulf Cooperation Council) oil exporters used investment more efficiently . . . These countries have better rule of law . . . and they have better environments for investment and growth
>
> (World Bank, 2011: 29)

It is worth comparing the Iranian macroeconomic performance with oil exporters in the region although IMF's revised projection of Iranian data over 2009–11 are considered overoptimistic by close observers of the Iranian economy as well as those interested in the impact of sanctions on the economy (see Habibi, 2011). A close examination of the IMF's projections of the Iranian growth data by Habibi indicates that the August 2011 'economic growth projections for Iran for 2009–2011 were revised upward in comparison with the IMF's April 2011 projections that had been released only a few months earlier' (Habibi, 2011: 4). The earlier projections indicated a growth rate of 0.06 per cent, 1.02 per cent and –0.03 per cent for 2009, 2010 and 2011, respectively. These very low rates of growth projections, as several studies have shown, reflected IMF's pessimistic forecasts for non-OECD countries at the time. However the revised projection of around four to six percent growth for 2009 and 2010 also reflect overoptimistic assumptions about the economy. Habibi argues that the two factors accounting for the report's positive assessment are 'the prospects of Iran's non-oil sectors and the supposed success of the 2010 subsidy removal reforms' (Habibi, 2011: 4). A closer examination of these assumptions indicates that manufacturing as an important non-oil sector faced stiff competition from cheap Chinese imports that flooded Iranian markets. Hence it was not surprising that – as was mentioned earlier – the growth of manufacturing sector slowed down significantly over the period 2006–11.[9] Furthermore, the removal of subsidy proved more costly than was initially thought. The subsidy removal reform, introduced at the end of 2010, included the allocation of a proportion of savings from the subsidy removal to industrial plants to offset the higher costs of fuel and other inputs following the removal of subsidies. However, instead of helping the producers the government in line with its populist policies distributed subsidy savings to consumers while hurting producers. This in turn reflects the 'haphazard way in which the price liberalization and subsidy removal reforms have been implemented' (Habibi, 2011: 4). In other words non-oil domestic production faced severe difficulties following the removal of subsidies and the growth prospect of the economy has been more challenging than the optimistic IMF projections suggest.

Data presented in Table 3.2 contrasts Iranian growth projection with those of oil exporters and oil importers in the Middle East and North Africa, Pakistan and Afghanistan (MENAP), and the MENAP region as a whole over the period

Table 3.2 Real GDP Growth, 2000–11

	Average 2000–05	Average 2006–11	2005	2006	2007	2008	2009	2010	2011
Middle East and North Africa (MENAP)	5.2	4.5	5.8	5.9	5.8	4.5	2.7	4.8	3.4
Oil exporters	5.6	4.4	6	5.7	5.4	4.1	2	5	4
Iran	5.5	4.1	4.7	5.8	6.4	0.6	3.9	5.9	2
Oil importers	4.4	4.8	5.4	6.3	6.5	5.5	4.2	4.3	2.2

Source: IMF. Regional Economic Outlook, Middle East and Central Asia, various years, 2007–2013

Notes: IMF classifications: MENAP region includes countries in the Middle East and North Africa plus Pakistan and Afghanistan.

2000–11. As has been mentioned, earlier Iranian growth data for 2009–11 are considered overoptimistic.

Table 3.2 indicates that over the earlier period of 2000–5 (during the economic reforms of Mr Khatami's administration), annual real GDP growth in Iran averaged 5.5 per cent per annum – a comparable rate with the 5.6 per cent growth rate for oil exporters in region and slightly above the growth rate of the MENAP region as a whole. However the annual growth for Iran fell sharply in 2008 and remained volatile afterwards. Over the period 2006–11 Iranian growth was 4.1 per cent compared to 4.4 and 4.5 per cent for MENAP oil exporters and the MENAP region, respectively.

Furthermore, the growth trajectory differs for Iran compared with the MENAP oil exporters as a group. For the latter the sharp decline in growth in 2009 correspond to a severe fall in oil prices while for the former the severe decline came in 2008 at the height of booming oil prices. Furthermore the fall in the Iranian growth rate is much sharper than that for the MENA oil exporters. In the case of Iran the annual growth of 5.8 per cent and 6.4 per cent in 2006 and 2007 respectively falls to less than one per cent in 2008. Also the recovery afterwards is far patchier for Iran than for oil exporters in general.

Comparative data on consumer price inflation indicates that the rate of inflation increased from 13.5 per cent over 2000–5 in Iran to 25.4 per cent in 2008 and has remained high ever since. It is also clear that for both periods the rate of inflation was much higher in Iran than in MENAP oil exporters or MENAP countries as a whole (Figure 3.3)

The trends in Iranian growth and inflation over the period 2005–11 provide a textbook case for the study of populist policies where high growth in the early years is followed by lower growth and the high inflation later on (see discussion Dornbush and Edwards, 1991, above).

Iran's relatively lower growth and higher inflation during the administration of Mr Ahmadi-Nejad comes against a background of higher government expenditure (Figure 3.4) and higher liquidity (Figure 3.5) over the same period.

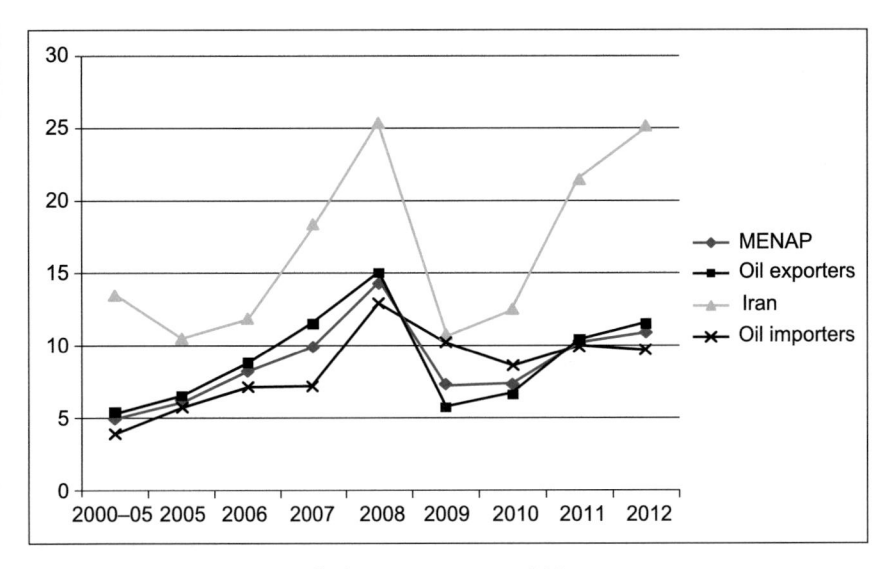

Figure 3.3 Consumer Price Inflation (Average Annual %)

Source: IMF. Regional Economic Outlook, Middle East and Central Asia, various years, 2007–2013

Notes: IMF classicfications: MENAP region includes countries in the Middle East and North Africa plus Pakistan and Afghanistan. Oil exporters and importers refer to those in the MENAP region.

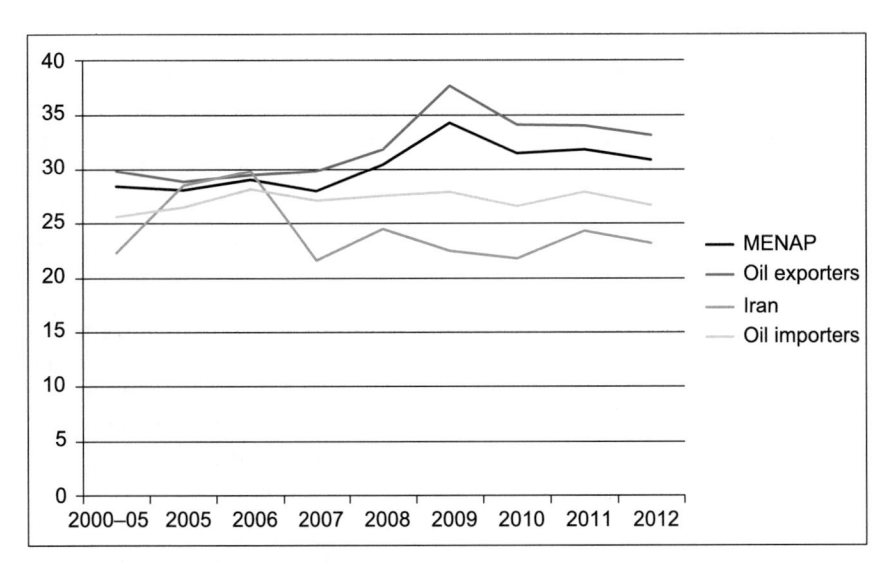

Figure 3.4 Government Expenditure (% of GDP)

Source: IMF. Regional Economic Outlook, Middle East and Central Asia, various years, 2007–2013

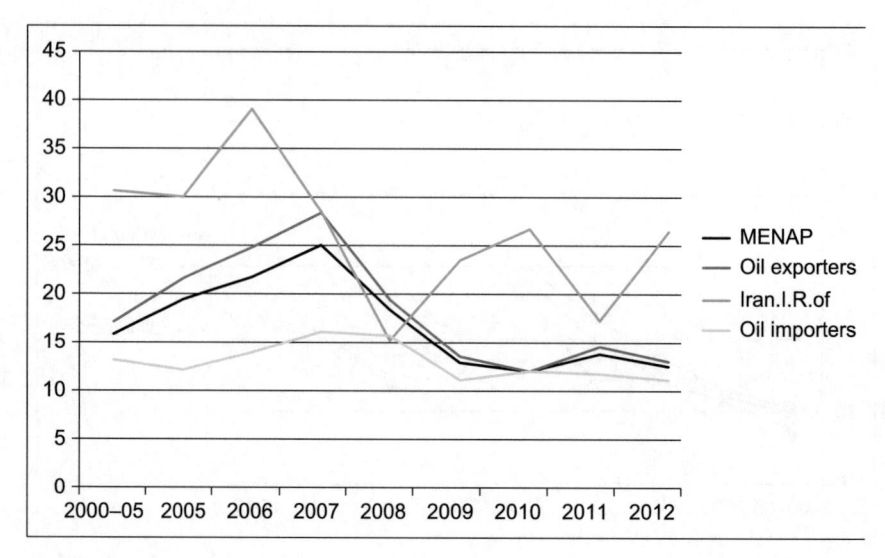

Figure 3.5 Broad money growth

Source: IMF. Regional Economic Outlook, Middle East and Central Asia, various years, 2007–2013

It can be seen that government expenditure/GDP ratio is lower for Iran than for MENAP oil exporters. Nevertheless, there is a sharp rise in government expenditure in 2006. The government expenditure/GDP ratio increased from 22.3 per cent of GDP over 2000–5 to virtually 30 per cent of GDP in 2006. This was accompanied by a sharp rise in the growth of broad money M3, as a good indicator of liquidity, from an annual average of 30.7 per cent over 2000–5 to 39.2 in 2006.

These data indicate that the growth of liquidity as well as that of inflation has been much higher in Iran compared to MENAP oil exporters, MENAP, or MENAP oil importers.

Privatization

Before the Revolution, Iran had a relatively large and modern private sector by regional standards which played a major role in the economy and particularly in the manufacturing sector. The large-scale nationalization of modern industries and services that followed the 1979 Revolution undermined the sanctity of private property. Instead, Article 44 of the Islamic Constitution focused on the importance of state ownership in basic or 'mother' industries. According to this article the economy is divided into three sectors: the state, cooperative, and private sectors. The state sector is to include all large-scale manufacturing industries, finance and banking, foreign trade, major minerals, telecommunications, utilities and transportation.

The cooperative sector is to include cooperative companies and enterprises concerned with production and distribution, in urban and rural areas, in accordance with Islamic criteria. The private sector consists of those activities concerned with agriculture, animal husbandry, industry, trade, and services that supplement the economic activities of the state and cooperative sectors.

(The Constitution of the Islamic Republic)

Prior to its amendment in 2004, Article 44 posed a major obstacle to attempts for large-scale privatization during Mr Rafsanjani's administration in the early 1990s. For instance, it faced opposition from sections of workers in nationalized industries as well as some political institutions. Hence not surprisingly consideration of 'economic justice' and anxiety over the potential leverage of the would-be private owners of SOEs over the workers provided a major setback for privatization (Behdad, 2000). Instead, in 1994 the Iranian Parliament, *Majlis,* 'passed a law to stop offering shares in these enterprises in the Tehran Stock Exchange until conditions could be determined for offering the shares first to the families of martyrs of the Revolution and veterans of the war' (Behdad, 2000: 129).[10] Limited privatization over this period benefited parastatal organizations including *Bonyads* and Revolutionary Guards as the guardians of the Revolution that had also benefited from the multiple exchange rate system during the war years.

However privatization policy acquired momentum following the unsustainable financial burdens posed by SOEs on government finances, concerns for efficiency of major industries and the lure of a possible boost to political legitimacy through 'share distribution'. The objectives of privatization were reflected in the amendment of Article 44 in 2004, which was concerned with the promotion of efficiency, equity and reduction public sector expenditure.[11]

The privatization policy required the government to privatize around 80 per cent of its assets in 'mother industries' or major sectors including heavy industry, downstream oil and gas, financial sector, energy and communications and foreign trade (Ehsani, 2009). Half of this was to be allocated to 'Justice Shares' (JS) for low-income families with another 40 per cent to be tendered through the Tehran Stock Exchange (TSE); the remaining 20 per cent was expected to be kept by the government.

The period 2006–11 witnessed large-scale privatizations of the SOEs (Figure 3.6). The number of SOEs privatized in 2010–11 increased to 177 companies compared to 50 in 2005–6. The annual proceeds from the sales of the shares in SOEs in current prices reached $24.9 billion in 2007–08, $21.4 billion in 2008–09 and $15.3 billion in 2010–11 compared with $76 million only in 2005–6. The total proceeds over the period 2005–11 amounted to more than $80 billion.

As was mentioned earlier two types of privatization were recommended. One was concerned with share distribution to low income families and the other concerned with the sale of shares through the TSE.

It is too early to evaluate the impact of the privatization scheme in terms of its own objectives. Nevertheless, a brief overview of the institutional set up for the distribution and operation of the Justice Shares may provide some insight into its potential impact. Similarly, we will also discuss privatizations through the TSE below.

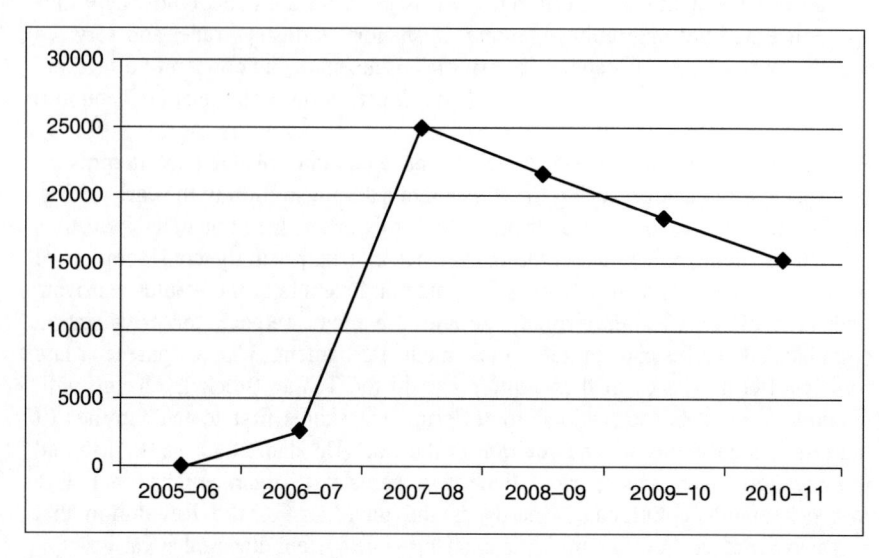

Figure 3.6 Proceeds of Privatization in Iran, 2005–2011 (annual proceeds, Million US$)

Source: Iranian Privatization Organization (IPO)

Privatization: Justice Shares (JS)

Another important component of populist policies over the period of 2006–11 was the mass distribution of shares through the so-called Justice Shares scheme. The existing evidence, nevertheless, indicates that JS has faced a number of major challenges including heavy bureaucratic and administrative costs for distribution of shares, the continued involvement of government in 'privatized' sections of SOEs and a heavy burden of dividend payment by government in the case of unprofitable companies.

In distributing JS the highest priority was given to the two lowest income deciles of the population 'who were offered 50 per cent discount on stock prices to be paid through 10-year instalments (Atashbar, 2011:7). The entitled families in the third to sixth deciles could also benefit paying through ten-year instalments but were not offered a discount on the price of shares. Those who obtained JS were also entitled to receive dividends.

For distribution of JS a complex web of state-controlled 'cooperative companies' were created in all provinces under the supervision of the government, parastatal organizations (Imam Khomeini Charity Committee), and the State Welfare Organization.[12] Table 3.3 provides data on the prioritization of targeted groups. The highest priorities were given to those identified by parastatal charitable organizations, followed by villagers and nomads, employees of the state companies and retirees and finally the war veterans. More than 36 million people, or nearly half of the total population, were considered entitled to JS and its benefits.

This 'mass privatization' however has been accompanied by heavy administration costs without reducing the role of the government in the privatized SOEs. In

Table 3.3 Privatization: the Justice Shares Scheme

Targeted groups	Number of people enrolled in cooperatives following entitlement to JS*	Share of targeted groups in the distribution of Justice Shares* (%)
1st group	6,993,860	19.3
Supported by charitable bodies		
2nd group	16,024,806	44
Villagers and nomads		
3rd group	12,048,685	33.2
Government employees and retirees		
4th group	1,140,006	2.9
War veterans		
Other groups	199,962	0.6
Total	36,407,319	**100**

Source: Atashbar (2011: Derived from Table 1).

an study of JS that was undertaken by Atashbar for the Iranian Parliament it has been argued that the designers of privatization established gigantic semi-government bureaucratic institutions, with the involvement of government stakeholders that led to 'the establishment of 30 provincial cooperatives, each of which had a managing board, inspectors, a general manager, and other executive and bureau employees with large expenses' (Atashbar, 2011: 10). Furthermore despite the privatization of a significant block of shares in SOEs 'the managing board positions are still occupied by government representatives' (2011: 10). In other words, mass privatization through JS, did not have any effect on the board of directors:

> The justice shares given to families simply cannot be considered to be privatization. The government is going to manage the equities which do not belong to it. Even if the government wants to be the representative of the stockholders in managing their equities and stocks, the stockholders have never given this authority to the government.
>
> (Atashbar, 2011: 10)

The continued presence of government representatives on the Boards of the 'privatized' firms contradicts one of the main objectives of privatization: the reduction of the role of the government in the economy. One of the reasons for privatization is to reduce the impact of principal-agent problem that affects the operation of SOEs far more than those of privatized firms. It is known that the 'principal' in the case of SOEs has virtually no control over the management and long-term goals of these companies. Instead, politicians can influence the operation of SOEs on the basis of political priorities. On the other hand, though the principal-agent problem is still present in the case of private firms (given the objectives of management usually differ from those of the shareholders) their objectives and management are not shaped by political expediency but by market criteria. Hence this form of mass privatization in Iran has not really addressed the principal–agent issue.

Another challenge was the payment of dividends to shareholders that created a huge burden on government resources as a large number of privatized SOEs were not profitable. Accordingly, as corporate profits are currently considerably low

> ... dividends are simply not payable, at least not during the next five years. Moreover, current difficulties for paying the promised dividends to the huge number of households from the small set of profitable companies participating in the plan have already forced the government to stop or delay paying any dividends
>
> (Atashbar, 2010:9)

It is too early to evaluate the impact of JS scheme on the rate of return and profitability of the firms concerned. Nevertheless, the existing evidence indicates that this highly populist policy of mass privatization was more focused on distributional aspects of share ownership than on profitability and efficiency, competiveness and long-term income distribution.

Privatization: The Tehran Stock Exchange

The other form of privatization of SOEs has been through the Tehran Stock Exchange, which is dominated by the IRGC, pension funds, social welfare institutions, various religious foundations and the municipalities. A study by Kevan Harrris (2010) indicates that parastatal organizations have been the main beneficiaries of these privatizations. For instance, over the period 2007–9, the shares of 82 firms worth $3.7 billion were transferred solely to parastatal organizations. The handover consisted primarily of shares from seven large state-owned companies. More than 45 per cent of the total shares were soley transferred to two parastatal organizations, namely the Social Security Investment Company (SHASTA) and Iranian Mehr Eqtesad, formerly the Basijian Group.

Due to complete opacity, accurate information about the size, functions and actual worth of the parastatal organization is not available. The structural characteristics of these organizations are well summarized by Vahabi (2011). Although Vahabi's description is about a particular *Bonyad* (*Bonyad-e Mostazafan va Janbazan* or the Foundation of the Oppressed and War Veterans), never-theless, his description is applicable to all parastatal organizations. Accordingly this organization operates like a giant holding encompassing many organiza-tions including manufacturing, mining, housing, trade, tourism, energy and communications. However the institutional set up of this giant holding is 'chameleon-like. It can change at will, acting as a private economy when buying privatised firms, but going "public" to control such "strategic" businesses as the national shipping line', (Vahabi, 2011: 15). The legal status of the foundations has been described as public, non-government institution with no shareholders, no public account and no accountability to government. 'However, as professed "charitable" organizations, they have been benefiting from tax exemptions, preferential bank credits, subsidies, and special "quasi-budgetary redistribution"' (Vahabi, 2011: 15–16).

This lack of accountability and transparency combined with their access to government resources makes it difficult if not impossible to make any evaluation of the potential efficiency and productivity of parastatal organizations.

Institutions, economic performance and governance

Unlike the pre-revolutionary system of political authority that was highly centralized, the post-revolutionary structure of power in the Islamic Republic has remained polycentric (Mohajer and Vahabi, 2011). It has been argued that such a defused structure of political power is rooted in Shi'a Islam that is dependent not on a single interpretation of Islamic law but on several personalities – *marja-e-taqlid* – and their version and understanding of Islam. Hence it differs from Sunni Islam that is based on one particular school (Beeman, 2004).

However, this polycentric structure is partly elected and partly unelected (Beeman, 2004; Karshenas and Moshaver, 2011). An elected Parliament and President operate alongside several unelected political institutions. The head of the army (which includes the Islamic Revolutionary Guards Corp), the judiciary, the head of the radio and television as well as members of two powerful conservative religious organizations, namely the *Guardian Council* and the *Expediency Council*, are all chosen by the supreme leader. A bill passed by the Parliament thus has to be ratified by the latter two organizations. This structure of power would not have been a problem except for the fact that unelected bodies that have veto power over the elected institutions 'are by and large the most conservative religionists in Iran' (Beeman, 2004: 2).

Above all, the power and influence of the unelected institutions have been rising continuously since the Revolution and particularly since 2005.

What distinguishes the period 2006–11 from the earlier period is the relative political harmony between the elected and the unelected institutions, at least up until 2011 (when the rift between Mr Ahmadi-Nejad and the supreme leader widened in response to the dire consequences of populist policies; see the concluding section below). This support was manifested in the unchallenged implementation of populist reforms by Mr Ahmadi-Nejad's administration during his first term of office as well as his re-election in the second term in 2009 despite widespread allegations of election fraud.[13] This is in contrast to the earlier period, when the administration of Mr Khatami was continuously challenged by conservative political institutions during his reign (1997–2005).

The support of unelected political institutions, particularly during the first term of Mr Ahmadi-Nejad's government, created an 'unrestrained executive' that undermined the relative independence of economic institutions including the Central Bank and the Management and Plan Organization as mentioned above. In other words attempt at de-politicization of economic institutions and the creation of 'rational' rather than 'ideological' economic institutions by the earlier reformist administrations were totally reversed over this period.

'Politicization' of economic policies has been accompanied by growing economic power of parastatal organizations which had the support of both elected and the non-elected institutions. These organizations, which are considered as 'cooperatives', increased their role and their assets enormously over this period through privatization of SOEs.

In other words, large-scale privatisations over 2006–11 have not been accompanied by the development of a vibrant private sector but by more involvement of the state and parastatal organizations in privatized SOEs. Despite the amendment in Article 44 and large-scale privatization over 2005–11 the opacity over the definition and boundaries of private property has in fact thickened over this period.

It has been argued that this ambiguity has its roots in the 'indeterminate' nature of confiscated property in Islam:

> Property rights in the parastatal sector are indeterminate; here, 'indeterminate' properties refer to booty from warfare and looting, or property confiscated during a revolution. Although this kind of property can be transformed into 'public, 'personal,' 'private,' 'combinatorial,' or other types of ownership, their initial status remains indeterminate. For 'indeterminate' properties, entitlement to property rights depends on the discretionary power of the coercive authority.
>
> (Vahabi, 2012)

Whether the opacity over the boundaries of private property is the reflection of the 'indeterminate' nature of confiscated property in Islam or it points to the presence of strong interest groups, the fact remains the control of the economy by the state and parastatal organizations has not been conducive to productivity growth and efficiency in the economy.

It has been suggested that the politicization of economic decision-making and delays in the implementation of economic reforms arise from the presence of 'latent social conflicts', combined with weak 'institutions of conflict management' (Rodrick, 1998). Accordingly, the speed of the implementation of economic reforms is negatively related to the intensity of pre-existing social tensions and conflict arising from, for instance, the high level of income inequality. On the other hand, the effectiveness and speed of reforms' implementation is positively related to the presence of strong 'institutions of conflict management' including democratic institutions, an independent judiciary and organizations that adjudicate distributional disputes within a framework of accepted rules.

It appears that the process of economic reform over the period 1997–2005 was more concerned with strengthening the institutions of conflict management – through opening political discourse – although this was severely challenged by conservative political institutions. On the other hand, populist policies over the period 2005–11 aimed at tempering the 'latent social conflict' through distributional policies. This also did not achieve its objectives as high inflation has severely undermined the purchasing power of the population and particularly the lower income group. Although the government's populist agenda has changed to accommodate extensive subsidy reforms since 2011 it appears that the crisis of the polycentric state has not yet been resolved.

Conclusion

A comparative analysis of Iran's economic performance over the two periods 1997–2005 and 2006–11 shows that growth and prosperity suffered in the latter period. This is in spite of inflated and over-optimistic IMF growth data that has been employed in this study for the second period.

Government policy during 2006–11 has certain prominent features that distinguishes this period from the earlier period of reform 1997–2005. Alongside the exceptional growth of oil income that fuelled petro populism 2006–11 also witnessed an unprecedented compromise between elected and non-elected political institutions which gave rise to the creation of an 'unrestrained executive'. This alliance between elected and non-elected political organizations was in sharp contrast to the hostility that the previous 'executive' faced over the period of reform (1997–2005).

The administration of president Khatami, though facing severe opposition for the introduction of democratic political reforms, implemented a host of economic reforms that improved the accountability and transparency of the economic system while simultaneously improving its growth and prosperity. The implementation of economic reforms however remained unfinished with the change of administration.

By contrast, over the latter period of 2006–11 the government of president Ahmadi-Nejad embarked on a host of populist policies, including the imposition of low interest rates below the rate of inflation, the prolongation of subsidies on basic commodities, the mass distribution of SOEs' share while maintaining control by the state – and particularly parastatal organizations – over privatized enterprises, with growing opacity over the institution of private property. For implementation of these polices the government that had the support of unelected political institutions succeeded in undermining the relative autonomy of economic institutions including the central bank and the MPO. These policies had unintended consequences, including high inflation, lower growth rates, growing financial costs of mass privatization (i.e. administrative costs as well as payment of dividends) and the prolonged costs of subsidies. Longer-term consequences of these policies are inefficiencies of investment, the lack of a vibrant private sector and growing opacity over the function and objective of parastatal organizations and the lack of transparency of the economic system.

However, the dire consequences of populist policies, with their potential implications for the spread of social unrest, have contributed to the growing conflict between the 'executive' and the 'legislature' since 2011. The severe rift between the government of Mr Ahmadi-Nejad, on the one hand, and the parliament supported by the unelected political institutions on the other, has dominated the political landscape in the last two years. This split has reinvigorated the polycentric structure of governance leading to growing political conflict between different political factions. Although since the 2011 reforms, aimed at the removal of subsidies, have been in progress the success and direction of future economic policies is far from clear.

Notes

1 For recent reviews of rentier state see Kamrava (2011) and Gray (2011).
2 The impact of the natural resource wealth on the performance of an economy has been tackled in the context of the 'curse of the natural resource' literature – focusing on the 'crowding out' of the tradable sectors at the cost of non-tradables and subsequent appreciation of the exchange rate (Dutch Disease), the impact of oil price volatility on government fiscal policies, corruption, etc. The most dramatic example of a major oil producer that has remained poor is Nigeria (Van der Ploeg, 2011; see also Frankel, 2010; Auty, 2001; Gelb, 1988; and Corden, 1984).
3 For a discussion of *Bonyads*, see Maloney (2000), and Saeidi (2004). For a discussion of Islamic Revolutionary Guards Corp (IRGC), see Vahabi (2011).
4 Ehsani (2009) argues that the Rafsanjani administration was trying to transform the state into a neo-liberal state.
5 On the issue of piety, see Milani (2007).
6 For an interesting discussion of this period, see Farzanegan (2009).
7 BBC (2007): http://www.bbc.co.uk/persian/business/story/2007/01/070103_mf_ka_budget.shtml.
8 High forward and backward linkages in the manufacturing imply that the growth of this sector is conducive to the generation of employment in sectors that are buying from or selling to the manufacturing sector. Also high productivity in manufacturing arising from 'learning by doing' and positive externalities in the sector is growth enhancing. Hence, shifting from manufacturing towards construction curbs future growth. For a discussion of the positive externalities in the manufacturing sector, see Van der Ploeg (2011).
9 Government's tolerance of Chinese imports was in part to reward Chinese's willingness to buy Iranian oil despite the American pressure and in part to appease domestic consumers in line with its populist policies. See Habibi (2011).
10 It appears that Mr Rafsanjani was not hesitant to offer a major stake in privatization to *Bazaar's* merchants or even ex-owners of confiscated nationalized firms in the early 1990s. Nevertheless, large factions of the conservative political elite and sections of workers in SOEs opposed the idea. For information on reforms over this period, see also Looney (2007).
11 Iranian Privatization Organization (IPO).
12 These companies were responsible both for gathering information on those eligible for access to JS and also for offering them membership in cooperatives (Atashbar, 2011).
13 Allegations of vote rigging were accompanied by a large protest movement in Iran followed by a severe clampdown of the reformist opposition.

References

Acemoglu, D., Johnson, S. Robinson, J. and Thaicharoen, Y., Institutional causes, macro-economic symptoms: volatility, crises and growth. *Journal of Monetary Economics*, 50 (1), 2003.
Acemoglu, D., Johnson, S. and Robinson, J., Institutions as the fundamental cause of long-run growth, *National Bureau of Economics Research*, Working Paper 10481: http://www.nber.org/papers/w10481, 2004.

Acemoglu, D., Egorov, G. and Sonin, K., A political theory of populism, *National Bureau of Economic Research*, Working Paper 17306, 2011.

Alizadeh, P., ed., *The Economy of Iran: Dilemmas of an Islamic State,* London: I.B. Tauris, 2000.

Alizadeh, P., Iranian Quandary: Economic Reforms and the Structural Trap, *The Brown Journal of the World Affairs*, Winter/Spring, 1X (2), 2003.

Alizadeh, P., Industrialization: the post-revolutionary period, 1979–2000s, in E. Yarshater, ed, *Encyclopaedia Iranica*, Centre for Iranian Studies, New York: Columbia University: 119–25, 2005.

Amuzegar, J., Iran's Oil Stabilization Fund: a misnomer, http://www.payvand.com/news/05/nov/1221.html, 2005.

Atashbar, T., Privatisation as proxy of distribution: is it possible?, (The Justice Shares mass privatisation: case of Iran), *Research Centre of Iran's Parliament, poverty and public policy*, 3 (4): http://www.psocommons.org/ppp/vol3/iss4/art9, 2011.

Auty, R. M., Natural resources, the state and development strategy, *Journal of International Development*, 9: 651–63, 1997.

Auty, R. M., The political economy of resource-driven growth, *European Economic Review*, 46: 839–46, 2001.

Bank Markazi Iran; www.cbi.ir/section/1372.aspx

BBC (2007): http://www.bbc.co.uk/pension/business/story/2007/01/070103_mf_ka_budget.shtml

BBC: Expanding business empire of Iran's Revolutionary Guards, *BBC Persian*, 26 July: http://www.bbc.co.uk/news/world-middle-east-10743580, 2010.

Beblawi, H., 'The rentier state in the Arab World,' in Beblawi, H. and Luciani, G., eds, *The Rentier State: Nation, State and the Integration of the Arab World*, London: Croom Helm, 1987.

Beblawi, H., 'The rentier state in the Arab World' in Luciani, G., ed., *The Arab State,* London: Routledge: 85–98, 1990.

Beeman W., Elections and governmental structure in Iran: reform lurks under the flaws, *The Brown Journal of the World Affairs,* X1 (1), 2004.

Behdad, S., From populism to economic liberalism: the Iranian predicament, in: Alizadeh (2000): 100–41, 2000.

The Central Bank of the Islamic Republic of Iran (Bank Markazi Iran), *Annual Report and Balance Sheet*, Tehran: various issues.

The Constitution of the Islamic Republic of Iran, http://www.iranonline.com/iran/iran-info/Government/constitution-1.html

Corden, W. M., Booming sector and Dutch Disease economics: survey and consolidation, *Oxford Economic Papers*, 36: 359–80, 1984.

Dornbusch, R. and Edwards, S., Macroeconomic populism, *Journal of Development Economics,* 32: 247–78, 1990.

Dornbush, R. and Edwards, S., eds, *The Macroeconomics of Populism in Latin America*, Chicago: University of Chicago Press, 1991.

Ehsani, K., Survival through dispossession: privatization of public goods in the Islamic Republic, *Middle East Report*, No. 250, 2009.

Farzanegan, M. R., Macroeconomic of populism in Iran, *MPRA Paper No. 15546*, http://mpra.ub.uni-muenchen.de/15546/, 2009.

Farzin, Y. H., 'The political economy of foreign exchange reform,' in Rahnema, S. and Behdad, S., eds, *Iran after the Revolution: Crisis of an Islamic state*, London: I.B. Tauris: 174–203, 1996.

Foroohar, R., The decline of the petro-Czar, *Newsweek*, February 14, http://www. thedailybeast.com/newsweek/2009/02/13/the-decline-of-the-petro-czar.html, 2009.

Frankel, J., The natural resource curse: a survey, *National Bureau of Economic Research*, Working Paper 15836, 2010.

Gelb, A. ed., *Oil Windfalls: Blessing or Curse?*, Oxford: Oxford University Press, 1988.

Gray, M., 'A theory of "late rentierism" in the Arab States of the Gulf', Georgetown University School of Foreign Service in Qatar, Centre for International and Regional Studies, Occasional Paper (CRIS), 7: 1–44. 2011.

Habibi, N., 'Is Iran's economy growing? An assessment of the IMF's 2011 report on Iran,' Crown Center for Middle East Studies, Middle East Brief, No. 57, December: http://www. brandeis.edu/crown/publications/meb/MEB57.pdf, 2011.

Hall, R. and Jones, C., Why do some countries produce so much more output per worker than others?, *Quarterly Journal of Economics*, 114: 83–116. 1999.

Harris, K., 'Pseudo-privatization in the Islamic Republic: beyond the headlines on Iran's economic transformation', available at: http://muftah.org/pseudo-privatization-in-the-islamic-republic-beyond-the-headlines-on-iran%E2%80%99s-economic-trans formation-by-kevan-harris/, 2010.

Helpman, E., *The Mystery of Economic Growth*, Cambridge, MA: Harvard University Press, 2004.

Helpman, E. ed, *Institutions and Economic Performance*, Cambridge, MA: Harvard University Press, 2008.

IMF, *Islamic Republic of Iran, Staff Report for 2002 Article 1V Consultation*, Washington: International Monetary Fund, 2002a.

IMF, *Islamic Republic of Iran, Selected Issues and Statistical Appendix, IMF Country Report No. 02/212*, Washington: International Monetary Fund, 2002b.

IMF, *Iran – The Chronicles of the Subsidy Reform,* (prepared by Guillaume, D., Zytek, R. and Farzin, M. R.) IMF working paper, WP/11/167, Washington: International Monetary Fund, 2011.

IMF, Regional Economic Outlook, Middle East and Central Asia, various years (2007–2013), Washington DC.

Iranian Privatization Organization (IPO): http://www.en.ipo.ir/index.aspx?siteid=83& pageid=800; and http://www.en.ipo.ir/index.aspx?siteid=83&pageid=822

Kamrava, M., ed, 'The political economy of the Gulf, Working Group Summary Report', Center for International and Regional Studies, Georgetown University School of Foreign Service in Qatar, *Summary Report No. 3.*, 2011.

Kamrava, M., 'The political economy of rentierism in the Persian Gulf', in Kamrava, M., ed, 2011.

Karshenas, M. and Hakimian, H., 'Dilemmas and prospects for economic reform and reconstruction in Iran', in Alizadeh, ed: Ch.2: 50–75, 2000.

Karshenas, M. and Moshaver Z., 'The political economy of rentierism in Iran' in Kamrava, M., ed, 2011.

Kaufmann, D., Kraay, A. and Zoido-Lobaton, P., 'Governance matters: from measurement to action', *Finance and Development*, 37 (2), Washington DC: International Monetary Fund, 2000.

Knack, S., 'Governance and growth: measurement and evidence', Paper prepared for the Forum Series on the Role of Institutions in Promoting Growth, IRIS Center and USAID, Washington DC, February, 2002.

Knack, S. and Keefer P., Institutions and economic performance: cross country tests using alternative institutional measures, *Economics and Politics*, 7: 207–27, 1995.

Looney, R. E., 'The re-emergence of Iranian petro-populism,' Gulf Research Center, Gulf Yearbook 2006–7: 417–27, 2007.

Mahdavi, H., 'Patterns and problems of economic development in rentier states: the case of Iran,' in Cook, M. A., ed, *Studies in Economic History of the Middle East*, Oxford: Oxford University Press: 428–67, 1970.

Maloney, S., 'Agents or obstacles? Parastatal foundations and challenges for Iranian development,' in Alizadeh, ed: 145–76, 2000.

Matsen, E., Natvik, G. J. and Torvik, R., 'Petro populism', Department of Economics, Norwegian University of Science and Technology, Working Paper series, Number 5/2012: www.svt.ntnu.no/iso/egil.matsen/Papers/petropopulism.pdf, 2012.

Mazarei. A., The Iranian economy under the Islamic republic: institutional change and macroeconomic performance 1979–1990, *Cambridge Journal of Economics,* 20 (3): 289–314, 1996.

Milani, A., Pious populist: understanding the rise of Iran's President, *Boston Review*: http://bostonreview.net/BR32.6/milani.php, 2007.

Mohajer, N. and Vahabi, M., Islamic Republic of Iran and its opposition, *Comparative Studies of South Asia, Africa and the Middle East*, 31 (1): 110–19, 2011.

North, D., *Institutions, Institutional Change and Economic Performance*, Cambridge University Press, 1990.

North, D. and Weingast, B., Constitutions and commitments: the evolution of institutions governing public choice in 17 Century England, *Journal of Economic History* 19: 803–32, 1989.

OPEC; Annual Statistical Bulletin, http://www.opec.org/opec_web/en/202.htm

Parenti, C., Hugo Chávez and petro populism, *The Nation*, 11 April: 15–21, 2005.

Pesaran, M. H., 'Economic trends and macroeconomic policies in post-revolutionary Iran,' in Alizadeh, ed, 2000.

Van der Ploeg, F., Natural resources: curse or blessing?, *Journal of Economic Literature,* 49 (2): 366–420, 2011.

Rahnema, S. and Behdad, S., eds, *Iran after the Revolution: crisis of an Islamic state*, London: I.B. Tauris, 1996.

Rahnema, S. 'Continuity and Change in Industrial Policy,' in Rahnema, S. and Behdad, S. eds (1996).

Rodrik, D., 'Where did all the growth go? External shocks, social conflict and growth collapses'. Centre for Economic Policy Research London, Discussion paper 1789, 1998.

Rodrik, D., Subramanian, A., and Trebbi, F., Institutions Rule: The Primacy of Institutions over Geography and Integration in Economic Development, *Journal of Economic Growth*, 9(2): 131–65, 2004.

Sachs, J., 'Social conflict and populist policies in Latin America,' Cambridge, MA: National Bureau of Economic Research, Working Paper 2897, 1989.

Saeidi, A., The Accountability of para-governmental organizations (*Bonyads*): the case of Iranian foundations, *Iranian Studies*, 37 (3): 479–98, 2004.

Salehi-Isfahani, D., 'Poverty, inequality, and populist politics in Iran,' *Journal of Economic Inequality*, 7 (1): 5–28, 2009.

Tisdell, C., Economic reform and openness in China: China's development policies in the last 30 years, *Economic Analysis & Policy*, 39 (2), September, 2009.

Vahabi, M., *'Soft budget constraint and the parastatal sector'*, MPRA Paper No. 37926, http://mpra.ub.uni-muenchen.de/37926/, 2011.

World Bank, Middle East and North Africa Region, *Economic Development and Prospects*, Washington, September, 2011.

4 Iran's free trade zones

Back doors to the international economy?

*Hassan Hakimian**

Introduction

For decades now, many governments around the world have sought to boost and exploit the economic power of their particular regions by designating them as 'special' or 'free' economic zones. This trend gained momentum in the last few decades with a rapid rise in the number of such zones. According to International Labour Office (ILO) estimates, by 2006 there were some 3,500 zones in 123 countries worldwide accounting for up to 60 million direct jobs (ILO, 2007).

Iran's interest in free zones can be traced back to the 1970s when the potential development of Kish Island as a flagship free trade zone in the Persian Gulf was first mooted. After the end of the war with Iraq and with economic reconstruction under way in the late 1980s, the first concrete steps were taken – under the auspices of the First Five-Year Development Plan (1989–93) – to realize this objective. In this first wave, three so-called 'Free Trade-Industrial Zones' (FTZs, hereafter) were announced: two of these – *Kish* and *Qeshm* – were islands situated in the Persian Gulf in the south, with a third – *Chahbahar* – also in the south but on the littoral of the Sea of Oman. The next decade and a half saw the establishment of three further zones: *Aras* and *Anzali* in the north (in the proximity of the CIS states) and *Arvand* in the south (bordering Iraq and Kuwait).

This initiative was followed up with another 16 zones set up throughout Iran, which are known as 'Special Economic Zones' (SEZs, hereafter). A number of the new SEZs have been given a 'special theme' indicating their specific industry or sectoral links (such as petrochemicals, shipping, minerals, energy, etc.).

The objectives of the FTZs and SEZs are, however, markedly different. The FTZs are more ambitious given that their principal aim has been to attract foreign direct investment (FDI) and ultimately to help generate a diversified industrial base by promoting Iran's non-oil exports. The SEZs, by contrast, were conceived for improving the supply and distribution networks in the country and to act as conduits and channels for goods in transit. As elsewhere, Iran's zones too have benefited from a raft of special economic incentives and facilities – from infrastructure to special rules and a legal framework – to encourage domestic and foreign investment and to accelerate the development of these zones.

Given the relatively recent history of Iran's zones and serious lack of available information, any attempts at full evaluation of their performance and impact is faced with major difficulties. What evidence is available, however, indicates a less than successful picture and a starting phase fraught with major challenges. In this chapter, we focus on two sets of challenges: micro-level factors – i.e. those relating to the design, operation and management of the zones, and macro-level issues – linking Iran's experience of the zones with the wider business climate and economic policies in the period under study.

We argue that Iran's 'pragmatic experimentation' with the free zone phenomenon has been marred by her inability to improve the wider business climate in the country in general, as well as her continued ambivalence towards her position in the international economy. With growing regional competition over foreign investment and capital, Iran's zones have thus been at a disadvantage given that policies pursued in the zones are largely decoupled from, if not at odds with, those in the mainland.

The structure of the chapter is as follows. After offering an overview of the rise of free zones globally, we focus on Iran's experience of setting up free zones since the late 1980s. This includes first a discussion of their characteristics, administrative set up, the general business environment and the legal framework adopted, followed by a critical examination of the outcomes and their track record. The chapter ends by offering an analysis of the challenges the zones have faced since their inception and their likely prospects in the years to come.

The rise of free zones

The introduction of Free Trade and Special Economic Zones[1] has featured as key components of many developing countries' outward-oriented policies in recent decades. This trend has been justified in several ways. First, free zones are considered by host countries as an essential plank of their strategy to attract FDI, promote manufactured exports and achieve long-term economic diversification and growth. Second, for countries suffering from unemployment, these zones are seen as spearheads for job creation and reducing unemployment in regional and national contexts. Third, an – albeit implicit – appeal of the zones has been that they offer a partial route to reforms and a more acceptable substitute for complete liberalization, which may be both practically and politically more daunting to achieve (Miyagiwa, 1993: 187; Madani, 1999).

According to the ILO, the number of countries with Export Processing Zones (EPZs) has risen steadily since the mid-1970s. By 2006, 130 countries were estimated to have set up a variety of different types of free zones (up from 27 in 1975) with a corresponding rise in the number of the zones globally (from 79 to 3,500) in the same period. In the decade of 1997–2006 alone, job creation in these zones trebled reaching a total of 66 million. Of these almost two-thirds (40 million) were accounted for by China (see Table 4.1).

Table 4.2 shows that EPZs are not just limited to the developing world alone. Despite a heavy concentration in Asia (particularly in China, as mentioned above), their outreach is now truly global: from Latin America and the Caribbean (with 6.3 million jobs) to the transition economies (with another 1.4 million jobs). In the

Table 4.1 Estimates of EPZs: countries, numbers and employment, 1975–2006

	1975	*1986*	*1997*	*2002*	*2006*
Number of countries with EPZs	25	47	93	116	130
Number of EPZs or similar types of zones	79	176	845	3,000	3,500
Employment (millions)	n.a.	n.a.	22.5	43	66
– of which China (millions)	n.a.	n.a.	18	30	40
– of which other countries with figures available (millions)	0.8	1.9	4.5	13	26

Source: ILO (2007: 1).

developed world, the United States and European EPZs account for about three-quarters of a million jobs (about one per cent of the total).

Such aggregate employment figures arguably underestimate the real contribution of EPZs to job creation in areas where they operate. First, their *indirect* contributions to job creation have to be taken into account as well as theire ability to create and support jobs in a range of ancillary sectors. Akinci and Crittle (2008: 34) estimate that taking into account the indirect employment effects, EPZs' job creation globally could go up to between 9.6 and 77 million jobs. Second, in some small island economies (such as Mauritius) small absolute numbers conceal the disproportionate contribution EPZs make to total local employment. Third, in some countries (such as in the Caribbean and small Central American states) EPZs tend to provide jobs mostly for the female workforce.[2]

In the Middle East and North Africa (MENA) region, too, free zones have a long history going back to the 1960s and 1970s.[3] The majority of these zones are, however, free trade zones and act as trading platforms rather than manufacturing zones for the host countries. This has severely limited the economic contribution of the MENA zones (with the exception of those in Egypt and Jordan, which have developed a manufacturing focus). Another exception is Dubai, where the

Table 4.2 Geographical distribution of export processing zones, 2006

Geographical area	*Employment*	*%*	*Number of zones*
China	40,000,000	59.7	
Asia (excl. China)	15,741,147	23.5	900+
Latin America	6,258,554	9.3	448
Middle East & North Africa	1,686,749	2.5	115
Sub–Saharan Africa	860,474	1.3	90+
United States	340,000	0.5	713
Transition Economies	1,400,379	2.1	400
Europe	364,818	0.5	50
Others (Pacific & Indian Oceans)	328,642	0.5	15
Total (estimated)	66,980,763	100.0	3,500+

Source: ILO (2007: 2).

government-developed Jebel Ali Free Zone has been established as a major regional distribution and logistics hub.[4]

Today, free zones are seen by many developing countries as pragmatic mechanisms for fostering their links with the international economy rather as spearheads for their globalization strategy. This perception seems to be summed up well by the World Bank that although 'EPZs are a second-best solution compared with generalized country-wide reforms, but ... where countrywide reforms are difficult to implement, they can be a useful weapon in the development arsenal' (Graham, 2004: 100).

Iran's experience with the development of free trade and special economic zones in fact reflects her ambivalent and contradictory approach to the international economy at large, which is the focus of this book, and fits well into this perception of the zones.

The development of free zones in Iran

History of FTZs and SEZs in Iran

Interest in setting up and operating free economic zones in Iran dates back to the 1970s, when the potential of the Kish Island as a flagship free trade zone in the Persian Gulf was first mooted. However, uncertainties following the revolutionary upheaval of the late 1970s and war with Iraq in the 1980s meant it was not for another two decades before interest in the subject was revived.

In the late 1980s, and with post-war reconstruction effort under way, the First Five-Year Development Plan (1989–93) laid down the foundation stones for Iran's so-called 'Free Trade-Industrial Zones'. Article 19 of the Plan stipulated three pioneering zones in Iran's southern shores: the two islands of Kish and Qeshm in the Persian Gulf, and Chahbahar at the far southeastern corner of the mainland bordering with the Sea of Oman (Table 4.3).

Table 4.3 Iran's FTZs

	Year established	*Area*	*Location*	*Nearby countries*	*International borders*
1. Kish	1989	91 sq km	Persian Gulf	GCC states	Gulf waterways
2. Qeshm	1990	480 sq km	Strait of Hormuz	GCC states	Gulf waterways
3. Chahbahar	1991	140 ha	Southeast	Pakistan, Oman, other GCC states	Oman Sea waterways
4. Aras	2003	97 sq km	Northwest	Azerbaijan, Armenia	Nakhchivan
5. Anzali	2003	3200 ha	North (Caspian Sea)	CIS, Caucasus	–
6. Arvand	2004	173 sq km	Southwest	GCC states	Iraq & Kuwait

Source: Compiled from Centre for Free and Special Economic Zones (Iran).

The momentum gathered pace soon after this when a number of other important steps were taken. First, a High Council was set up in 1992 entrusted with regulatory oversight and management and operational responsibilities for these and future zones. One of the first priorities of the Council was to devise and ratify the laws and regulations that were to govern the operation of free zones, a task which was completed by 1993–4. By the end of the plan period in 1993, all three zones had been established, marking this year as a watershed in Iran's quest for FTZs. This early initiative was then followed by another three zones in more recent years, raising the total to six. Two of the newly established zones – *Aras* and *Anzali* – are located in the north: the former is in the northwest bordering the Republic of Nakhchivan (in the proximity of Azerbaijan and Armenia), the latter on the shores of the Caspian Sea with good access to the CIS states. A third FTZ, *Arvand*, is in the southwestern province of Khuzistan bordering Iraq and Kuwait (Table 4.3).

The economic context in which Iran's experience of FTZs originated deserves some attention. Given the isolationism of the post-revolutionary period as well as the ravages imposed by the Iraq war during the harsh decade of the 1980s, these zones were seen as attractive 'back doors' to the global economy, whilst the vexed question of the Islamic Republic's position in the wider international economy could be deferred. The war years had been particularly harsh for their impact on an economy starved of imported consumer goods, industrial inputs and intermediate products. Whilst the benefits of FTZs were officially articulated in terms of their potential contribution to addressing Iran's endemic economic problems (widespread capital shortages, low productivity, run-down public resources, highly limited non-oil exports, low level technology and management skills levels and practices; see below), an unstated attraction of the zones was, no doubt, their potential contribution to alleviating Iran's appetite for imports at the time. It was thus not surprising that the early zones were selected principally for their good access to Iran's international waterways in the south and were seen as gateways to the wider international economy.

Another important provision under the First Plan was the establishment of SEZs throughout the country. If facilitating access to imported goods was only partially important for setting up Iran's FTZs, it was an even more explicit motivation behind the establishment of SEZs. Even before the Revolution and in the heyday of the 1970s' oil-boom, various industrial units had experienced costly delays in sourcing their industrial inputs and intermediate products from abroad. To address this, special facilities had been set up by Tehran's Customs Office to facilitate the importation and storage of such goods. The need for these was heightened in the 1980s with the disruptions caused by the Iraq war.

Article 20 of the First Five-Year Development Plan recognized the need for the so-called '*protected customs areas*' but introduced a two-pronged approach whereby the zones in the mainland were managed by the Customs and those on the shorelines were under the supervision of the Ports and Shipping Organization. Under this Plan, the first SEZ was established in Sirjan in 1992 (in Kerman province, north of Bandar Abbas) under the official title of 'protected customs area'. The status was later changed as Sirjan was officially designated an SEZ. This was then followed by a second zone in Sarakhs on the old silk route connecting Iran's northeastern province of Khorasan to the Central Asian states through a newly established railway line (Mashad–Sarakhs–Tajan).

The number of SEZs in Iran steadily increased thereafter with a third zone set up in the port of Anzali (which was later changed into an FTZ), and a fourth one was also designated in an existing FTZ area of Qeshm (embracing the non-FTZ areas of this island). The momentum gathered pace in 1997 when several new SEZs were introduced. Moreover, new zones with a 'special theme' were established such as a petrochemicals zone in Bandar Khomeini, followed by an energy SEZ (oil and gas) in Pars (1998), a mining zone in Lorestan (1999), an electronics zone in Yazd (1997) and a shipping zone in Bushehr. There are currently a total of 16 SEZs in Iran (see Annex A for details).

Objectives and administrative set-up

As stated above, most free zones are set up with a set of explicit or stated objectives. The most common ones are: to attract FDI and to promote manu-facturing exports, to create jobs, to upgrade domestic technological capability, managerial skills and know-how, and to regenerate deprived and stressed areas and regions. Many zones have implicit or unstated objectives, too. The two most common ones being: to reduce anti-export bias (while keeping the protective barriers elsewhere in the economy intact); and to act as experimental laboratories for trialling new policies (such as financial, legal and labour policies) before considering their application elsewhere in the economy (Akinci and Crittle, 2008: 12; Madani, 1999: 16–17).

In the case of Iran, too, free zones have had both a policy and infrastructure rationale combining most of the above goals and objectives. For the Free Trade-Industrial Zones, in particular, the principal stated objective was to help reduce Iran's isolation from the international economy by promoting both domestic investment and FDI to boost manufacturing exports. As we have seen, this explains their location in areas with good, strategic links with major waterways and key regional markets. A further, albeit implicit, attraction of these entities in the Iranian context has been the promotion of non-oil exports and greater economic diversification in the absence of a more comprehensive, nationwide, but vexed, programme of economic liberalization.

The objectives of the SEZs are rather different. These zones are far more dispersed throughout the country and are expected to play a more active role in regional policy, for their potential role in revitalizing designated regions, as well as in improving the country's distribution system and supply network. Given the physical size of Iran and its logistical problems with the supply and distribution of imported inputs and intermediate products, it is not surprising that the SEZs have the added attraction of facilitating imported goods in transit and improving the industrial inventory system, whilst simultaneously generating income and revenue for the SEZ authorities and creating local jobs.

FTZs and SEZs in Iran have markedly different governance structures. Governance matters pertaining to the Free Trade Zones are defined by '*The Law on the Administration of Free Trade-Industrial Zones*', As mentioned above, this law was first passed in 1993 under the auspices of the First Five-Year Development Plan and was subsequently amended in 1999. It comprises 28 Articles and eight Notes, covering all aspects relating to operations, management and governance in the zones (Free Zones Regulations).

According to this law, all plans for the establishment of new zones and their boundaries are subject to proposal by the government and have to be ratified by the Islamic Consultative Assembly. Moreover, each zone is administered by an Authority organized as a company, with an autonomous legal status, whose capital shall belong to the government.[5] Management is through a Board of Directors, which consists of three to five persons appointed by the Board of Ministers. The Managing Director, who is also *ex officio* chairman of the Board, is appointed by the President of the Republic from amongst the members of the Board of Directors and is the highest executive authority in the economic affairs and infrastructure of a zone. To facilitate the coordination of the zones' activities, a High Council was established, which is chaired by the President and its membership is made up of various Ministers and the Secretary of the High Council of Free Trade–Industrial Zones.[6] The Council in turn has a Secretariat, which is administered by the Secretary, who is appointed by President of the Republic.

Most significantly, perhaps, the Board of Ministers has under Article 138 of the Constitution, delegated all powers for the management of the zones to the Secretariat. This means that in the case of the FTZs, clear guidelines and legal powers exist which define their operation and management.[7] This is deemed necessary to avoid inconsistencies and conflicts between different departments and the management of these zones.

This contrasts with the operation of the SEZs, which were set up and are managed in different circumstances. Until 2005, these zones were governed according to Article 25 of the Second Five-Year Development Plan (1994–9). In 2005, The Expediency Council intermediated between the *Majlis* and the Guardian Council to finalize the set of rules for these zones commonly known as '*The Law on the Establishment and Administration of Special Economic Zones in the Islamic Republic of Iran.*' This law comprises 25 Articles and 12 Notes and covers all aspects relating to operations, management and governance in these zones.[8]

As we shall see below, there are numerous similarities between these rules and those governing the operations and management of the FTZs. However, one of the main differences relates to the general governance and administration of these zones. Unlike the FTZs, the establishment and operation of SEZs is not subject to a clear cut and universal template. First, the administration of SEZs is open to both state and non-state entities unlike the FTZs, which can only be administered by state bodies. Second, a decentralized administration system is in place which subjects each special zone to the constitution and rules of its own home organization (see Annex A for details on the relevant authority for each SEZ). In practice, this means there is a multiplicity of decision-making bodies and one corollary of this is that the budget for each zone is determined by its parent organization rather than centrally by the Secretariat Authority, which oversees all FTZs.

It is common for most free zones to enhance their geographic and locational advantages by offering additional concessions to foreign investors. In Iran, too, the quest for establishing free zones has seen the introduction of a number of incentives to promote business and particularly FDI into designated areas. These are briefly discussed below.

Business environment

Economic incentives

A wide range of economic incentives is on offer in Iran's zones to encourage domestic and foreign investment. The most common measures are: 15 years' tax exemption for operators within the FTZs (this does not apply to SEZs); duty exemption for raw materials and machinery imported for production and manufacturing in the zones; no taxes are levied on re-exports and exported goods from the zones to the mainland; and provision of competitive infrastructure facilities and ancillary services.

Additionally, all zones boast good availability of skilled and semi-skilled manpower and highlight Iran's abundant energy resources (crude oil and natural gas). Several of them benefit from warm climates which, combined with Iran's strong historical heritage, can act as major attractions for tourism.

To complement these incentives, a special legal framework and special labour laws have also been adopted to increase the attractions of doing business in the zones. The former aims to offer a streamlined bureaucracy and a set of business friendly rules and regulations for enticing investors, and the latter greater flexibility of employment in the zones.

Legal framework

The 'Law on the Administration of Free Trade-Industrial Zones' offers a raft of special rules and regulations designed to attract new enterprises to the FTZs. These include full protection and guarantees offered to foreign investors. For instance, joint ventures are allowed with no limits on investment. It is thus possible to set up a wholly owned foreign enterprise in the FTZs (in the SEZs, a limit of 49 per cent applies to foreign ownership). Other concessionary provisions include:

1. no currency restrictions;
2. 100 per cent of capital and profit may be repatriated (to other Iranian Free Zones or to other countries);
3. non-Iranians can lease land (Iranians can also buy and sell land);
4. business set up and company registration is streamlined and bureaucracy is simplified;

5.   foreign nationals do not require visas for entry into the FTZs; and finally,
6.   special employment and labour regulations apply in the zones (discussed below).

In general, some rules are commonly applicable to both FTZs and SEZs. Chief among them are:

1.   goods produced, as well as those in transit, are exempt from customs duties when exported to the mainland;
2.   both zones benefit from complete freedom of entry and exit for capital (including foreign capital);
3.   in both zones, land can only be leased to foreigners (Iranians can buy and/or lease land);
4.   special labour and employment laws apply in both zones (see below); and finally,
5.   employing foreign labour is allowed in both zones (with a limit of 10 per cent of the workforce in the enterprise).

There are, however, some differences, too. The main ones being:

1.   there is a 15-year tax exemption for businesses in the FTZs (Iran's general tax rules, however, apply to the SEZ enterprises);
2.   foreign nationals are exempt from visa entry requirements for the FTZs (in the SEZs, mainland visa entry requirements apply);
3.   in the FTZs both Iranians and foreign nationals can engage in retail transactions (in SEZs only the latter are allowed this facility);[9]
4.   there is no limit for foreign ownership in FTZs (a ceiling of 49 per cent applies for joint ventures in SEZs);
5.   FTZs benefit from full off-shore banking facilities including free market exchange rates (in SEZs, only domestic banking services and exchange regulations applicable to state banks are in force).

Labour laws

Probably the most important factor differentiating the business environment in the zones from the rest of the country concerns their respective labour laws. The labour laws applicable in both FTZs and SEZs, as well as in Iran's Science and Technology Parks, are known as '*Regulations of Employment of Human Resources, Insurance and Social Security in the Free Trade – Industrial Zones.*'[10] These were developed at an early stage according to *'The Law on the Administration of Free Trade-Industrial Zones'* and are under the supervision of the zones' authorities. Elsewhere and in the rest of the country, Iran's Labour Code applies (Iran Labour Code, 1990). This was adopted in 1990 and is jointly overseen by the Ministry of Labour and Social Affairs (MoLSA) and the Ministry of Justice.

Despite their many commonalities, the regulations are more flexible and permissive compared to the Code in such key provisions as suspension or termination of employment and other aspects of working conditions.

Probably the most significant difference in the two documents relates to rules regarding termination of employment. The Code limits employment termination to six events:

1. the worker's death;
2. the worker's retirement;
3. the worker's total disability;
4. the expiry of a fixed-term contract;
5. the completion of work under a contract concluded for a specified assignment; and
6. the worker's resignation (Article 21 of Iran's 'Labour Code').

It is virtually impossible for employers to dismiss a worker for any other reason in Iran. By contrast, the regulations take a more flexible view by permitting the employer and the employee to agree and stipulate other reasons for termination, for instance for *'economic, technological, and organizational reasons'* – an arrangement not allowed in the Code.[11]

Similarly, the Labour Code establishes much more generous severance payments in case of contract termination – generally defined as one month's salary entitlement for each year of service.[12] According to the regulations, however, severance payments are negotiated individually. If the dismissal of the worker is judged acceptable by the Board of Settlement of Disputes, the board shall confirm the dismissal, and shall oblige the employer to pay only half a month's salary (15 days) to the employee for each year of service (Article 33 of the 'Regulations').

There are no significant differences in respect of minimum wages in both provisions, as the regulations stipulate that these shall not be less than the minimum legal wages elsewhere in Iran.[13] Despite this similarity, however, the regulations are less generous in respect of employees' entitlements for annual leave. For instance, the Labour Code provides for one month's entitlement for paid annual leave (in addition to the official holidays observed by the country).[14] The regulations are also more flexible in relation to the number of regular working hours.[15]

And last, but not least, the regulations only vaguely cover issues such as occupational safety and health, and provision of training; they do not cover issues relating to workers' and employers' organizations, collective bargaining and agreements; or workers' welfare services.

In general, the regulations provide far more flexible work arrangements based on individualized labour contracts, and less generous entitlements, such as annual leave, overtime bonuses, or welfare benefits in the zones compared to the mainland. This is in sharp contrast to the Labour Code, which is notoriously more prescriptive, especially with regards to its provision for suspension or termination of an employment contract; remuneration; or working conditions for vulnerable groups, such as women and youth.

In what follows below, we shall see whether the adoption of the above stimuli measures – economic incentives combined with legal and regulatory privileges – were adequate and effective to attract new investment to the zones, helping them achieve their stated objectives.

Track record

A full assessment of the free zones' record requires a careful study of their respective incremental benefits and costs. Benefits are customarily categorized into static and dynamic benefits (Akinci and Crittle, 2008: 32–3). Static benefits consist of the zones' direct employment and income creation, export growth and diversification, foreign exchange earnings, foreign direct investment, and government revenues. Dynamic benefits consist of their contribution to indirect employment creation, upgrading of skills, female empowerment, technology transfer, positive demonstration effects associated with the adoption of best practices, and regional development and regeneration. In general, it is easier to measure the static benefits, although the dynamic benefits may be much more important in the longer term.

There are also significant costs associated with the set up and maintenance of the zones. Relevant costs are: salaries of the government employees in the zones, operating costs of the zone authorities, infrastructure development outlays, and any tax incomes forgone from the domestic firms which relocate from the mainland to the zones. For both costs and benefits, only incremental values should be taken into account, i.e. those additional costs and benefits that could be attributed to the zones and would not have been incurred otherwise (Akinci and Crittle, 2008: 33).

A full assessment of Iran's free zones is, however, hampered by two factors. First, as we have seen, many of the zones are relatively new creations and therefore lack sufficient history and track record. Second, there is a pervasive – almost institutionalized – dearth of evidence relating to the experience of the free zones in Iran. For instance, only the Kish Free Zone Organization publishes some quantitative information on certain aspects of its operations and even this information is limited in scope and highly selective in nature. In any case, the partial evidence and inadequate data that is available seem to point to serious shortcomings so far and point to very limited achievements of the zones in the Iranian context.

Tables 4.4–6 provide data on three key aspects associated with the static benefits for the three principal zones of Kish, Qeshm and Chahbahar for which some data is available: trade and contribution to exports, investment (including FDI), and employment creation. Below, we examine these briefly.

As stated before, one of the main objectives behind the establishment of the FTZs was to help diversify Iran's non-oil exports and to act as a springboard for exporting manufactured goods. On the contrary, evidence suggests that the zones have developed into mainly import platforms. This is evident from Table 4.4, which shows a huge disparity between the zones' import and export volumes in

Table 4.4 Imports and exports – Iran's FTZs, 1993–2004 (million $)

	Kish		Qeshm		Chabahar		Total	
	Imports	Exports	Imports	Exports	Imports	Exports	Imports	Exports
1993–2000							2,494	56.9
2001	136.6	4	247.8	9.5	100	0.06	484.4	13.6
2002	135.2	3	445.3	11.5	102.3	0.3	682.8	14.8
2003	82	4	194.5	114	73.8	0.2	350.3	118.2
2004	68.2	6.3	162.4	40.5	105.3	0.2	335.9	47.0
2001–04	422	17.3	1050	175.5	381.4	0.76	1,853.4	193.6

Source: Secretariat of the High Council of the Free Trade-Industrial Zones (1380) and (1383).

the three pioneering FTZs in the first seven years of their establishment (1993–2000) followed by the next four years (2001–4). It can be seen that during the early years, imports outstripped exports by a staggering import/export ratio of 44:1. Although the gap has declined to 10:1 in more recent years, it is clear that the zones still have a long way to go to meet their exports and foreign exchange earnings expectations.

There are also significant disparities marking the experiences of these three zones. In Chahbahar, exports have been virtually non-existent. In the case of Qeshm Island, in 1998, imports amounted to $480 million, compared to exports earnings of $1 million only. It has been argued that of the 145 companies registered on the Island, only a handful could be considered to be engaged in any meaningful export business or activity (Hedayati-Zadeh, 2007). Moreover, the total combined exports of Kish and Qeshm Islands for the entire period 2001–4 amounted to $193 million only. That is just a fraction of Iran's non-oil exports (with an average annual figure of about $5.6 billion for the same period) (Hakimian, 2011: 864). It is thus clear that the zones' 'success' to date has been limited to acting as platforms for meeting Iran's appetite for consumer goods imports rather than acting as export platforms.

The zones also score very low in respect of another one of their original objectives. Table 4.5 gives the volumes and trends for domestic and foreign investment for the same three principal zones since 2003. It can be seen that despite an increasing trend in more recent years, overall foreign investment remained very modest: amounting to a total of $2.8 billion for all three zones combined over more than a decade since they were set up (1993–2004). The lion's share is apportioned by Kish (accounting for just under 60 per cent), followed by Qeshm (under 40 per cent) with a mere two per cent going to Chahbahar. Similarly, domestic investment has risen over these years with Kish accounting for more than four-fifths of all investment (81 per cent), followed by Qeshm (14.3 per cent), with again a modest performance by Chahbahar (less than five per cent).

But even this point – indicating the zones' success in attracting *domestic* investment – has to be qualified by the fact that some of this represents a diversion

Table 4.5 Domestic and foreign investment in Iran FTZs, 1993–2004

	Kish		Qeshm		Chahbahar		Total	
	Foreign	Domestic	Foreign	Domestic	Foreign	Domestic	Foreign	Domestic
	(m $)	(Bn Rls)	(m $)	(Bn Rls)	(m $)	(Bn Rls)	(m $)	(Bn Rls)
1993		4.31		116.5			0	120.8
1994		26	0.33	109.6			0.3	135.6
1995		116	2.6	83.2		5.1	2.6	204.3
1996	29.3	305	43.75	57		68.7	73.1	430.7
1997	130	335	61.7	183.6		75.97	191.7	594.6
1998	118	172	100	276.6		134	218	582.6
1999	120	253	142	330.6	1	114	263	697.6
2000	115	312	125	478.75	1	10.7	241	801.5
2001	218	2553	160	585	0.3	5	378.3	3143.0
2002	315	3398	143	600	1.2	4	459.2	4002.0
2003	302	7649	217	649	1.2	109	520.2	8407.0
2004	300	8296	100	670	53.5	838	453.5	9804.0
Total	1647.3	23419.31	1095.38	4139.85	58.2	1364.47	2,800.9	28,923.6
(% of Total)	58.8	81.0	39.1	14.3	2.1	4.7	100	100

Source: Secretariat of the High Council of the Free Trade-Industrial Zones (1380) and (1383).

of investment from elsewhere in the economy reflecting incentives on offer in the zones. As mentioned above, it is the incremental benefits that should be considered and although available data do not make it clear to what extent domestic investment in the zones reflects diversionary investment, considering the costs (both direct incentives and infrastructure provided) would qualify the extent of such success.

Table 4.6 sheds light on employment creation in these three zones during the first nine years of their operation (1993–2001). Starting from very low bases, it is evident that all three zones have experienced rapid growth in employment (reflecting the size of the Island, Qeshm accounts for the largest workforce). In absolute terms, however, the contribution of any one zone or even their combined effect – amounting to a total workforce of just over 45,000 – is very modest for a country the size of Iran, with an official unemployment rate of about 11.5 per cent (World Bank, 2007).[16] It is further reported that employment in the private sector companies operating in Qeshm as of March 2008 amounted to 1,144 employees only. Most are concentrated in small-scale consumer goods industries with an average employment size of fewer than 25 persons (Hakimian, 2011: 865).

Female employment creation – another common attraction of the free zones in the global context as we saw earlier – is again very weak in the Iranian experience. Although detailed employment figures by gender are not available, the limited

Table 4.6 Employment in Iran's FTZs, 1993–2001 ('000 persons)

	Kish		Qeshm		Chahbahar		Total	
		% Change		% Change		% Change		% Change
1993	1.2		1				2.2	
1994	3	150%	5.4	440%	0.5		8.9	305%
1995	5	67%	7.7	43%	1.7	240%	14.4	62%
1996	7.4	48%	14.2	84%	3	76%	24.6	71%
1997	7.6	3%	18.8	32%	4.5	50%	30.9	26%
1998	8.7	14%	21	12%	5.5	22%	35.2	14%
1999	9.1	5%	22	5%	7	27%	38.1	8%
2000	9.4	3%	24	9%	8	14%	41.4	9%
2001	10.5	12%	26.5	10%	8.5	6%	45.5	10%

Source: Secretariat of the High Council of the Free Trade-Industrial Zones (1380) and (1383).

demographic data on the Kish Island indicates a highly skewed gender composition of the population in favour of males, indeed.

Table 4.7 shows the demographic growth and expansion of the Island in the last half century since Iran's first census was conducted in 1956. It is clear that, despite a quick growth spurt in the oil-boom days of the mid-1970s, the Island's population remained small throughout the 1980s. It was not until after it was officially established as a free zone in the mid-1990s that its population began to increase noticeably. According to Iran's latest census, there were some 20,000 inhabitants in the island in 2006 (up from nearly 3,000 in 1986). This indicates that over the past decade, both the population and the number of families living on the Island have trebled. Furthermore, as mentioned above, the gender composition is highly

Table 4.7 The population of Kish Island by gender and number of families (1956–2006)

Date	Population			No of families
	Men	Women	Total	
Nov 1956	377	383	760	*
Nov 1966	457	428	885	*
Nov 1976	3,916	1,676	5,592	*
Oct 1986	1,473	1,358	2,858	*
Oct 1996	5,148	2,274	7,422	1,818
Nov 1997	9,688	2,959	12,647	2,953
Dec 1998	11,087	4,139	15,226	3,883
March 2000	11,133	5,368	16,501	4,454
March 2004	13,767	7,998	21,765	6,316
2006	12,381	8,541	20,922	6,168

Source: Kish Free Zone Organization.

biased in favour of males (with a 60:40 ratio). This indicates the sizeable presence of single, male internal migrants who are attracted to the zone in search of jobs.

As stated above, data limitations make it impossible to conduct a more detailed assessment of the zones' track record. However, even the limited data available for Iran's flagship free zone – Kish – suggests that this island has emerged as a major centre for domestic trade and tourism.[17]

Challenges and prospects

For over a decade and a half, Iran's free zones have (officially at least) sought to act as special havens for attracting capital investment and spearheading Iran's quest for economic diversification in an international context. Offering incentives and facilities – from infrastructure to special rules and a dedicated legal framework – they have tried to entice domestic and foreign investors to create jobs and to promote Iran's non-oil exports.

The discussion in the last section has, however, indicated that despite these incentives, Iran's experience has been anything but a success: the free zones have failed to achieve their principal stated objectives of attracting FDI, diversifying the economy and contributing to employment creation. Even Kish has emerged at best as a centre for domestic trade and tourism, a far cry from the zones' original objective of helping Iranian exports reach international markets.

Viewed from a broad perspective, such a limited and unsuccessful experience with the free zones is at odds with Iran's greater *potential* to emerge as a centre of regional and international importance. Iran commands great geographic and geo-political significance in the Middle East and the Persian Gulf context and benefits from rich natural and human resources. With a landmass three times the size of Spain, and with a population of over 70 million, Iran is one of the largest MENA countries. She is the fourth largest oil producer in the world (the second largest in OPEC) with natural gas reserves that account for about 15 per cent of the world's total – placing it second after Russia. Iran has a developed educational infrastructure and a health-care system that offers abundant supplies of literate and technically trained personnel. Moreover, its rich culture and history as an ancient civilization offer unique tourist attractions enhancing its potential as an important gateway between 'East and West'.

Placed in this broad context, Iran's free zones could, in theory at least, have benefited from Iran's potential attractions as a hub for regional business and commerce. As we have seen, the FTZs have good access to major air, sea and land transportation routes at the local, regional, and international levels. This puts them in proximity to the regional markets, which facilitates importation of raw materials and intermediate or manufactured goods and provides easy access to local and neighbouring markets – principally those of the CIS and Central Asia in the North and the Persian Gulf and the GCC states in the South (the so-called North-South route).

Against these potentially positive factors, however, Iran's experience of setting up and operating free zones – as seen in the last section – has been marred in practice by at least two sets of factors. At one level, some design and operational issues – micro-level factors – have diminished their success. Much more importantly however, macro-level factors too have played their part in limiting a successful outcome. These relate in the main to the uncertain business and investment climate in Iran coupled with ambiguities towards foreign investment during much of the post-revolutionary period, and growing regional competition in recent decades – all thwarting the success of Iran's experimentation with the free zones. We shall discuss these two sets of factors in turn below.

It is clear that there are some important operational and design lessons to be learnt from Iran's experience of the free zones. Chief among these are lack of sufficient focus on, and clarity of, objectives, governance matters, and resourcing issues.

For instance, the customs rules adopted for the early FTZs had much to do with an outcome that witnessed their emergence as a main source of domestic tourism and commerce – a most notable feature in the case of Kish Island – as seen above. One important reason behind this related to the customs rules adopted since early stages in the zones. In a bid to draw in visitors and to increase the zone's attractiveness for business and commerce, the rules allowed domestic travellers to the zones to take back with them to the mainland (import) goods according to Iran's general customs and excise regulations (i.e. such goods were treated as imports from abroad and benefited from customs duty free allowances). Given that Iran had just emerged from the consumer goods 'hunger' of the war years in the late 1980s, and the higher costs of travelling abroad, the rule gave Kish an edge in its appeal to Iranian travellers keen to exploit commercial opportunities for purchasing foreign goods at competitive prices. This encouraged Kish from early on to become a major conduit for imports of consumer goods which sprang up on the back of growing domestic tourism, a practice which was contrary to the spirit of setting up FTZs as export platforms.[18]

Customs rules aside, other factors too have diminished the potential success of Iran's free zones. For instance, the proliferation of SEZs has been confusing. Under a decentralized system of governance adopted, each SEZ is subject to the rules and regulations of a different organization or Ministry under which it is set up. Despite the intended greater flexibility, in practice this means there can be as many zone authorities as there are special zones with each Ministry or organization in charge setting and following their own objectives. There have also been resource implications as these zones' budgets are subject to the financial considerations of their parent organizations, which in practice limits their ability to raise revenue.

In the wider scheme of things, however, macro-level factors have posed much more serious challenges for the success of the zones. Here, a generally weak investment and business climate tainted by great political upheaval and uncertainty in much of the post-revolutionary period have been compounded by statist and inward-looking economic policies at large raising the bar against investment in general and foreign investment in particular. Iran has faced these challenges at a time of growing regional competition over FDI further thwarting its experience with free trade zones.

It is widely acknowledged that since the 1979 Revolution, Iran has pursued ambivalent and contradictory economic policies at home characterized by the state and parastatal domination of the key economic sectors. This has combined with a largely isolationist course in the international economic and political arena leading to a weak overall investment climate in which both domestic and foreign investors have been disinclined to engage in long-term productive investment in the country (see Chapter 2 of this book).

Political isolation and Iran's fraught international relations have further exacerbated challenges for investors who have been navigating an economic landscape tainted by revolutionary political upheaval, internal strife and far-reaching institutional changes since the 1979 Revolution. On the one hand, foreign investors have been deterred by official ambivalence – if not open hostility – towards investment from abroad. On the other hand, economic sanctions – albeit targeted and focused on particular sectors – have dissuaded foreign capital from taking a direct interest in Iranian markets. Even before the more recent nuclear stand-off with the West, which has led to financial sanctions against Iran, the US trade sanctions since 1996, have aimed to deter foreign investors away from Iran's key energy sectors (see Chapter 7 of this book and Salehi Esfahani and Pesaran, 2009: 207–11).

In this context, luring foreign capital into Iran or into the free zones has not been an easy task. In the face of significant political and economic uncertainty, the government's pro-business policies and incentives offered in the zones have lacked credibility, flying in the face of inward-looking policies in force elsewhere, which are broadly seen as unwelcoming to foreign interests.

Experience seems to suggest that the most successful zones have been able to capitalize on their links with the mainland.[19] In Iran, on the contrary, the pursuit of free zones and mainland policies have been largely decoupled from, if not at odds with, each other. Thus, despite the best efforts in the zones, their ability to attract investment is curtailed by adverse external perceptions of Iran as an investment destination and internal imperatives dispelling such investment.

Additionally, Iran has faced growing competition within the region. The recent successes of smaller, resource-rich Gulf States and emirates such as Dubai and Qatar with a clearly established lead in exploiting their free zone advantages, makes it that much harder for late-comers like Iran to succeed. Even larger economies in the region seem to have established a clear lead over Iran in their appeal to foreign investors: Saudi Arabia is determined to push ahead with far-reaching economic reforms and setting up new and large economic cities; and Turkey has sought to exploit its links with Europe and a to make a virtue of the economic difficulties its neighbour – Iran – faces vis-à-vis the rest of the international economy.

What is clear is that even if the overall investment climate in Iran were to improve and some of the obstacles to foreign investment were to disappear overnight (with better external relations, internal political and macroeconomic stability, and greater willingness for foreign investment), tough regional competition would still mean Iran faces an uphill struggle for years to come.

Conclusion

Iran's experience of free zones in the past decade and half has failed to achieve its principal objectives of attracting FDI, diversifying non-oil exports and generating new jobs. Apart from certain design and operational issues, this paper has highlighted a number of important factors that have diminished the success of these zones: international sanctions; an uncertain business and investment climate in Iran during much of the post-revolutionary period; general ambiguities towards foreign investment; and growing regional competition in recent decades. Despite offering major economic and legal incentives as well as improved infrastructure, Iran's generally weak appeal as an investment destination has severely curtailed the zones' overall attraction for foreign investors. The zones appeal to domestic investors, too, has arguably been mainly due to diversion of investment from elsewhere in the economy (to take advantage of incentives on offer), thus qualifying their overall *net* contribution to diversification and jobs creation in the economy.

For as long as Iran's FTZs continue to be seen as mere 'back doors to the international economy', prevailing perceptions of Iran as an uncertain and unwelcoming investment destination will continue to thwart their success. Unless economic sanctions are eased and Iran's mainland policies in relation to foreign investment and general economic reform can be streamlined and brought into line with those it aims to promote in the free zones, the latter's ability to succeed will be curtailed and Iran's uphill struggle in the international economic arena will continue.

Notes

* I am grateful to Homa Katouzian, Editor of *Iranian Studies*, where this chapter was originally published (November 2011) for permission to include it in this book.

1 For a typology of different types of free zones, see Akinci and Crittle (2008: 10–11).

2 According to the ILO, the following countries had the highest proportion of female employment in their EPZ operations in 2006: Jamaica 90 per cent, Nicaragua 90 per cent, Bangladesh 85 per cent, El Salvador 85 per cent; Sri Lanka 78 per cent, Honduras 75 per cent, the Philippines 74 per cent; Madagascar 71 per cent, Republic of Korea 70 per cent (see ILO, 2007).

3 Egypt, Syria, Israel and Jordan, for instance, established government-run zones at about the same time that zones were first set up in the Philippines, the Dominican Republic, the Republic of Korea, and Taiwan (see Akinci and Crittle, 2008: 28).

4 Dubai has also pioneered the development of specialized zones, such as 'Internet City', 'Knowledge Village' and 'Media City' (see Akinci and Crittle, 2008: 28–9).

5 'The Authority and its affiliates and subsidiaries shall be exempt from the laws and regulations governing state-owned companies and from other general regulations decreed by the government . . . these companies shall be subject to the Commercial Code' (Article 5).

6 Membership is as follows: Ministers for Economic Affairs and Finance, Commerce, Interior, Labour and Social Affairs, Industries and Mines, Roads and Transportation, Petroleum, Energy, Housing and Urban Development, Culture and Islamic Guidance, the Head of Management and Plan Organization, the Governor of the Central Bank of the Islamic Republic of Iran, Head of the Environment Protection Organization and the Secretary of the High Council of Free Trade–Industrial Zones.

7 For instance, Article 27 clearly enshrines the executive powers of relevant departments to the chairpersons and managing directors of these zones. This means that both in principle and in practice the heads, chiefs and the acting directors of all government departments in the zone are appointed with the joint recommendation of the Chairperson and Managing Director of the free zone and ordinance of the highest official of the relevant government executive department.

8 A Farsi version of this Law is available from: http://www.seez.ir/upload\Establishment% 20and%20Management%20of%20. . . . pdf For an English version, see: http:// amirabadport.pmo.ir/specialeconomiczone-page5249-page5251-en.html

9 This applies only to the first thee FTZs (Kish, Qeshm and Chahbahar).

10 Available from: http://www.alaviandassociates.com/documents/labourregulations1.pdf

11 Whether the dismissal of a worker is acceptable (if disputed) is judged by the Board of Settlement of Disputes in the zones. Moreover, both the Code and Regulations allow for open-ended and fixed-term labour contracts. However, whereas in the Labour Code, the maximum duration of the fixed-term contracts is determined by the MoLSA, no such limits are mentioned in the regulations.

12 If the termination of an employment contract is the result of total disability or retirement of the worker concerned, as well as of the completion of a fixed-term contract, the employer shall pay the worker an amount equal to the last monthly wage for each year of completed service (two monthly wages for each year of service if the disability is work related, and 1.5 monthly wages in case of unlawful dismissal; Articles 31, 32 and 165 of Iran's 'Labour Code').

13 It has been estimated that in Iran, the total costs of employing a worker receiving the minimum wage are equal to 54 per cent of average value-added per worker (of which 44 percentage points are a minimum wage, and 10 percentage points are non-wage costs). The World Bank contends that at this relatively high rate many private firms (especially those in low-tech activities) cannot afford to comply with the minimum-wage law, and as a result, the poor continue to work in informal activities for only a fraction of the mandated minimum wage (World Bank, 2007: 48).

14 It also stipulates that every worker is entitled to take one full month of paid leave and one month of unpaid leave once during his/her working life in order to perform the pilgrimage to Mecca (Article 67 of 'Labour Code'). The Regulations, in contrast, set the limit to an employee's annual paid leave as 20 days (Article 24 of the 'Regulations').

15 The code limits these to 44 hours per week (Article 51). The Regulations take a more flexible route by allowing 176 hours per four consecutive weeks (parties are free to negotiate the actual working hours per day or week within this limit; Article 16 of the 'Regulations').

16 The ILO's EPZ database updates Iran's total free zone employment for 2005–6 at just under 70,000 (ILO, 2007: 7).

17 In 2006, a quarter of all air passenger traffic was attributable to foreign journeys (up from about 5 per cent in 1998). A study of the origins and destination of passengers in the same year shows that about two-thirds of all domestic passengers were attributed to Tehran (68 per cent), followed by Shiraz, Isfahan and Mashhad (each with 7–9 per cent). For external passengers, Dubai was in a commanding position with 80 per cent of all, followed by Sharjah (18 per cent) and Abu Dhabi (2 per cent). The growing volume of air passengers from the UAE indicates bristling business with the neighbouring emirate but also a growing number of Iranians living and working in

the Gulf emirates who maintain business and family ties with those living on the opposite side of the shore (Hakimian, 2011: Table 8).

18 This was subsequently abandoned after 2003, when Iran set up its three new zones (Zakeri, 2006: 3–4).

19 This is, for instance, the case of successful free zones in China, Mauritius and the Philippines (Madani, 1999).

References

Akinci, G., and Crittle, J., '*Special economic zones: performance, lessons learned, and implications for zone development*', Washington DC: The World Bank.

Centre for Free and Special Economic Zones (Iran); website http://www.freezones.ir/ and http://www.freezones.ir/Default.aspx?tabid=282

Esfahani, S. H. and Pesaran, M. H., 'The Iranian economy in the twentieth century: a global perspective', *Iranian Studies*, 42, 2009.

Free Zones Regulations, Centre for Free and Special Economic Zones; available from: http://www.freezones.ir/Default.aspx?tabid=230

Graham, E. M., 'Do export processing zones attract FDI and its benefits? The experience from China', *International Economics and Economic Policy,* 1 (1): 87–103, 2004.

Hakimian, H., 'Iran's free trade zones: back doors to the international economy?', *Iranian Studies*, 44 (6): 851–74, 2011.

Hedayati-Zadeh, R., 'Maziyat-e Mantaghe Azad-e Aras dar Hedayat-e Tavan-mandihay-e Keshvar be Samt-e Saderat' (the Potential Role of Aras Free Zone in Export Promotion), paper presented at the 'First Conference to Identify Investment Opportunities in Aras', Aras Free Zone, 10–12 Aban 1385; available from: http://www.arasfz.ir/fa/papers. htm, 2007.

ILO, 'Database on export processing zones – (Revised)', International Labour Office, Sectoral Activities Programme, Working Paper No. 251; Geneva, April, 2007.

Iran Labour Code (1990), Islamic Republic of Iran; available from: http://www.ilo.org/ dyn/natlex/docs/WEBTEXT/21843/64830/E90IRN01.htm

Kish Free Zone Organization, http://www.kish.ir/HomePage.aspx?TabID=4489&Site= DouranPortal&Lang=en-US

Madani, D., 'A review of the role and impact of export processing zones', World Bank Development Research Group Policy Research Working Paper 2238, Washington DC, 1999.

Miyagiwa, Kaz, 'The locational choice for free-trade zones, rural versus urban options', *Journal of Development Economics*, 40: 187–203, 1993.

Secretariat of the High Council of the Free Trade-Industrial Zones (1380) and (1383), 'Gozaresh-e Amalkard-e Manategh-e Azad' (A Report on the Performance of the FTZs), Tehran.

World Bank, 'Islamic Republic of Iran – Employment and Labour Markets Study', Social and Economic Development Group Middle East and North Africa Region, The World Bank, Washington DC, December, 2007.

Zakeri, A., 'Forsatha va Zarfiathay-e Sarmay-e Gozari dar Mantaghe Azad-e Aras', (Opportunities and Capacities for Investment in the Aras Free Zone), paper presented at the 'First Conference to Identify Investment Opportunities in Aras', Aras Free Zone, 10–12 Aban 1385, 2006.

Annex A Iran's Special Economic Zones (SEZs)

SEZ (Year established)	Area	Responsible authority	Location in Iran	International links	Theme
1. Sirjan (1991)	1700 ha	Kerman Development Organization	North of city of Sirjan	300 km North of Bandar Abbas	Multi-purpose
2. Salafchegan (1997)	2000 ha	Tossa'e va Omrani Qum Company	Near Qom (185 km from Tehran)	No direct link	Multi-purpose
3. Sarakhs (1996)	5200 ha	Astan-e Ghods Razavi	Northeast (165 km from Mashhad)	Turkmenistan	Multi-purpose
4. Petrochemical Special Economic Zone	1770 ha	National Petrochemical Industries Company Organization	Southwest, (Mahshar a district of Bandar Khomeini)	Persian Gulf shores	Petrochemicals
5. Bandar Bushehr	41 ha	Ports and Marine Organization	Southwest (Bushehr port)	Persian Gulf shores	Shipping and Port facilities
6. Arg-e Jadid (1997)	2000 ha	Arg Development Company	10 km from Bam	No direct link	Multi-purpose
7. Pars Special Economic Energy Zone	10000 ha	Pars Special Economic Energy Zone Company	South (between Bandar Abbas and Bandar Bushehr)	Persian Gulf shores	Energy (gas, oil and petrochemicals)
8. Bandar Shaheed Rajaee (1999)	20 sq km	Ports and Marine Organization	South	Persian Gulf shores	Shipping
9. Bushehr (1998)	2034 ha	Bushehr Development Company	South	Persian Gulf shores	Energy (gas, oil and petrochemicals)
10. Shiraz Electric and Electronics SEZ (2000)	300 ha	Fars Industries and Exports Promotion Company	Central (near Shiraz)	No direct link	Electrical and electronic
11. Bandar AmirAbad Behshahr (1997)	60 ha	Ports and Marine Organization	North (Mazandaran)	North-South (Sari-Bandar Abbas)	Port and shipping services

Annex A *(Continued)*

SEZ (Year established)	Area	Responsible authority	Location in Iran	International links	Theme
12. Payam (1992)	3600 ha	Payam Aviation Services Company	50 km west of Tehran	–	Air cargo, postal transportation, storage and time sensitive goods
13. Yazd Textile SEZ (2000)	570 ha	Yazd Industrial Parks Company	Central Iran	No direct link	Textile
14. Keshti Sazi Khaleej Fars		Persian Gulf Shipbuilding & Offshore Industries Complex Company	South	Persian Gulf shores	Shipbuilding
15. Lorestan	71 ha	Industrial Towns Company	Western Iran	No direct link	Stones and quarry
16. Persian Gulf Mines and Metals SEZ (1997)	1200 ha	National Iranian Steel Company NISCO	South (near Bandar Shaheed Rajaee)	Persian Gulf shores	Steel

Source: Compiled from Centre for Free and Special Economic Zones.

5 The role of government in the Iranian banking system, 2001–11

Sima Motamen-Samadian

Introduction

The Iranian financial system appears to have made considerable progress since the establishment of a number of private banks in 2001 and has become more effective in mobilizing funds across the economy. In this respect, private banks appear to have played a positive role in pushing forward with modernization of the banking system and raising the level of private sector financial savings, non-cash financial transactions and e-commerce.

Non-bank financial institutions and markets have also grown to some extent and attracted both private and public participants. For instance, the considerable rise in share prices in the Tehran Stock Exchange (TSE) could be seen as an indication of such participation. Despite these improvements, however, the Iranian economy continues to remain predominantly cash-based, and the range and depth of financial products, markets and institutions within the financial sector remain well behind those of the developed markets. That is to some extent because the private sector remains sceptical about the riskiness and the level of liquidity of various financial assets. This is particularly in view of reports of a number of major corruption and fraud scandals in recent years that have adversely affected public trust in the safety and sound functioning of financial institutions.

Financial development in Iran has arguably been adversely affected by a number of factors:

1. limited development of financial institutions and markets, which is closely linked to inadequate information and transparency of the activities of financial institutions;
2. inefficient property rights and bankruptcy laws;
3. lack of trust in the judicial system;
4. continuous government intervention in the financial sector and the central bank; and
5. the *Sharia* law.

In addition to the above, government's various policies such as subsidy reform and the nuclear programme (which has led to significant international sanctions against Iran) have all contributed to continuous high inflation and economic uncertainty, and in one way or another adversely affected the private sector's activity and financial decision-making. Nevertheless, the banking industry continues to be the main financier of private investments in Iran and appears to be the most profitable sector of the economy compared with other sectors.

In 2005, following the election of Mr Ahmadi-Nejad to the presidency, the government announced its determination to make major changes in the economic environment. In particular, it aimed at reducing unemployment, stimulating private investment, controlling inflation and dealing with the endemic problem of corruption. To implement the above objectives the government adopted the following strategies:

1. To reduce unemployment and stimulate investment, the government adopted an industrial strategy that was supported by an expansionary monetary policy and an expansionary fiscal policy. As far as monetary policy was concerned, banks were instructed to reduce their loan interest rates, and expand their credits to SMEs or the so-called 'businesses with quick returns' in particular to those who invested in small labour intensive projects. The above programme was apparently adopted following the successful example of India's industrial policy after the 1950s when successive governments tried to promote SMEs. Expansionary fiscal policy in Iran was primarily financed by an increase in oil revenues and a rise in its share of government's income. In this respect the rise in the price of oil particularly helped Mr Ahmadi-Nejad's government.
2. To tackle corruption, the government adopted an anti-corruption strategy which was later referred to as the 'silent coup' and involved changing almost all members of the cabinet, mangers of all banks including private banks, and the top officials of a large number of public institutions, and replacing them with a new group of people who were supposedly loyal to Mr Ahmadi-Nejad and Ayatollah Khamenei but had neither the direct education or training related to the offices to which they had been appointed nor the necessary management skills required for running those high offices.
3. To reduce inflation, the government tried to promote imports to increase the supply of goods hoping to reduce inflationary pressures.

Within a short period of time, all the above strategies proved unsuccessful. The government's industrial strategy, though initially appearing to be successful in reducing the rate of unemployment, failed to deliver a long-term fall in the jobless rate. That was partly due to the fact that a large number of borrowers misused the borrowed funds and spent it on either short-term speculative projects, or unrelated expenditure. The failure of the above industrial policy was also partly blamed on the global recession of 2008–9, which affected almost all countries, including the Gulf States such as the UAE with which Iran had a fairly strong trade relation. Hence by 2009–10 the rate of unemployment was rising again. There was also the news of a continuous rise in the level of overdue loans that created serious concern about the safety of banks and their ability to survive. The government's industrial strategy also faced frequent opposition from the Central Bank that was concerned about its adverse impact on the level of liquidity and inflation leading to the resignations of two central bank governors.

The anti-corruption strategy of the government also appears to have failed at two levels with a significant rise in the level of bribery in various state offices and repeated reports of large banking and non-banking frauds in the country. The most important of which was the news of a number of large bank embezzlements and fraud that involved state-owned banks and a large number of officials.

The anti-inflationary strategy of using imports to fill the excess demand gap has also failed to achieve its objectives. That is partly because it led to a fall in the domestic supply due to the closure of a number of domestic producers of import substitutes who could not compete with cheaper imports. It is also partly because the international sanctions on oil exports and the financial sector have considerably reduced the oil export revenue and increased the cost of imports. The combination of the above two has put pressure on the domestic currency to depreciate significantly adding to inflationary pressures.

This chapter discusses the role of government in the banking sector. It aims to shed some light on some of the conflicts that emerged between the objectives of the government and those of the Central Bank, and to show how this adversely affected the ability of the Central Bank to achieve its objectives.

The organization of the paper is as follows. Section 2 provides a brief background to the structure of the banking sector and looks at the recent developments that have taken place. Section 3 examines the extent of independence of the Central Bank and its ability to control inflation. Section 4 discusses the problem of overdue loans and the soundness of the Iranian banking system as a whole. Section 5 sheds light on the extent of financial deepening, and finally section 6 offers some concluding remarks. The study will focus on the policies that were implemented between 2001 and 2011, which covers the period both before and after Mr Ahmadi-Nejad's presidency. Due to unavailability of the latest data in some cases, the study does not cover the whole of this period.

The structure and operation of the banking system in Iran

Following the Revolution, the government nationalized all private banks and insurance companies, merged a number of newly nationalized banks and introduced an Islamic banking system. Accordingly, the number of state-owned commercial banks was reduced to three,[1] specialized banks were reduced to six,[2] and the number of representative foreign banks dropped from 70 prior to the Revolution to 30 in 1987,[3] and further to only five in 2011 due to the international sanctions.[4]

In 2004, Article 44 of the Constitution that determined the structure of ownership of economic entities in Iran was amended and allowed for privatization of some state-owned institutions and the establishment of private enterprises. According to new amendments, 80 per cent of state-owned institutions were to be privatized, and only 20 per cent of each industry was to remain under the state control. Consequently, the TSE was re-launched in 2004, and four private investment institutions were established in 2006.[5] These were engaged in both retail and wholesale banking as well as universal banking where the banks themselves were investing in various economic activities and institutions.

The process of privatization was further enhanced in 2007, when Ayatollah Khamenei asked the government to speed up the process of privatization. Accordingly, the director of privatization programme announced on 11 July 2007 the government's intention to privatize five state-owned banks.[6] By 2012 the number of private banks had increased to 18[7] (see Table 5.1 for the number of banks and the structure of the banking system in Iran before and after the Revolution).

It is important to point out that following the establishment of private banks, the number of bank branches rapidly increased in Iran and by 2012 their number rose to 20,000 which is much higher than those of other countries in the region such as Turkey where bank branches are around 6,000.[8]

The payment systems

Until 2001 the payment system and bank clearing arrangements in Iran were highly underdeveloped and lagged behind other developing countries. Following the limited financial liberalization of 2001 and the rise in competition among banks, private banks began to introduce debit cards and their own ATMs, and more recently some have also introduced their own credit card.

In 2002, the government introduced the SHETAB system (Interbank Information Transfer Network), which is an electronic banking clearance network that requires all bank ATMs and POS (Payment at Point of Service) machines to adhere to its standards.

Between 2005 and 2008, the Central Bank of the Islamic Republic of Iran (CBI) reached an agreement with the Central Banks of Bahrain, UAE, Qatar, Kuwait and China to connect their ATMs to the SHETAB system. This enabled Iranian travellers to have direct access to their accounts in Iran. A number of

Table 5.1 The structure of the banking system before and after the revolution

Type of banks/ No. of banks	Commercial banks	Specialized banks	Savings and loan associations	Regional banks	Foreign banks
Prior to the Revolution in 1978/79	24	12	3	3	70
	Commercial government-owned banks	State-owned specialized banks	Private commercial banks	Private investment banks	Foreign representatives
1978/9–2012	3	6	18	3	5

Source: Curtis and Hooglund (2008).

banks have also made arrangements with retailers and suppliers of electronic and durable goods and businesses in service sectors such as hotels and restaurants to accept their debit and credit cards and to accept POS. Nevertheless, most of those institutions that accept POS tend to be in big cities and their number remain rather low in the country.

An increasing number of banks are also introducing online banking. The SHETAB system is particularly important for the development of e-commerce, which has grown considerably over the last decade. The above developments have helped somewhat to reduce the reliance of the public on cash transactions. This is evident from the fall in the ratio of notes and coins to M1, which was reported in the CBI Annual Review (2010–11) to have fallen from 32 per cent in 2010 to 29.7 per cent in 2011.

In addition to the SHETAB system, 2010–11 also witnessed the launch of three new payment systems. These were TABA (the Scriptless Securities Settlement System), which is for placement and settlement of various securities, PAYA (the automated clearing house system) responsible for processing individual and multiple payment orders, and connection of the SHETAB to ATMs and POS Switch systems for the acceptance of international bank cards, and SHAPARAK which is an electronic card payment system responsible for the centralization and reorganization of all POSs and acceptance of interbank cards.

Despite the above developments, the public continues to rely heavily on cash payments. A number of factors are responsible for this trend:

1. a high rate of inflation which creates a high level of uncertainty about the future purchasing power of money;
2. a low percentage of retailers that hold POS machines;
3. high concentration of bank branches in big cities and limited access to bank branches in rural areas;
4. public distrust of financial institutions;
5. as well as religious beliefs that associates bank operations with usury.

The latter is despite the changes that have taken place in banking regulations after the Revolution and the fact that all Iranian banks offer interest free deposits called gharz-al-hassaneh accounts. These accounts, while enabling depositors to enjoy safekeeping of their funds by banks, offer no interest on deposits, instead entitling the depositor to win a prize through a prize draw. In this respect they are similar to the British Premium Bonds, where the account holder receives no interest but is entitled to win prizes in the weekly prize draws. While Premium Bonds are primarily used for financing the Public Sector Borrowing Requirement (PSBR) in the UK, gharz-al-hassaneh accounts in Iran are partly used by public banks and partly by private banks to provide low interest loans or credits to those that are determined by the government. In general, gharz-al-hassaneh deposit accounts are highly profitable for banks, as they do not pay out any interest. Hence banks enter into a kind of non-price competition to attract customers, and offer prizes such as cars or household goods that can be won through prize draws. In practice, banks may give the prizes to only about four per cent of their customers.[9] In most cases, the financial value of prizes is very small and only very few large prizes such as automobiles are given. These prizes are paid out of the profits that banks make from working with those deposits and the frequency of prize draws varies among banks.

The attraction of prizes, however, appears to have outweighed the religious incentives of such accounts in recent years and encouraged the public to frequently move their deposits from one bank to another. After coming to presidency in 2006, Mr Ahmadi-Nejad instructed banks to reduce the ceiling of their prizes to discourage the profit motive for opening such accounts. Also as the frequency of movement of funds from one bank to another adversely affected both the banks and the central bank's ability to control the liquidity, banks were issued a decree in 2008 to have only two prize draws a year. Moreover, to discourage continuous movements of funds, the draws should not be more than ten days apart from that of other banks.

According to the CBI reports in 2008–9, total gharz-al-hassaneh deposits accounted for 7.8 per cent of the total liabilities of specialized banks (including agricultural banks), 3.2 per cent of the total public banks' liabilities, but only 0.5 per cent of total liabilities of private banks. The above differences in the share of gharz-al-hassaneh accounts of different banks' liabilities reflects the extent of religious public's view about the involvement of private banks in usury. The CBI data in Economic Trends (2008–9) also show that in that year, gharz-al-hassaneh deposits accounted for 29.3 per cent of M1, which is more or less the same percentage as the share of notes and coins in M1.

Along with the above deposit accounts there are also gharz-al hassaneh loans that act as interest free loans that banks extend to borrowers. These loans account for about five per cent of the total loans extended by all commercial and specialized banks. Additionally, there are also about 6,000 small-scale unofficial funds called 'gharz-al-hassaneh' funds that are involved in raising funds at a zero interest rate and providing interest free loans to lower income borrowers. These are not registered anywhere and hence are not subject to any reserve requirement or supervision of the central bank. According to an IMF report in 2004, there were also over 1,000 registered credit cooperatives, which were very small, and their total asset was below 0.1 per cent of GDP. The *Bonyads* also have established some quasi-banking institutions that are supervized by them.

In addition to the above, there are also numerous lenders in the unofficial kerb markets, which offer short-term loans at very high interest rates.[10] Their presence in practice reflects the private sector's difficulty in raising funds through the official banking and financial markets.

The independence of the Central Bank

Historically central banks are considered to have two very important objectives: maintaining the purchasing power of money both at home and internationally, and ensuring the sound operation of the financial system and maintaining the public's trust in that system. In order to achieve these objectives, central banks should have the ability to adopt appropriate measures to control inflation, prevent excessive depreciation of the domestic currency and keep a watchful eye on the safe conduct of the financial institutions.

Meeting the above objectives, however, might not always comply with governments' objectives, which may be more politically motivated especially when seeking popularity for re-elections. Hence the problem of 'time inconsistency' might arise between the monetary and fiscal policies that central banks might approve and those that governments might wish to adopt. That is why it is considered important for central banks to be independent (see, for example, Fischer, 1995; Alesina and Gatti, 1995; Franzese, 1999; Eggertsson and Le Borgne 2003; Ahsan *et al.*, 2006 and 2009; Agrawal, 2010; and Bernanke, 2010). The events of the 2007–8 global financial crises, however, have compelled some to question the merits of full central bank independence in cases of economic recession or a considerable fall in public trust in the safe conduct of the banking system (Agrawal, 2010, and Gorby, 2012).

In Iran, the independence of the Central Bank has been seriously undermined since the presidency of Mr Ahmadi-Nejad in 2005, as not only the President but also the parliament started to intervene in determination of interest rates and monetary policy – both supposed to be in the Central Bank's domain of responsibility. Indeed, according to Article 10 of Iran's Law of Money and Banking, the CBI is responsible for the design and implementation of monetary and credit policies of the country in line with the country's macroeconomic policy.

In the case of Iran one might identify four cases where the government's objectives and programmes have adversely affected the CBI's ability to control inflation and to exercise strong monitoring and supervisory power over the operation of the banking system. These are:

1. The government's decision and the parliament's approval of increasing the proportion of oil revenues in government budget. A policy that used up a large proportion of foreign exchange reserves and led to a significant rise in the level of liquidity and inflation.
2. The government's decision to adopt expansionary monetary policy and instruction to all banks to lower their interest rate on loans and to increase their lending to businesses with 'quick return' in order to reduce unemployment and stimulate the economy.
3. The government's removal of subsidies on fuel and some consumer goods that led to a sharp increase in prices and closure and bankruptcies of a large number of factories.
4. The government's stand-off with the West over its nuclear programme which has led to severe international sanctions and a rise in the rate of inflation and significant depreciation of the currency.

The first conflict of objectives between the CBI and the government emerged in 2006 when Mr Ahmadi-Nejad, following his pre-election promises of distributing a greater proportion of the country's oil revenue to the poor people, submitted a bill to the Parliament asking for an increase in the size of oil revenue in the government's budget to US$ 40 billion. The above amount was to come out of the Oil Stabilization Fund, which had been set up in 2002 to moderate fluctuations in foreign exchange revenues from oil exports. The Parliament subsequently approved the government's bill despite the fact that in the Fourth Development Plan the amount of oil revenue that was envisaged to be allocated to the budget was only US$15 billion. The significant increase in the use of oil revenue by the government led to an unprecedented 34.3 per cent rise in the level of liquidity in 2005–6 and rising to 39.4 per cent the following year (see Figure 5.1). This move by the government and Parliament met with strong objection by the Central Bank governor who considered the actions irresponsible and highly inflationary.[11]

The second conflict emerged in 2006, when the government asked the Parliament to approve a cut in banks' lending rates. Once again despite the Central Bank's strong objections, the Parliament approved the President's request and instructed private and public banks to reduce their interest rates by five and three per cent, to 17 and 14 per cent, respectively (see Table 5.2, column 7 under 'expected rate of return on facilities').

At the same time, the government instructed the public banks to allocate IRR80,000 billion (approximately 8 billion dollars) of their credits to 'small businesses with quick return.' The above amount was envisaged to increase to IRR1,000,000 billion by 2010 (approximately 100 billion dollars based on the exchange rate prevailing in 2006–7).[12]

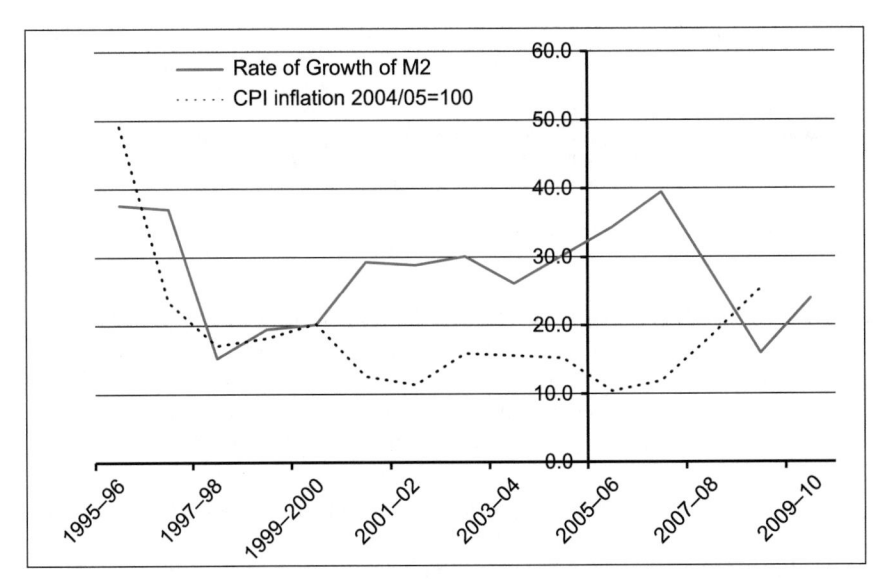

Figure 5.1 Rate of Growth of M2 and Inflation (Consumer Price Index, 2004/05=100) 1995/96–2010/11

Source: Calculated from the CBI Economic Time Series Data Base (2012).

Table 5.2 Percentage of profit shares paid on demand and time deposits

		Public banks		Private banks		Expected rate of return on facilities[a]	CPI inflation
		Demand Deposits (DD)	5 years fixed	One month	5 years		
1380	2001/02	7	17	n.a.	n.a.	16–18	11.34
1381	2002/03	7	17	n.a.	n.a.	13–17	15.74
1382	2003/04	7	17	n.a.	n.a.	13.5–18	15.60
1383	2004/05	7	17	10–12	20.5	13.5–18	15.34
1384	2005/06	7	17	12	19.5–20.5	13.5–18	10.40
1385	2006/07	7	16	14	17–18.5	17	11.87
1386	2007/08	7–8	16	10–13	15–17.5	13	18.38
1387	2008/09	9–10	17–19	9	17.5–19	12	25.38
1388 [b]	2009/10	9–10	17.5	9	17.5	12	10.75
1389 [c]	2009/11	6–11	17	6–11	17	12–14	12.41
1390 [d]	2011/12	6–10	15	6–10	15	11–14	21.47

Source: CBI Economic Trends, various issues from 2005/06 to 2011/12.

Notes:
1. Rate of return on the facilities extended for transactions (non-participatory) contracts.
2. As of March 2009, four public banks (Saderat Iran, Mellat, Tejarat and Refah Kargaran) have been classified as private banks.
3. Based on the Supervisory-Policy Package of the Banking System in 1389 (2009/11), the lending rate for transaction contracts with maturity of less than two years was set at 12 per cent and for more than two years, 14 per cent. Moreover, the lending rate on the facilities extended for instalment sale contracts in the housing sector is 12 per cent.
4. According to the Monetary, Credit and Supervisory Policies of the Banking System in 1390 (2011/12), the lending rate for non-participatory contracts is set at 11 per cent for credits up to two years maturity and 14 per cent for credits of longer term maturity. Moreover, the lending rate on the facilities extended for Islamic contracts under Mehr Housing Programme in housing sector is set at 11 per cent for the construction period of the new projects and 12 per cent for instalment sale after the completion of projects.

In 2007, Mr Ahmadi-Nejad called for a further cut in interest rates to 12 per cent and the harmonization of the private and public banks' lending rates. The Monetary and Credit Council of the CBI [13] and the Governor of the Central Bank considered these recommendations to be inflationary and objected to it. Nevertheless, in order to push forward with these, Mr Ahmadi-Nejad dissolved the Money and Credit Council and argued that high bank interest rate was a kind of usury, and hence against the *Sharia* law. Moreover, it was argued that the economy was mostly cash-based and private savings were not highly interest elastic. In a sign of protest to Mr Ahmadi-Nejad's action, both the Governor of the Central Bank and the Secretary of State for Economic Affairs and Finance resigned in 2007. Within a short period of time, the combination of the above policies led to a rapid increase in the rate of inflation from 11.87 per cent in 2006–7 to 25.38 per cent in 2008–9 (see Figure 5.1).

In 2008, Mr Ahmadi-Nejad asked the Central Bank to instruct all public and private banks to reduce the loan rate to borrowers in housing, agriculture, industry and mining sector to 10 per cent, and keep it at 12 per cent for borrowers in the services and trade sector. This was despite the fact that in its package of 'Policy and Monitoring', the Central Bank had indicated that the interest rate should be set at a level that was compatible with the rate of inflation. Yet the head of auditors of the Ministry of Economic Affairs and Finance rejected the Central Bank's earlier recommendation and announced that 'the government does not see any link between banks' interest rate and inflation'.[14] This was despite the CBI's earlier report of a rise in liquidity and inflation following the earlier cut in interest rate in the previous year and the rise in inflation to 18.4 per cent in 2007–8. Consequently, the above conflict between the government and the CBI led to the resignation of the second Central Bank governor within two years.

The cut in lending rates not only was inflationary, but it also adversely affected private banks that had to pay between 18 and 22 per cent interest rates on their long-term deposits against the 12 per cent only they could now charge on the loans they made. Accordingly, they strongly objected to the government's low interest rate policy. They argued that while public banks could reply on government's financial support, private banks had to mostly rely on deposits as their main source of funds. Therefore, they could not reduce their deposit rates, as that could have diverted depositors away from banks. Hence reducing loan rates without any change in deposit rates pushed banks to the verge of making a loss. Indeed, following the above controversies between the government and private banks, the share price of private banks dropped sharply and bank shareholders rushed to sell their shares. Consequently the TSE share index dropped sharply in 2007/08 (Figure 5.2).

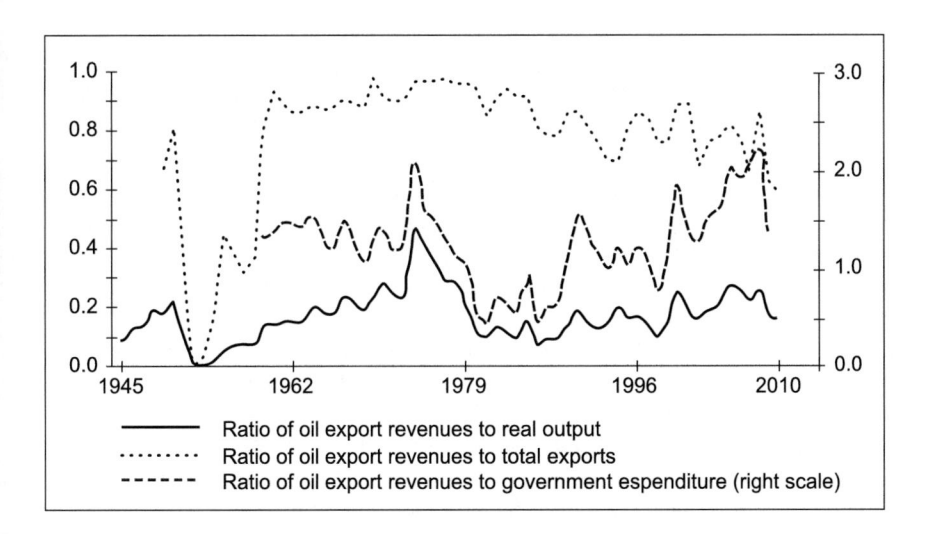

Figure 5.2 Tehran Stock Exchange performances 1999–2011

Source: CBI Economic Trend, various issues between 1999/2000–2011/12.

Table 5.3 Economic indicators[a]

	2001/02	2004/05	2005/06	2006/07	2007/08	2008/09	2009/10	2010/11	2011/12
M2 Growth rate (%)	29.3	26.1	30.2	34.3	39.4	27.7	15.9	23.9	26.1
Inflation measured by CPI (2004/05=100) (% change over the previous year)	12.8	15.3	10.4	11.9	18.4	25.4	10.8	12.4	n.a.
Unemployment rate (%)	15.7	10.3	12.1	12.1	11.9	10.4	11.9	13.5	11.8
M2/GDP with oil	0.48	0.47	0.50	0.57	0.57	0.56	0.66	0.47	0.50
M2/GDP without oil	0.57	0.62	0.69	0.78	0.80	0.75	0.83	0.62	0.69
Total GDP growth rate (% annual)	5	6.4	6.9	6.6	5.0	0.8	3.0	5.8	6.4
Non-oil GDP growth rate (% annual)	4.5	6.8	7.8	7.0	5.4	1.2	3.7	6.1	6.87
Imports/Non-oil GDP	18.5	23.7	23.7	n.a.	n.a.	n.a.	n.a.	n.a.	n.a.
Non-oil Exports/ Non-oil GDP	7.5	7.4	8.0	n.a.	n.a.	n.a.	n.a.	n.a.	n.a.

Source: CBI Economic Time Series Data Base (2012).

Note: All data are based at Constant 1997/98 Prices, except M2/GDP and rate of growth of M2 which are based on current prices and CPI which is based on 2004/05 prices.

It is important to point out that 2008 and 2009 were in fact the years when the Iranian economy was experiencing a recession and the real GDP growth rate had dropped to 0.8 per cent (Table 5.3). In other words, those were the years when the Iranian SMEs along with those of other countries in the world were experiencing a downfall in economic activities, and the central banks of most developed countries and regions, such as those of the United States, the UK and the EU had adopted Quantitative Easing (QE) to encourage banks to lend to businesses that were suffering from the recession.

Therefore, what the Iranian government was doing appeared to be in line with global practice. The difference, however, was that while Western countries were adopting a serious contractionary fiscal policy, the Iranian government was pursuing an expansionary fiscal policy that was mostly financed by oil revenues and was spent on public consumption rather than long-term investment. Moreover, while the rate of inflation in the rest of the world was in low single digit and falling, that of the Iranian economy was high (in double digits) and rising. Furthermore, those who were borrowing in the name of investing in 'businesses with quick return' were not exactly investing in productive sectors. Indeed according to a study that was carried out by a team of central bank researchers in collaboration with the Ministry of Labour more than 38 per cent of those loans were used for purposes other than the projects for which the loans had been granted (BBC Persian, 2008; Rahemi, 2008).[15] The study, which covered 8,000 institutions, also showed that there was a major problem of asymmetric information between the banks and the borrowers in that a number of private borrowers of loans, used the funds for a variety of unrelated purposes such as purchase of land, building of apartments, purchase of shares of privatized institutions, etc. Some also had simply deposited the funds in private or public banks that paid high interest rates, or even deposited the borrowed funds in gharz-al-hassaneh accounts before prize draws. Moreover, some of the private borrowers had managed to borrow much larger amounts than were initially envisaged. Thus in practice a large number of the above businesses failed in achieving their initial objectives and repaying their loans. Indeed, according to a report by Donya-e-eqtesad (2013), after examining three government and non-government reports the Parliament Research Centre announced that more than 60 per cent of 'businesses with quick return' had failed in achieving their initial objectives.

There was also growing evidence of loans default and non-payments. In a number of cases the borrowers claimed that the businesses in which they had invested were experiencing a loss and hence were not able to repay the bank loans. Therefore, they were asking for both an extension to the maturity of loans, and an additional loan to recover their business. But according to anecdotal evidence, the majority of borrowers refused to repay the loans simply because they could earn a much higher rate of return on speculative business than the interest rate they had to pay on their loan.

Having considered the above cases where government's actions interfered with the Central Bank's responsibilities of controlling inflation, it is also interesting to point out a case where the independence of the Central Bank became subject of a curious controversy between the Parliament and the governor of the Central Bank. In 2010, the research centre of the Parliament announced that their study had shown that the Central Bank was enjoying a very low level of independence. It had been argued that the government's repeated interference in the activity of banks had led to a rise in the level of overdue loans, and increased use of oil revenue to fund government expenditure had led to a rapid rise in liquidity and inflation. These had in turn compromised the ability of the Central Bank to prevent erosion in the purchasing power of money. Accordingly, it was suggested that some of the regulations governing the operation of the Central Bank should be reconsidered in order to improve its independence and its ability in controlling the value of money. Following the above report the Parliament received a proposal in November 2010, to change the membership of the General Council of the Central Bank from five to 11 members.[16] Under the new bill, the President was to move out of the Council membership and instead seven expert economists were to be added to the Council (each for a period of ten years). The membership of the above seven had to be approved by the Parliament.

The above bill was strongly opposed by the Governor of the Central Bank and the Minister of Economic Affairs and Finance. The Governor of the Central Bank argued that inclusion of seven representatives of the private sector against the four representatives of the government seriously undermined the independence of the Central Bank and would not be to the benefit of the country. Similarly the Minister of Economic Affairs and Finance argued that, 'The council of the central bank is the council of shareholders and all around the world shares of the central bank belong to the government. Hence it is natural that the council of shareholders should be a government council.'[17]

The above views of the Iranian Central Bank Governor and the Minister of Economic Affairs and Finance were contrary to the general views and practices of central bank governors in many Western countries who strongly believe in the importance of the independence of the Central Bank.[18] Yet the Governor of the Central Bank of Iran argued against the inclusion of expert economists from the private sector on the grounds that their inclusion undermines the Central Bank independence and threatened to resign if the new arrangements were put in place. In line with his view, 50 members of the Parliament objected to the bill and asked for it to be reconsidered and amended by the committee that decided the implementation of the Parliament bills. By December 2012, the website of the Central Bank still continued to show the composition of the General Council as it used to be in the past with only five members.

The impact of the removal of subsidies on inflation

Another case where government's actions adversely affected the Central Bank's ability to control inflation is related to the removal of subsidies. Following the IMF recommendation of price reforms and approval of the 'Subsidy Targeting Act'[19] by the Parliament in 2010, the government started to implement the gradual removal of subsidies on 16 items including fuel and some foodstuffs. To ease the pressure of price rises, however, it was decided to replace subsides with some kind of cash subsidy or income support to lower income groups. The subsidy on fuel, water, flour, bread, wheat, rice, oil, milk, sugar and postal and transportation services were expected to be phased out within five years by 2015. The retail prices of petrol, gasoline, heating oil, kerosene, liquefied petroleum gas (LPG) and fuel oil are envisaged to rise to no less than 90 per cent of the Persian Gulf FOB prices.

According to various reports, the government has been spending between US$90 billion and US$100 billion per year on subsidies, of which between US$35 billion and $45 billion was related to subsidies on fuel.[20] The reform of energy prices was expected in the first year to increase government revenues out of the sale of fuel items by about US$20 billion of which 50 per cent was to be spent on income support or cash subsidy, and 30 per cent on support for the 70,000 vulnerable institutions that were going to be adversely affected by the removal of subsidies, and the rest on various long-term investments by the government.

In December 2010, contrary to the initial plan that envisaged only 50 per cent of population would be entitled to receive cash subsidy, more than 90 per cent of the population (72 million people) registered for it and each member of the household received IRR405,000 each month which later increased to IRR445,000.

Consequently almost all government revenues out of increased prices were used up for cash subsidy and almost no fund reached the affected industries. To ensure the public about the payment of cash subsidies the government paid the cash subsidies about two months prior to the time when the funds could be withdrawn. The public was also advised not to withdraw all the deposited cash subsidies in one go and were encouraged to leave them in banks and use them once they received the higher utility bills. Banks were also prohibited from using the deposited funds as a base for lending, but were also instructed not to pay any interest on the cash subsidies that the government had deposited in public's accounts. Thus it was hoped that the above regulations would prevent a rise in liquidity. To enable the public to access the rest of the money in their account, however, people were allowed to transfer their own funds to other short- or long-term accounts that earned interest.

Nevertheless, despite the Central Bank's efforts to restrain inflation, following the removal of subsidies the price of various items such as petrol and gasoline rapidly increased by 75 and 2,087.5 per cent respectively. The prices of other items also increased within a year by between 10–300 per cent. In 2011, the government reduced the number of recipients of cash subsidies by 10 million and, to account for inflation, the size of the cash subsidy was envisaged to increase to IRR735,000 per person (from IRR445,000) in the second phase (Hassanzadeh, 2012).

The removal of subsidies, and in particular fuel subsidies, was an important policy that was long overdue and had to be implemented given the fact that oil is an exhaustible resource and its price should reflect its scarcity. Nevertheless, it is also true that the removal of fuel subsidy has a cost-push inflationary effect which, on the one hand, can quickly transmit the price rise to all other goods including those that were not directly in receipt of subsidy, and on the other hand, might lead to the disappearance of some of the producers that cannot cope with higher fuel and utility prices. In the long run, however, prices could fall if higher prices attract more efficient suppliers into the market and replace less efficient ones that can no longer survive in the new environment. Accordingly supply can rise in the long run and put a downward pressure on prices. For this to happen, it is important for the government to have an industrial policy that allows and encourages entry of such suppliers in to the market. Unfortunately, with high level of red tape, bribery and uncertainty that prevails about the future value of the currency at the moment, the majority of entrepreneurs shy away from long term investment and are only interested in undertaking short-term or speculative investment. Therefore, the success of the subsidy programme depends heavily on government's ability in eliminating uncertainties and restoring confidence in the economy.

During the first two years of subsidy reform, between 2010 and 2012, a sharp rise in prices together with significant pressures from international sanctions seriously affected the country's productive capacity and led to the closure of a large number of factories (Nader, 2013). Consequently, in 2012 the Parliament demanded a temporary stop on the process of subsidy eliminations, and the second phase was halted.

The impact of international sanctions on the financial system

The increased scope and severity of international sanctions on Iran has significantly reduced the demand for Iran's oil exports and hence the supply of foreign currency. Sanctions on Iran's international financial transactions have also increased the cost of imports and raised the demand for foreign currencies. The combination of these factors has created an acute excess demand for foreign currency and a huge pressure on domestic currency to depreciate. This in turn has further fuelled the inflationary pressures. The financial sanctions, in particular, have not only restricted investors' access to international markets for both imports and exports, they have also seriously reduced long-term investment opportunities due to the high level of uncertainty about future prices of inputs.

Between 2007 and 2011, 23 Iranian public and private banks and their affiliates went under US sanctions. In May 2012, the Society for Worldwide Interbank Financial Telecommunication (SWIFT) cut its ties with Iranian banks that are subject to EU sanction and excluded them from the international banking transfer system. This in practice has made it very difficult for Iranian banks to engage in global financial transactions,[21] and has significantly increased the cost of imports. That is because importers have to engage in a number of extra transactions to bypass the effects of sanctions. It has also increased the level of uncertainty and expectations of further currency depreciation and led to considerable capital outflows. Some of these capital outflows take place through exporters of non-oil goods who keep all or part of their export proceeds out of the country. Some are also done through importers who are able to receive foreign currency at a lower exchange rate from the government for their imports than the rate that prevails in the black market. To receive the cheaper foreign currency they submit an import bill with higher prices for their imports than the actual price. Once the foreign currency is received, the difference between the actual price and the fake higher prices may be kept out of the country for a variety of purposes including the sale of foreign currency at a higher price in future.

The sharp depreciation of the currency in 2011–12 has also increased the public's demand for safe assets such as gold and strong foreign currencies such as the US dollar and the Euro. The extent of this was reflected in a statement by the Governor of the Central Bank, on 17 November 2012, who said, 'currently there are between 12 and 18 billion US dollars that are held by the public in Iran'.[22]

Reflecting this trend, there were several episodes of sudden public rush to purchase gold and dollars with the exchange rate changing on an hourly basis. Consequently, the Central Bank was forced to repeatedly intervene and set a limit on the official amount and price of gold and the dollar that could be purchased from banks. To overcome the international sanctions, the Central Bank Governor also announced in February 2012 that Iran is prepared to accept non-dollar payments for its trade and countries could pay either in their own currency or gold. Thus, Iran has reportedly accepted Indian rupees, Chinese renminbi and gold from Turkey in exchange for its oil and gas exports.[23]

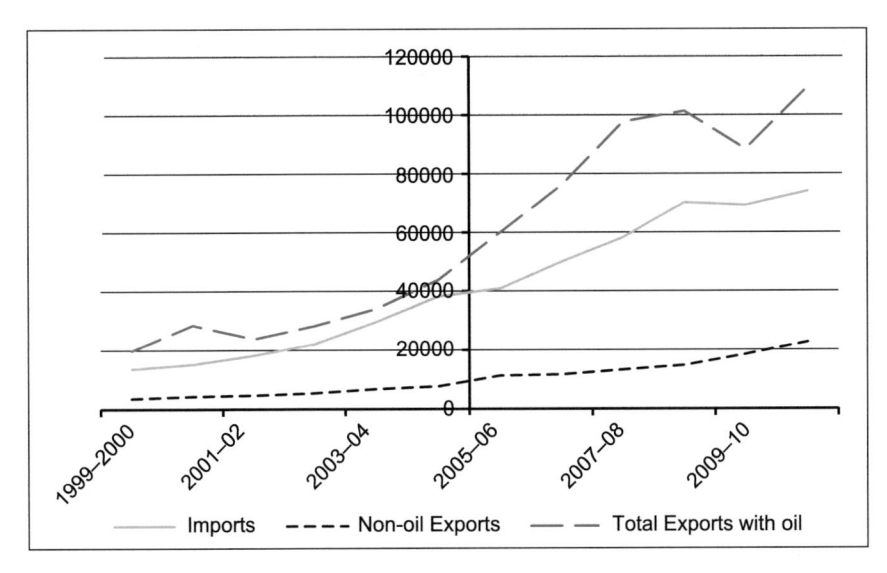

Figure 5.3 Exports and Imports (million US dollars).

Source: Author's calculation using the data reported in various issues of the Central Bank of the Islamic Republic of Iran (CBI) from 1999/2000–2011/12.

The uncertainty about the price of foreign exchange has had a particularly inflationary effect in Iran, as the level of imports had significantly increased in recent years. That is because with the rise in the price of oil, the government was trying to control inflation by increasing the supply of cheaper imported goods (see Figure 5.3).

The above policy, though might have been helpful in reducing inflation at a time when the current account was in surplus, has proved very problematic in recent years, once the level of oil exports declined and the currency started to depreciate. That is because when the current account was in surplus and the currency was strong, cheap imports pushed a number of domestic producers out of business and reduced the domestic supply of many goods. Following the rise in international sanctions in July 2012 and the significant cut in demand for Iranian oil exports, however, the current account moved into deficit and the domestic currency began to depreciate precipitously. Consequently, the size of imports could not be maintained and began to fall. This has created an excess demand for goods and added to inflationary pressures. According to data published by the Iranian Customs Office and reported by the BBC Persian service (04.01.2013), imports have dropped by nearly US$5 billion during the first nine months of the Iranian calendar 1391 (between March 2012 and January 2013). This significant drop in the level of imports has clearly contributed to the rise in inflation in 2012 that has been reported by the CBI consumer price report (2012).

The depreciation of the currency has also been adversely affecting many Iranian industries that heavily rely on imports of raw material and intermediate goods and are dependent on imported inputs. Moreover, the price elasticity of demand for such imports is very low. The output of the industries that use imported inputs, however, is not competitive in the international markets. Therefore, while depreciation of currency is supposed to increase their competitiveness in the international markets, it also increasing the costs of their imported inputs and to some extent cancels out the overall impact of currency depreciation on the final price of these goods. Therefore, while the demand for these goods might rise slightly,[24] their potential in earning higher exports revenue is rather limited and not sufficient in the short run to compensate for the significant fall in oil exports, which has declined from over 2.7 million barrels a day in 2006–7 to around 800,000 barrels a day in 2012, and improve the trade balance. Hence it is likely that the Iranian Rial might continue to depreciate in the future and contribute to greater inflation.

Some might argue, however, that such currency depreciation is taking place with the implicit approval of the government and the central bank. That is because it can help in reducing the demand for imports over time and creating a strong switching effect leading to the growth of domestic import substitutes in the long run, in particular when the country faces severe international sanctions. Some also argue that the government is deliberately allowing the currency to depreciate as it can sell its foreign currencies at a higher price and use the proceeds to finance the cash subsidies. Such a policy, however, is contrary to the remits of the Central Bank that is responsible to prevent the erosion of the value of the domestic currency against foreign currencies. Also because it cannot continue for long, as the depreciation of the currency will further feed inflationary pressures, which is also contrary to the objectives of the Central Bank.

Central bank supervision and overdue loans

One area of concern about the soundness of the Iranian banking system is related to the strength of the Central Bank's supervisory role.

Over the years, the Central Bank was known to have exercised a strong supervisory power over the activity of Iranian banks. One example of the above power was demonstrated in 2006 when Mr Shaibani (the then Governor of the Central Bank) dismissed the executive director and all members of the board of directors of the Parsian Bank (which was a private bank) and replaced them with a new board of directors whose members were all appointed by the Central Bank. The above actions were in fact taken following an announcement by Mr Ahmadi-Nejad about his determination to deal with corruption within the banking system. In explaining the above dismissal, Mr Shaibani announced that prior to the dismissal the CBI had issued a number of cautions to the Parsian Bank about the irregularities in their activities but the bank appeared to ignore all the cautions and disregarded them. According to the banking laws, no bank is allowed to lend more than 20 per cent of its capital to any actual or legal person. That is because such a high level of lending to one borrower would increase the bank's liquidity risk, and might adversely affect all bank depositors. Yet the Parsian Bank appeared to have exceeded that limit. In 2010–11 there were a number of other irregularities were also reported that put the supervisory power of the CBI under question.

One of the problems that central banks usually face is the problem of moral hazard, which arises when there is a need for rescuing a bank that might have excessively exposed itself to the possibility of bank failure by investing in risky assets. In such cases the central bank's rescue package might entice a particular bank or other banks to continue taking undue risks. The question that arises here is what appropriate measures should the central bank take to reduce the problem of moral hazard?

To address the above problem it is important to determine the following points; a) whether the bank at risk is a private or public bank; b) whether the rise in bank exposure has arisen due to internal decision-making by bank managers or due to some external instruction by the government; and c) whether the problem has arisen due to a problem of asymmetric information between the borrowers and lenders or due to corruption within the bank or other parties.

In the case of Iran, in fact most of the banks that are suffering from the problem of overdue loans are public banks that had extensively lent to borrowers of projects of 'quick return'. Moreover, the loans were mostly lent under the instruction of the government. Nevertheless, bank managers in some cases must have been given private incentives by both borrowers and government officials to grant the loan to specific borrowers. As mentioned earlier, it is also true that there was a serious problem of asymmetric information between the public banks and private borrowers where the borrowed funds were not used in the projects for which the funds had been initially granted. But in any case, bank managers had the responsibility of overseeing the soundness of the position of the borrowers and the actual value of their guarantee documents. Therefore, given that most of the banks in difficulty were public banks, the Central Bank could not use the argument of moral hazard and allow those banks to go under. But it should have at least exercised a strong monitoring and supervisory role to ensure the sound functioning of banks. This is yet another of those cases where the independence of the central bank has been severely affected by various interventions on the part of the government, or elite groups close to various power factions in Iranian politics. What is particularly curious is the fact that in a number of cases the banks in difficulty have not even taken the necessary legal actions against the biggest borrowers to recover their overdue loans.[25]

In the case of Iran, the soundness of the banking system and the central bank's supervisory role was in fact seriously questioned after 2008 when there were repeated reports of a rise in the number of bank loan delinquencies, and later, bank frauds. At first in 2005 the amount of overdue loans were announced to be around US$10 billion. Within the next three years, the size of the overdue loans increased by 75 per cent to US$17.8 billion in 2008. By 2009, the above figure rose by another 100 per cent to US$38 billion, and by 2012 it exceeded US$57 billion.[26]

As pointed out by Mr Pour Mohammadi, the head of the General Inspections Organization (GIO),[27] which is an institution responsible for regular control and supervision of various state-run institutions and companies, the above amount of delinquency was particularly alarming as the total size of banks' capital stood at US$20 billion, and the overdue loans on average accounted for over 15 per cent of all state banks' loans, which was much higher than the international standard of three to five per cent.[28] The GIO head blamed the banks for the problem and asked them to adopt adequate measures to recover the loans. In addition, to prevent a possible bank failure the government proposed a bill to repay government's debt to banks, and the head of GIO called on the parliament to approve the bill as soon as possible as banks appeared to be in desperate need of money.

In addition to the above recommendations, in 2012 the Central Bank put a limit of nearly US$ 15,000 on daily cash withdrawals by the public. The limit was supposedly set to control money laundering. But according to anecdotal reports, it was set because some of the largest banks and lenders, such as Bank Melli and Bank Mellat, were on the verge of bankruptcy (Risk Watchdog, 2010).

One of the explanations given for the overdue loans was that a large number of borrowers were suffering from the economic recession and were unable to repay their loans. This was indeed a similar phenomenon to the one experienced by businesses in other parts of the world. In a number of cases, where the Iranian borrowers were in need of extra borrowing to manage their business, the government encouraged banks to extend further loans to them to overcome their short-term cash flow problem. However, a number of businesses did not show any sign of recovery and the extra loans further increased the size of overdue loans and exerted more pressure on banks.

Another explanation given was that a large number of borrowers were public institutions whose businesses were suffering for a variety of reasons including international sanction and rising costs and their managers did not feel the pressure to repay the loans. But there was clearly a serious problem of asymmetric information between the banks and their borrowers as well as corruption among the lenders. According to a report by the Press TV (2009), 90 individuals who already had a record of US$27 billion overdue loan had collectively managed to secure US$ 8 billion further facilities from the banking system. The problem was further accentuated since, due to the recession, banks were not able to sell the assets that were used as loan guarantees. Therefore, to tackle the problem of overdue loans the government prepared a list of more than 6,000 institutions that were in difficulty and asked banks to extend the maturity of their loans by an extra year and extend further loans to the existing borrowers to enable them to continue their operation. The above measures, however, not only did not help in reducing the problem of overdue loans, they rather added to their size. The total size of overdue loans in 2012 increased to IRR 700,000 billion which, at the official exchange rate in January 2013, amounted to approximately US$ 57billion.

The above developments, though partly due to economic recession, also demonstrated the weakness of the Central Bank monitoring and auditing system and their lack of independence from the government and other influential political power points in Iran.

Banking frauds

Another development that demonstrated the weakness of the supervisory system was noted in 2010 when the head of the General Inspection Office (GIO) announced the news of a very large bank embezzlement that amounted to around US$ 2.8 billion. It was later reported that the fraud involved seven state-owned and private banks and a large number of non-bank institutions and executives and bank officials, including senior members of Bank Melli (the largest public bank), and Bank Saderat and Arya Group (a financial conglomerate). The Arya group is said to have used its influence and government officials' cooperation to obtain forged letters of credit and huge bank loans that far exceeded the value of their assets (see Harris, 2011).

This scandal was not a unique case, as in 2012 Mehr News Agency (2012) reported another banking fraud that amounted to hundreds of millions of Euros' and dollars' worth of loans that were extended to private companies by a state bank without the backing of necessary collateral. Such discoveries once again reveal the extent of the involvement of officials in public banks in various fraudulent activities and the weakness of the CBI in monitoring and supervizing the system.

Financial repression

Despite some degree of financial liberalization, the banking system in Iran is characterized by a high level of financial repression in the form of frequent government intervention in the determination of interest rates, high inflation rates yielding negative real interest rates, directed credit rationing and high reserve requirements of between 10–15 per cent. The latter, however, might be justified given the extent of public's reliance on cash transactions and limited number of money markets from which banks can borrow.

In 2001 the government allowed public banks to independently determine the profit share on time deposits of two to four years within the range of 13–17 percent. This range provided a low but positive real interest rate compared with the official CPI inflation rate based on 2000 prices. In practice, however, the unofficial rate of inflation was rising much faster than the official rate and the deposit rates remained unchanged till 2005–6 generating negative rates of return. It should be pointed out, however, that private banks were paying a higher positive interest rate compared with the public banks (Table 5.2). This appears to have helped in mobilization and channelling of funds within to the private sector. This is evident in Figure 5.4, where it can be seen that from 2001–2 onwards, both private sector deposits and loans from banks continuously increased. This was particularly pronounced from 2005–6 onwards, when President Ahmadi-Nejad encouraged banks to lend to projects with a 'quick return,' bearing in mind that during the first 18 months of his presidency, the real rate of interest was still positive.

The establishment of private banks in 2001 also helped financial deepening, raising the ratio of M2 over GDP (with oil and without oil). As Figure 5.5 shows, financial deepening measured by M2 over GDP appeared to be rather constant until 2001 (hovering between 0.4 and 0.5). However, it increased consistently after 2001 reaching around 0.82 by 2010. The privatization of three public banks in 2006 also further contributed to the rise in the ratio of M2/GDP.[29]

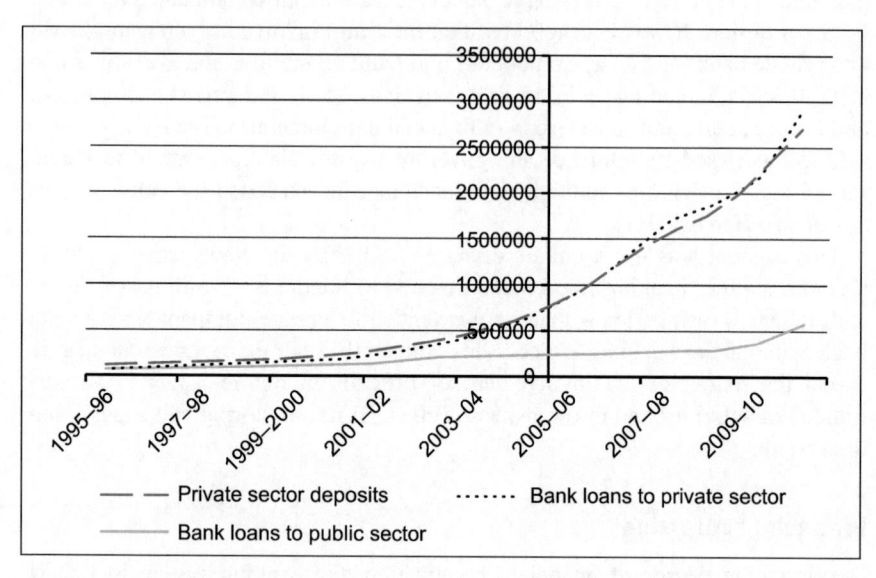

Figure 5.4 Private Sector Deposits and Loans and Total Bank Claim on Public Sector (billion Rials, 1995/96–2010/11).

Source: CBI Economic Trends, issues 16–65.

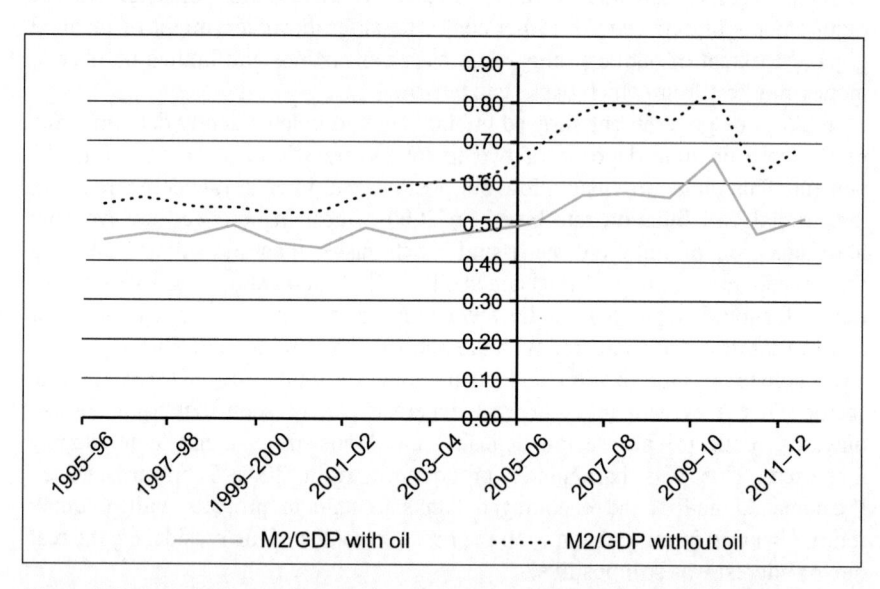

Figure 5.5 Financial Deepening (M2/GDP with and without oil) (1995/96–2010/11)

Source: Calculated from CBI Economic Time Series Data Base (2012).

As it is evident from Figure 5.5, once the effect of oil exports and oil price fluctuations are removed one can see that the economy has experienced a high degree of financial deepening. In other words, financial deepening measured by the ratio of M2 over non-oil GDP increased from 0.57 in 2000–1 to 0.83 in 2009–10, but declined again to 0.69 in 2011–12. Nevertheless, there are numerous factors that adversely hamper the transmission of financial deepening into long-term private sector investment. Most important among these are: the high level of uncertainty about government policies and economic environment, numerous red tapes and the presence of some elite groups close to political power points that tend to monopolize various profitable ventures.

Conclusion

This chapter has shown that the Iranian government's industrial strategy relying on low interest rates has not exactly delivered its objectives. Indeed, the lowering of interest rates seriously affected the position of private banks and pushed some of them to the verge of bankruptcy. Moreover, extension of credit to the so called 'small businesses with quick return' not only did not achieve its prime objective of enhancing growth and reducing unemployment, it led to a number of new problems such as rapid increase in liquidity and inflation, significant misuse of funds and large amounts of loan delinquencies. We have also demonstrated the extent to which the government's intervention in the activity of the banking sector and its various programmes (such as the subsidy reform and nuclear programme) has undermined the independence of the Central Bank and its ability to control inflation and maintain the sound functioning of the banking system.

We have seen that despite a number of developments in the Iranian banking system and some improvement in the level of financial deepening over the last decade, the financial system remains predominately repressed and suffers from frequent government intervention.

Finally we have shown that the low interest rate strategy pursued by Mr Ahmadi-Nejad suffered from a number of shortcomings. The success of low interest rate policies of Japan and South Korea in the post-Second World War era was partly due to the fact that both countries strongly supported the export sector and private investors in their path of industrial development. This was in sharp contrast to the experience of Iran, where high levels of red tape and arbitrary government intervention led the private sector mostly to engage in short term speculative activities. Consequently Mr Ahmadi-Nejad's strategy of low interest rate growth, although leading to a rise in the level of private sector borrowing and appearing to have contributed to a rise in the level of financial deepening, failed to achieve its objective of promoting long-term investment by the private sector.

Notes

1 The three public commercial banks are: Bank Melli, Bank Sepah and Post bank of Iran.

2 The six specialized banks are: The Agriculture Bank, The Housing Bank, Bank of Industry and Mines, Export Development Bank of Iran, Cooperative Bank, Gharz-al-hassaneh Mehr Iran Bank.
3 Foreign banks were excluded from retail banking in the mainland, and were only allowed to work as representative offices liaising between their respective parent bank and companies involved in trade. Among them, French banks were totally excluded from activity in Iran in 1983, and German, Swiss, Japanese and British banks financed around 30 per cent of total trade.
4 The five representative offices are allowed to operate only in Tehran and Kish free trade zone.
5 The four investment institutions are: Amin Investment Bank, New Enterprise Investment, Pasargad Investment Bank and Turqoise Investment Partners.
6 These were Bank Tejarat, Mellat, Refah, Saderat, and Post Bank although the latter continued to remain under the state control.
7 The 18 private banks include the following 12 banks: Eghtesad Novin Bank, Parsian Bank, Saman Bank, Karaferin Bank, Bank Pasargad, Sarmayeh Bank, Sina Bank, Tat Bank, City Bank, Day Bank, Ansar Tourism Bank, Iran Zamin Bank.
8 Bozorgmehr (2011).
9 The number of winners tends to be between 200,000 and 300,000, which is very small compared with the five to seven million people who hold such accounts.
10 According to anecdotal evidence, the loan rates in these markets might rise to between 30–45 per cent.
11 See http://www.bbc.co.uk/persian/business/story/2006/05/060518_v-ka-cbi-shaybani-iran.shtml
12 See http://www.bbc.co.uk/persian/business/story/2006/01/printable/060110_pm-ka-unemployment.shtml
13 The Money and Credit Council is the highest banking policy making body of the Central Bank. Its members include Minister of Economic Affairs and Finance, Governor of the CBI, Head of State Management and Planning Organization (before it was dissolved in 2007), two Ministers elected by the Council of Ministers, Minister of Commerce, two monetary and banking experts to be nominated by the Governor of the CBI and confirmed by the President, Attorney-General or his deputy, President of the Chamber of Commerce, Industries and Mines, President of the Chamber of Cooperatives, Representatives of the Economic Affairs and Plan and Budge and Account Commissions of the Islamic Consultative Assembly (one from each) as the overseers, to be chosen by the parliament (CBI website, 2012).
14 See http://www.bbc.co.uk/persian/business/story/2008/05/printable/080523_bd-interest-rate.shtml
15 The report was published in BBC Persian (2008) http://www.bbc.co.uk/persian/business/story/2008/09/080927_ka-jahromi-cbi.shtml
16 The council members originally included the President, Minster of Economic Affairs and Finance, Head of the State Management and Planning Organization, Minster of Commerce and one more minster selected by the Council of Ministers.
17 The above comments were reported by the BBC Persian (15.11.2010): http://www.bbc.co.uk/persian/business/2010/11/101115_138_iran_central_bank_reax.shtml
18 For example, in the UK the Monetary Policy Committee (MPC), which decides the Bank of England's base rate, includes nine members, of whom six are from the private sector. Its membership includes: the Governor of the Bank of England, two deputy governors, two bank executives and four external members appointed by the Chancellor from experts in monetary and financial economics.
19 The information about the Subsidy Targeting programme is provided in the Fifth Five-Year Development Plan (2011–15) and has been extracted from the website of the President Deputy Strategic Planning and Control website in Persian, see: http://www.spac.ir/Portal/File/ShowFile.aspx?ID=90fa4381-ca1c-4d41-885a-8e889d572e3d

20 See Christian Science Monitor http://www.csmonitor.com/
21 In May 2012, the EU expanded the Sanctions against Iran under International Sanctions Act (ISA). The Act increased the number of mandatory sanctions to the following:

   a) A prohibition on 'foreign exchange' transactions subject to the jurisdiction of the United States by the sanctioned person;
   b) A prohibition on 'banking transactions' defined to mean 'transfers of credit or payments' between, by, through or to 'any financial institution' that are subject to US jurisdiction; and
   c) A prohibition on 'property transactions' (thus effectively blocking assets of the sanctioned party to the extent such assets are subject to US jurisdiction).

22 This news was reported in the BBC Persian on 17th November 2012. See http://www.bbc.co.uk/persian/business/2012/11/121117_l23_cb_iran_currency_dollar_outside_iranian_banks.shtml
23 According to a report by FT (2012a and 2012b) in May 2012, Iran imported nearly US$1.4 billion worth of gold from Turkey (see the FT, http://www.ft.com/cms/s/0/c74e6f00-620d-11e1-807f-00144feabdc0.html#axzz2ENRYTpG7, and CNN, http://edition.cnn.com/2012/11/29/world/meast/turkey-iran-gold-for-oil/index.html
24 According to a report by the Iranian Customs Office, during the first nine months of the Iranian calendar in 1391 (between March 2012 and January 2013), non-oil exports rose by US$462 million. This must have been in response to the currency depreciation. The above news was published on the BBC website on 04.01.2013: http://www.bbc.co.uk/persian/business/2013/01/130104_l45_iran_customs_report.shtml
25 BBC Persian reported 6 January 2013 that 'The Minister for Economic Affairs and Finance announced that the amount of overdue loans have reached 70,000 billion Tomans' http://www.bbc.co.uk/persian/business/2013/01/130106_ka_majlis_hosini_bank.shtml?print=1
26 The above amounts were reported in the CBI Annual Review various Issues between 2008–9 and 2010–11, the central bank Governor press releases on various dates that were also reported by the BBC Persian on the following websites.

   http://www.bbc.co.uk/persian/business/2008/11/081127_ka_bank_iran.shtml
   http://www.bbc.co.uk/persian/business/2008/11/081128_ka_bank_cbi_bahmani.shtml
   http://www.bbc.co.uk/persian/business/2009/09/090901_ka_centralbank_bahmani.shtml
   http://www.bbc.co.uk/persian/business/2010/01/100103_ka_finance_crisis.shtml
   http://www.bbc.co.uk/persian/business/2013/01/130106_ka_majlis_hosini_bank.shtml?s
   http://www.eghtesadeiranonline.com/vdcexw8zwjh8xpi.b9bj.html

27 According to the Constitution, GIO is in charge of regular control and supervision of executive bodies, military and disciplinary forces, state-run institutions and companies, municipalities and their subsidiaries, public notary chambers, foundations of public utility, revolutionary organs, and institutions whose financial resources totally or partially belong to the government. http://www.payvand.com/news/09/nov/1019.html
28 See Press TV (October 2009), http://edition.presstv.ir/detail/108239.html
29 In 2007 the government announced its intention to privatize five state banks. These were Mellat, Sadert, Tejarat, Refah and the Post Bank. The first four banks were privatized later but the last one remained a state-owned bank.

References

Agrawal, A., *Central bank Independence: A Major Victim of The 2007 Crisis*, STIC Primary Dealer Ltd., 2010.

Ahsan A., Skully M. and Wickramanayke, J., Determinants of central bank independence and governance: problems and policy implications, *Journal of Administration & Governance* (JOAAG), 1 (1): 47–67, 2006.

Ahsan, A., Skully M. and Wickramanayake, J., A critical analysis of central bank independence and governance in Australia and Bangladesh, *Journal of Administration & Governance*, 4 (1): 11–28, 2009.

Alesina, A. and Gatti, R., Independent central banks: low Inflation at no cost?, *American Economic Review*, 82 (2): 196–200, 1995.

Bank Pasargad Iran, http://bpi.ir/saving

BBC Persian (27.09.2008), '38 per cent divergence in activity of "businesses with quick return"', http://www.bbc.co.uk/persian/business/story/2008/09/080927_ka-jahromi-cbi.shtml

BBC Persian (15.11.2010), 'Reactions to the Parliament's bill regarding the central bank', http://www.bbc.co.uk/persian/business/2010/11/101115_l38_iran_central_bank_reax.shtml

BBC Persian Website (04.01.2013), 'Drop of nearly 5 billion dollars in imports': http://www.bbc.co.uk/persian/business/2013/01/130104_l45_iran_customs_report.shtml

BBC Persian (06.01.2013), 'The Minister for Economic Affairs and Finance announced that the amount of overdue loans reached 70,000 billion Tomans': http://www.bbc.co.uk/persian/business/2013/01/130106_ka_majlis_hosini_bank.shtml?print=1

Bernanke B. C., 'Central bank independence, transparency and accountability', Speech at the Institute for Monetary and Economic Studies International Conference, Bank of Japan, Tokyo, Japan, May 25, 2010, Board of Governors of the Federal Reserve System: http://www.federalreserve.gov/newsevents/speech/bernanke20100525a.htm, 2010.

Bozorgmehr N., 'Scandal puts Iranian banks on the defensive in Tehran', *Financial Times*, 7 December 7 2011: http://www.ft.com/cms/s/0/8b7ebbde-14ff-11e1-a2a6-00144feabdc0.html#axzz2EdmZKAjj, 2011.

Business Monitor International, 'Is Iran's banking sector in crisis?', Feb 3, 2010: http://www.riskwatchdog.com/2010/02/03/is-iran's-banking-sector-in-crisis/, 2010.

Central bank of the Islamic Republic of Iran (CBI) website, various pages (2012): http://www.cbi.ir

Central bank of the Islamic Republic of Iran Economic Trends, 2005/06 to 2011/12 (Issues No. 16–65), Tehran, issued by the central bank of Islamic Republic of Iran (CBI): http://www.cbi.ir/Category/EconomicTrends_en.aspx.

Central bank of Islamic Republic of Iran (2012), Consumer Price Index for All Urban Consumers Shahrivar 1391, Economic Statistics Department, Mehr 1391 (October 2012), www.cbi.ir

Central bank of the Islamic Republic of Iran Economic Time Series Data Base (2012), http://tsd.cbi.ir/DisplayEn/Content.aspx

Christian Science Monitor (2010), http://www.csmonitor.com/

Crean S., Goyal R., Mobarak A.M. and Sab R., Financial sector development in the Middle East and North Africa, *IMF working Paper*, WQP/04/201, 2004.

Curtis G. E. and Hooglund, E. eds, *Iran a Country Study,* 5th edition, Washington DC, Federal Research Division Library of Congress Country Studies/Area Handbook Program, 2008.

Donya-e-eqtesad, http://donya-e-eqtesad.com/Default_view.asp?@=332001, 2013.

Eggertsson G., and Le Borgne, E., A political agency theory of central bank independence, *IMF Working Paper,* WP/03/144, 2003.

Fischer, S., Central bank independence revisited, *American Economic Review*, 85 (2): 201–6, 1995.

Franzese, Partially independent central banks, responsive governments, and inflation, *American Journal of Political Science*, 43 (3), 1999.

Gorby, P. E., Time to admit it: independent central banking has been a failure, *Business Insider*, 24 May 2012, http://www.businessinsider.com/why-are-central-banks-independent-2012-5, 2012.

Harris, K., 'Pseudo-privatization in the Islamic Republic: beyond the headlines on Iran's economic transformation', MUFTAH: http://muftah.org/pseudo-privatization-in-the-islamic-republic-beyond-the-headline-on-iran's-economic-transformation-by-kevan-harris, 2010.

Harris, K., 'Iran's massive bank scandal', United States Institute of Peace, Iran Premier, 16 October 2011: http://iranprimer.usip.org/blog/2011/oct/16/iran's-massive-banking-scandal, 2011.

Hassanzadeh, E., 'Recent developments in Iran's energy subsidy reforms', International Institute for Sustainable Development (iisd), *Policy Brief*, October 2012. http://www.iisd.org/gsi/sites/default/files/pb14_iran.pdf, 2012.

IMF, 'Islamic Republic of Iran', *IMF Country Report* No. 04/308, 2004.

Mehr News Agency, http://www.mehrnews.com/en/, 2012.

Nader A., 'Iran faces a rough 2013', in Real Clear World website http://www.realclearworld.com/articles/2013/01/03/iran_faces_a_rough_2013_100447-2.html, 2013.

The New York Times, 'Governor of Iran's central bank resigns', 27 August 2007: http://www.nytimes.com/2007/08/27/world/middleeast/27iran.html?_r=0, 2007.

Payvand Iran News, http://www.payvand.com/news/07/jul/1131.html, 2007.

Press TV, http://edition.presstv.ir/detail/108239.html, 9 October 2009.

Rahemi, M., 'Central bank's different report on business with quick return', *Bank and Development*, http://bank-to.blogfa.com/post-190.aspx, 2008.

Risk Watchdog, 'Is Iran's banking sector in crisis?' 3 Feb 2010, http://www.riskwatchdog.com/2010/02/03/is-iran's-banking-sector-in-crisis/

6 The development of Iran's auto industry in a comparative perspective

*Parvin Alizadeh**

Introduction

The development of the auto industry in emerging markets has been informed by two distinct trends. The first trend has emphasized the implementation of a 'national car project' and has been concurrent with substantial government-backed investment to upgrade a country's technological capability to enable the national design of a wide range of vehicles. The second path has focused on expansion into the global markets with emphasis on specialization. The two trends are, however, not mutually exclusive and the distinction between them is largely a matter of emphasis placed on any single strategy. The Iranian auto industry, alongside those of South Korea and Malaysia, belongs to the first group while the car industries in Thailand, Turkey and Indonesia belong to the second.

This chapter provides an analysis of the structure of the auto industry in Iran since the 1960s. It provides a comparative analysis of the development of the auto industry in the above mentioned countries to highlight the similarities and differences in their responses to globalization, rationalization and cost pressures since the 1980s.

It is shown that the Iranian auto industry has been one of the fastest growing industries in terms of output and manufacturing value-added (MVA) since the mid-1990s. The total number of vehicles produced increased to 1.65 million in 2011 from 179,500 in 1997. The spectacular growth of the industry has turned it into the second most important industry in Iran after oil and gas. Government protection and promotion of the industry, almost entirely state- or parastatal-owned and controlled, typifies the government's industrial policy of achieving self-sufficiency and autarky since the mid-1990s. Government attempts at complete indigenization of the industry, which is dominated by two major firms 'Iran Khodro' and 'Iran Saipa', has been paralleled by the development of a national car project, *Samand*, that is considered a nationally designed and manufactured car.

However unlike South Korean's national car project that was transformed into a major global export, the Iranian auto industry is primarily oriented towards the domestic market with insignificant levels of exports. In this respect, its development diverges from virtually all other countries in this study that, following the trade liberalization of the 1980s and 1990s, have ventured into export markets. The expansion of emerging markets' auto production into export markets is paralleled by growing cost pressures and overcapacity in industrialized countries. However, in spite of its remarkable growth the Iranian auto industry has failed to benefit from globalization of the industry. For one thing, Iran is not yet a member of the WTO or other regional trade organizations, a trend that has been growing fast in the last two decades.

The structure of this chapter is as follows. I shall first provide a brief discussion of the key features of the international auto industry including the importance of economies of scale, competition among major producers, growing cost pressures and overcapacity in the industry, regionalization trends and the rapid growth of auto production in emerging markets. The next section provides an analysis of the development of the industry in Iran since its inception in the 1960s. This section also includes the evolution of the industry since the Revolution including the role of government policy in the implementation of the national car project. Comparative developments of the industry in selected countries – Malaysia, Thailand, Indonesia, South Korea and Turkey – will be discussed afterward.

Finally, discussion focuses on the performance of the sector in these selected countries. It is argued that all countries in this study pursued an import substitution policy in the 1960s that included protection for their infant auto industry. Nevertheless, the structure of the auto industry in selected countries except for South Korea and Iran was fragmented between different models and producers and in most cases it was dominated by foreign capital and control. However, a rationalization response by these countries in the 1990s has resulted in two distinct development trends. The first trend has emphasized the implementation of a national car project along a diluted version of the Korean model. The second path has focused on expansion into the global/ regional markets with an emphasis on specialization. Also all countries in this study except for Iran have undertaken a significant trade liberalization initiative mainly in response to joining a regional trading bloc since the 1990s. It is shown that Iran has remained an under-exporter of automobiles with substantial potential for the expansion of auto exports. Furthermore, while the growth of domestic production since the mid-1990s has been spectacular, Iranian auto industry has maintained a very limited openness to international trade.

Key features of the international auto industry

The auto industry is one of the most globalized industries with an oligopolistic structure that is dominated by a small number of leading companies (Humphery and Memedovic, 2003; Sturgeon *et al.*, 2009). Barriers to entry in the industry include leading companies' ownership of technology and the process involved in the design and development of the vehicles and their parts as well the presence of significant economies of scale (EOS) in production. The minimum efficient scale (MES, or the range of output over which long run average costs are minimized) is around 100–250 thousand units for passenger cars, although it is lower in assembly than in other manufacturing processes including pressing of the body parts and manufacturing of engine and mechanical parts (Husan, 1997).

The production of motor vehicles in developing countries starts with the assembly of parts and components that are imported in the form of a kit, called complete knock-down (CKD) – meaning all parts and components are totally separated and should be assembled locally – or semi-knocked-down (SKD). Assembly is the first phase of production and is far less subject to economies of scale (EOS) than manufacturing of more technologically sophisticated parts including the body and the engine. Furthermore, the structure of motor industry consists of two parts: terminal producers that are involved in the assembly/ manufacture of the body, and component producers that produce a large number of pieces ranging from simple items like batteries to sophisticated parts such as an engine. The in-house capability of terminal producers varies across firms. However a close collaboration between terminal producers and component producers dominates the industry particularly because parts and components are specific to a particular model.

In the early phase of an industry's development the domestic industry is involved in assembly from CKD/SKD and production of certain technologically simple components. These easily made parts are called 'hang-on parts' and include items such as batteries, radiators and upholstery. Vertical integration of the industry, however, means gradual domestic production of more technologically sophisticated parts such as the body of the vehicle and engine. These parts are far more susceptible to EOS and their production involves high fixed costs of machinery and equipment. The final stage of integration includes design of the vehicle including parts and components and involves high costs in Research and Development.

Economies of scale are also considerably lower in the production of commercial vehicles compared to cars. The production efficiency of the auto industry hence depends on its ability to achieve EOS by expanding into export markets as well as continuous technological upgrading concerning auto design and the design and functioning of parts and components.[1]

A marked feature of the industry is the rapid expansion of production in emerging markets which has outpaced the growth of output in the Triad region – North America, Japan and Western Europe – (Humphrey and Memedovic, 2003). Graph 6.1 provides data on major auto producers (i.e. those producing more than one million vehicles) in the Triad region and in emerging markets in 2000 and 2011. The total production of vehicles in China in 2011 was 18.4 million, that is more than the overall production in the United States and Japan put together. South Korea, India, Brazil and Mexico have also emerged as new players in the market followed by smaller producers including Russia, Iran, Thailand, the Czech Republic and Turkey. In fact, there is a visible decline of production in the Triad region while production in emerging markets has been rising fast. Expansion of production in the emerging markets has been driven partly by their industrialization

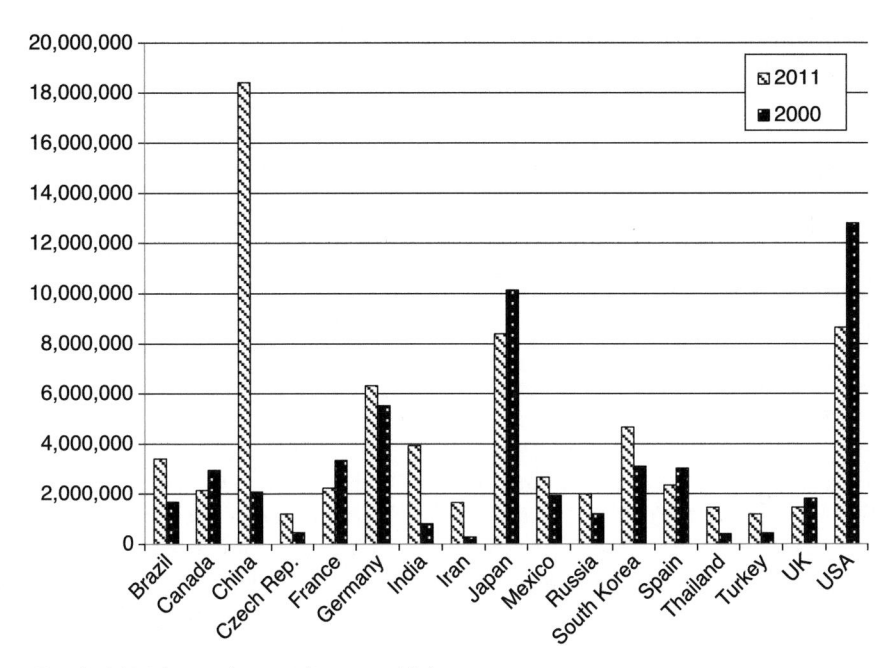

Graph 6.1 Major producers of motor vehicles.
Source: Atiesh Bakar, 2005 and OICA (The International Organization of Motor Vehicle Manufacturing known as the "organisation internationale des constructeurs d'automobiles" (OICA).

drive and partly by the relocation of production away from the Triad region in response to their rising labour costs and environmental regulations.

Another aspect of the development of the industry is growing regionalization of the industry. This in turn has been facilitated by significant trade liberalization and economic reforms in Asia, Latin America and Eastern Europe since the mid-1980s and the formation of trading regional blocks such as the ASEAN (1992), MERCOUSUR (1992) and NAFTA (1994).

Other important characteristics of the industry are intense competition, persistent overcapacity and cost pressures (Humphrey and Memedovic, 2003; Doner *et al.* 2006). This has led to a significant consolidation of the global auto industry since the 1990s. Global producers such as Volvo, Nissan, Mazda and Chrysler are no longer independent producers as they have been pushed into mergers with other firms in response to intense competition and the constant threat of bankruptcy.

Iran's auto industry

This section highlights the development and the evolving structure of the auto industry in Iran since its inception in the 1960s. It provides an analysis of the market structure, output growth and government policy both before and after the Revolution.

The Iranian auto industry in historical perspective: the 1960s and 1970s

The assembly of cars and commercial vehicles (CV) from CKD kits started in the early 1960s. This was concurrent with the implementation of an import-substitution policy based on the protection and promotion of domestic producers (Alizadeh, 1985).

To assist the transition of the industry from assembly operations to a more integrated domestic industry, the government imposed import content regulations, called the 'mandatory list' in the mid-1960s. Items on the 'mandatory list' consisted of simple items such as radiators and upholstery (called 'hang on' parts) as well as manufacturing of the body of the vehicle – highly susceptible to economies of scale. Vehicle producers were officially obliged to procure items on the mandatory list from local sources. The inclusion of the body of the vehicle on the mandatory list was aimed at increasing local content to 45–50 per cent (Alizadeh, 1985).

Furthermore in the late 1960s and early 1970s, the government – in cooperation with the largest development bank, the Industrial and Mining Development Bank of Iran (IMDBI) – and foreign auto producers initiated the establishment of joint ventures in diesel engines and engine components for CVs. IMDBI also provided a package loan in 1972 to the largest passenger car producer, the Iran National Company, to expedite the company's integration into the production of engines and other mechanical parts for passenger cars. This policy was expected to add another 25 per cent to the local content of the industry increasing it to around 75 per cent by the late 1970s.

By the mid-1970s, two terminal assemblers/manufacturers dominated the industry, producing passenger cars and commercial vehicles. There were also a number of smaller assembler/ manufacturers that were producing vehicles.

The dominant producer in the field of passenger cars, buses and mini-buses was 'Iran National Company', accounting in 1978 for 68 per cent and 86 per cent of the total domestic production of passenger cars and buses respectively (Table 6.1). The company was wholly Iranian-owned and produced the Hillman Hunter model under the trade name of Peykan, under license from Chrysler UK which was taken over by Peugeot in 1979. The company also had a licensing agreement with Daimler-Benz of Germany for the production of buses and mini-buses. The second major producer in the industry, which was the leading truck producer in the 1960s and 1970s, was 'Khavar Company', which in 1978 accounted for 67 per cent of total domestic production. This company was also wholly Iranian-owned and was operating under license from Daimler-Benz. Although there were a number of joint ventures in the industry, they were small producers.

Foreign capital was, however, prominent in the component producing sector, particularly for those that required technical sophistication. Joint ventures were dominant in producing tyres and tubes, auto glass, diesel engines and engine parts such as ball bearings, pistons, spark plugs, etc. Wholly Iranian-owned producers were involved in the production of more simple items ranging from radiators to body accessories (Alizadeh, 1985).

Table 6.1 Iran domestic vehicle producers and their share in domestic production (1968 and 1978)

Passenger Cars and Jeeps (%)	1968	1978	Trucks (%)	1968	1978
Iran National	64	68	Khavar Company	53	67
Citroen, Iran	7	15	Kaveh Company	11	12
Jeep, Iran	22	7	Zamyad Company	12	11
General Motors, Iran	–	7	Leyland Company	24	10
Moratab Company	5	3			
Iran Syika	2	–			
Market Share of wholly Iranian Owned Producers	91	78	Market Share of wholly Iranian owned Producers	53	67
Share of Producers with Foreign Equity	9	22	Share of Producers with Foreign Equity	47	33
			Buses and Minibuses		
			Iran National	85	88
			Khodrosazan	14	8
			Leyland Company	–	4
			Market Share of wholly Iranian Owned Producers	86	88
			Share of Producers with Foreign Equity	14	12

Wholly Iranian owned producers operating through licensing agreement with foreign firms
– Iran National (Peugeot)
– Khavar company (Daimler-benz)
– Mortab company (Land Rover, UK)
– Jeep Iran (American Motor)

Source: UNIDO (1971); IMDBI (1978).

The nominal import duties that were imposed during the 1960s and 1970s for the protection of completely built up (CBU) passenger cars were in the range of 200–237 per cent, rising progressively with the price of the car (Atieh Bahar, 2005). Import duties on CVs were considerably lower ranging from 20 to 50 per cent, reflecting the natural protection that CVs enjoyed due to very high transportation cost.

The main driving force for the growth of the industry in Iran was the rapid growth of domestic demand. Production of passenger cars increased from fewer than 3,000 in the mid-1960s to more than 120,000 by 1977, reflecting the impact

Table 6.2 Vehicle market in Iran – passenger cars and jeeps (1963–77)

Year	Production (Units)	Imports (Units)	Exports (Units)	Import share%*
1963	1,927	9,895		83.7
1964	2,332	15,437		87.0
1965	2,152	14,081		86.7
1966	2,458	15,655	6	86.5
1967	8,218	11,794	2	58.9
1968	20,278	12,026	9	37.2
1969	29,002	4,407	46	13.2
1970	30,351	3,353	217	10.0
1971	39,912	3,710	188	8.5
1972	50,528	2,545	226	4.8
1973	50,572	10,837	144	17.6
1974	73,125	29,635	69	28.9
1975	89,504	59,687	64	40.0
1976	102,167	57,429	27	35.9
1977	123,543	62,476	NA	33.6

Source: Foreign Trade Statistics of Iran, various issues; Alizadeh (1985).

Note: Total Market = Production + Imports – Exports.

of the increased oil income that was injected into the economy through expansionary fiscal and monetary policies (Table 6.2).

Production of motor vehicles was almost totally geared towards the domestic market although Iran exported a limited number of buses to Russia and the Ukraine. In fact the very small share of exports virtually disappeared after oil prices rose in 1974 that led to the explosion of domestic demand and rapid rise of imports.

Despite government efforts to promote vertical integration of the industry, the local content programme was only partially successful. By the late 1970s, the local content achieved by the two largest terminal producers, Iran National and Khavar Company, was in the range of 47–50 per cent while smaller producers were mainly involved in assembly and the production of 'hang on parts' (Alizadeh, 1985).

The Iranian Auto industry since 1979

The emphasis on self-reliance in industrial policy in Iran was born out of the Revolution in 1979 and was later solidified in response to the eight years' war with Iraq. All auto firms, alongside other large modern manufacturing and financial companies, were nationalized after the Revolution. The implicit industrial policy of the 1980s was self-sufficiency to reduce Iran's dependence on imports, both of vehicles and their parts (Atieh Bahar, 2005). However the 1980s was a period of decline and stagnation for the Iranian economy. This was partly due to dwindling oil revenues and a substantial reduction of foreign exchange quotas to meet the import requirements of domestic industries (Rahnema, 1996) and partly due to the war with Iraq. As a highly dependent industry on imported parts and components the terminal manufactures operated considerably below capacity over this period. Car production by the largest vehicle producer, Iran Khodro (previously called Iran National) declined from 90,866 in 1977–8 to 9,686 in 1987–8 (Atieh Bahar, 2005). During the war with Iraq, the industry redirected its activities to support the war effort.

However, the automotive act of 1993 laid the foundation for the development of a national auto industry. With the end of the war in 1988, and following the growth of domestic demand which led to a sharp increase in vehicle imports in the early 1990s, the government placed emphasis on 'the reconstruction and renovation of the automotive industry' (Atieh Bahar, 2005). The Automotive Law of 1992, enacted in 1993, underlined the importance of a nationally integrated auto industry capable of exporting to the world. Also the performance standard was set out to promote increased local content and success in export markets.

Moreover, the structure that has evolved in the Iranian auto industry since the mid-1990s shares a strong element of continuity with the past. This is particularly true as regards the level of concentration of the industry that is dominated by two major firms, Iran Khodro and Iran Siapa (Table 6.3).

Both these firms have developed a substantial in-house capability for producing parts and components. Iran Khodro is the largest auto manufacturer. The firm has a long-term relationship with PSA Peugeot Citroen going back to the late 1970s and produces a number of models under license from this firm. The company has also collaborated with other European and Asian companies including Renault and Suzuki. It is one of the main shareholders in Renault Pars Company that is in charge of engineering, quality control and marketing services for Renault products in Iran.

The company's national car project produced 'Samand' in early 2003 – based on the Peugeot 405 platform. It has made trucks and buses under licence from Mercedes-Benz and was planning to produce 900-class Mercedes-Benz engines before its relations with its foreign collaborators became severely strained due to the tightening of economic sanctions in recent years. Iran Khodro has also established a factory with a capacity to produce 5,000 Samand Sedans in Syria and has signed agreements with China, Senegal, Azerbaijan, Ukraine and Venezuela to set up factories for producing the same car.[2] Nevertheless all these projects are currently suspended as a result of intensified sanctions (see below on more recent developments).

Iran Saipa, a small car company in the pre-revolutionary period, has captured a significant share of the market since the 1990s when it concluded an agreement with Kia Motors of South Korea to manufacture Pride cars in hatchback and saloon models (Atieh Bahar, 2005). The rather low costs of the vehicle enabled it

Table 6.3 Passenger cars production (1998–2005)

	Company	1998–99	1999–2000	2000–01	2001–02	2002–03	2003–04	2004–05
Iran Khodro	Paykan (1600cc)	90,219	90,214	110,393	128,468	145,238	145,537	156,599
	Paykan 2000 (2000cc)	—	—	26	—	—	—	—
	Peugeot 405 (2000cc)	15,063	15,948	14,759	23,269	11,922	—	—
	Peugeot 405 Injector engine	—	—	—	—	28,051	64,403	102,724
	Peugeot Pars (2000cc)	—	30	5,278	7,843	16,940	23,874	27,140
	Peugeot[1] RD (1600cc)	1,258	20,015	27,320	29,501	23,908	20,315	—
	Peugeot RD Injector engine	—	—	—	—	—	34,730	55,299
	Peugeot Station (2000cc)	—	977	808	117	173	612	—
	Peugeot 206 (1400cc)	—	—	—	14,511	32,668	60,231	76,256
	Peugeot 206 (Automatic)	—	—	—	—	1,902	334	4,315
	Samand (X7)	—	—	—	1,345	21,136	58,197	72,931
	Samand (limousine)	—	—	—	—	—	—	11
	Samand (Gas Burner)	—	—	—	—	—	—	66
Saipa & Pars Khodro	Kia Pride (1300cc)	43,259	44,023	66,838	83,341	136,191	209,263	234,471
	Sepand (1100cc)	4,201	10,190	12,446	10,576	12,472	20,214	20,596
	Nissan Maxima	—	—	—	208	2,908	3,278	2,682
	Citroen Xantia	—	—	—	3,370	3,692	4,694	11,947

Kerman Khodro	Daewoo Cielo (2000cc)	2,988	5,350	6,129	11,516	16,554	3,128	841
	Daewoo Matiz (800cc)	—	—	4,041	4,931	6,990	306	1
Others	Sinad	—	—	200	238	—	327	221
	Mazda 323 (2000cc)	61	1,042	838	1,948	2,304	3,309	4,008
	Proton Sedan	—	—	—	—	—	390	509
	Proton Hatchback	—	—	—	—	—	420	542
	Volkswagen Gol	—	—	—	—	—	—	296
	Hyundai (Verna)	—	—	—	—	—	—	3,309
	Total	157,049	187,789	249,076	321,199	462,049	653,562	774,764

Source: Atieh Bahar (2005).

to compete successfully with Iran Khodro. Saipa has also another significant agreement with the Peugeot/Citroen to assemble the 'Citroen Xantia'.[3] Similar to Iran Khodro, Saipa has been involved in exporting cars and components to Syria and several other neighbouring countries.

As can be seen from Table 6.3, in addition to these two large firms there are a number of smaller producers that operate as joint ventures with European firms such as Fiat or with Asian companies like Kia, Hyundai, Daewoo and Nissan.

The most remarkable aspect of the auto sector development in Iran since the mid-1990s is the rapid expansion of domestic production that has increased from a very low level in the mid-1990s to more than 1.6 million in 2011, up from a figure of 179,500 only in 1997 (Graph 6.2). The spectacular growth of the industry has turned it into the second most important industry in Iran after oil and gas.

By 2011 Iran had rose to the thirteenth largest producer in the world (Graph 6.1). Iran's production of vehicles in 2011 exceeded those of Thailand and Turkey, not to mention the United Kingdom.

However, the sanctions had a major negative impact on the industry after 2006 and particularly since 2011 (see Habibi, Chapter 7 of this volume). Foreign firms have substantially cut back or terminated their presence in Iran in response to the intensification of sanctions. This has led to a substantial drop in vehicle output: in April 2012 it was 32 per cent smaller than April 2011. It appears that PSA Peugeot Citroen has halted shipments of vital components to Iran Khodro. Similarly, Hyundai has halted its business relations with Iran, where it had a joint venture.

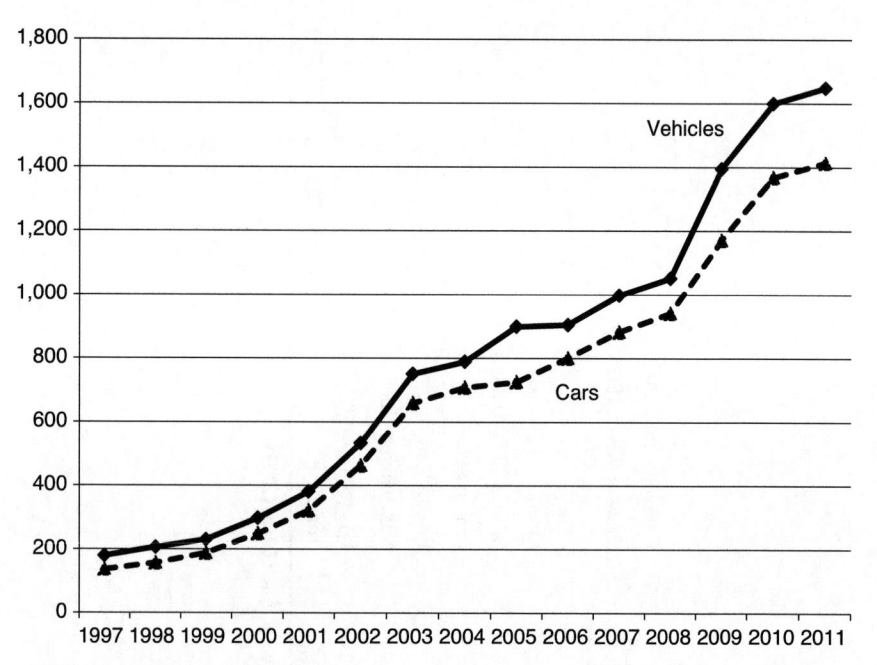

Graph 6.2 Iranian motor vehicles output.

Source: The same as graph 6.1.

According to reports in the Iranian media, more than 110 auto component makers have shut down and many workers have lost their jobs since 2012. 'Moreover, Iran's two largest state-run carmakers, Iran Khodro and Saipa, are reportedly now suffering from overstaffing – or "hidden unemployment", as the domestic media call it – due to the decline in output' (FT, 2013).[4]

National car project and export-oriented auto industry

The development of the auto industry in emerging markets has been informed by two trends. The first trend has emphasized the implementation of a national car project and has been concurrent with government-backed substantial investment in the auto industry to upgrade a country's technological and engineering capability and to promote the establishment of a large network of component-producing industries to enable the national design of a wide range of vehicles (Doner, 1991; Wad, 2009; Amsden, 1989). The second path has focused on expansion into the global/regional markets with emphasis on specialization. The two trends are not mutually exclusive and overlap, as will be discussed later on. However the distinction between them reflects the degree of emphasis placed on any single strategy. Korea, Malaysia and Iran belong to the first group while Thailand, Turkey and Indonesia belong to the second.

Both trends were designed to rationalize the industry either via deepening the process of vertical integration into the indigenization of vehicle design, or specialization for and expansion into the global market.

This section provides a comparative analysis of the evolution of auto industry in selected countries to highlight the prospects and constraints of the Iranian auto industry.

The Auto industry in a comparative perspective: economic nationalism and market fragmentation (1960–80)

South Korean experience provides a successful example of a national car project. It is widely recognized that the development of the auto industry in South Korea during the 1960s and 1970s was highly state-centric, combined with a very strong dosage of economic and technological nationalism (Amsden, 1989). The government strategy in the early 1960s, when the Automotive Industry Promotion Law was enacted, was the 'unitarization' of the industry: that is, the creation of a single producer with the objective of achieving economies of scale in production. However, the weakness of creating a monopoly with the potential for generation of inefficiency and economic rent became clear to the government and by the late 1960s there were four assemblers of passenger cars including Hyundai and Kia (Amsden, 1989; Ravenhill, 2001). The next effort at rationalization of the industry was concurrent with the implementation of economic reforms in 1973 to facilitate transition from import substitution to export-oriented industrialization (EOI). Furthermore, the government put severe limitations on foreign control in the industry as only minority foreign share holdings were allowed to operate.

Hence auto production in Korea remained under tight national control as Korean-owned firms were given export targets by the government. The Hyundai Pony, the first Korean-developed passenger car, was built in 1975. The Pony was a collaborative effort, comprising the design from Italdesign, transmission and engine from Mitsubishi and technology for the body and other parts from several other European and Japanese companies. The Pony was exported to Ecuador in 1976 and later to the US market.

Given the significant barriers to entry in the auto industry and rapidly changing product and process technologies, Hyundai's design and mass production and exports of the Pony was very unique. This was in contrast to the experience of other developing countries. For instance, the centrality of the state and econ-techno nationalism was far less pronounced in the development of the auto industry in Thailand, Malaysia, Indonesia and Turkey.

The birth of the auto industry in Thailand, Malaysia, Turkey and Indonesia also dates back to the 1960s and was concurrent with the implementation of an import substituting industrial policy that included the usual package of protection and promotional policies.

There were substantial structural similarities between the Malaysian, Thai and Indonesian auto industries during the 1960s and 1970s. The auto industries in all these countries were fragmented between different makes and models and were dominated by joint ventures in Thailand and Malaysia although domestic producers were more prominent in Indonesia (Doner, 1991). It is also clear that the scale of production was limited in all these countries. Table 6.4 provides information on market structure, ownership, actual local content achievement and the scale of the production of the auto industry in these countries by the late 1970s.

The number of assembly plants producing vehicles in Malaysia increased from six in the late 1960s to 11 by 1980. A local content policy in 1972 required incorporation of 35 per cent local content by the early 1980s. The industry, however, was highly fragmented in terms of the number of models and was dominated by Chinese ethnic and Japanese joint ventures and was subordinated to the strategies of Toyota, Nissan and Honda which dominated the industry (Wad, 2009).

Also in Thailand, Japanese joint ventures dominated a market that was highly fragmented amongst several models. Similar local content requirements to those in Malaysia were imposed on domestic producers in Thailand in the mid-1970s (Doner, 1991; Rasiah *et al.*, 2008). In Indonesia, under government protection assembly operation expanded in the late 1960s. An import ban was imposed on CBU vehicles in 1971, and by 1972 there were 22 assemblers, mainly joint ventures, producing more than 50 models (Aswicahyono *et al.*, 1999). The local content programme was introduced in 1977 with the specific target of incorporating locally produced parts.

In Turkey, American and European joint ventures entered the market in the 1960s and 1970s although foreign ownership and control was far less prominent than in the case of Thailand and Malaysia (Wad, 2009; Doner, 1991). In the early 1970s, the government imposed an 85 per cent local content requirement on auto

Table 6.4 Market structure in the auto industry of selected countries in historical perspective (1960s and 1970s)

	Thailand	*Malaysia*	*Indonesia*	*South Korea*	*Turkey*	*Iran*
Start of domestic production	1961	1967	1968	1960	Early 1960s	1962
Source	Wad, (2009)	Wad, (2009), Jomo (2003)	Aswicahyono et al (1999); Doner (1991)	Amsden (1989); Doner (1991)	Yuzal & Sari (2008); UN Comtrade	Alizadeh (1985)
No of firms	15 assemblers 1980	11 assemblers 1980	22 assemblers 1972	6 assemblers/ manufacturers late 1970s	9 assemblers/ manufacturers late 1970s	12 assemblers/ manufacturers late 1970s
Market structure	Market fragmentation	Market fragmentation	Market fragmentation	Market concentration	Market fragmentation	Market concentration
Total car production Late 1970s	81,235 (1979)	170,230 (1979)	54,586 (1978)	145,784 (1977)	84,010 (1976)	123,543 (1977)
Local content (LC) requirement	40% target for 1981	NA	20–50% LC By 1984	National car project to indigenize all processes and parts	85% LC after 5 years of production.	75% LC by the late 1979s
Local content achievement	15–20% Limited	15–20% Limited	11–20% Limited	Indigenization	15–35% Partial	15–50% Partial
Ownership	Mainly Japanese joint ventures.*	Ethnic-Chinese- Japanese Joint–ventures.	Indonesian and joint ventures with Japanese.	Korean	European Joint-ventures.	Iranian
Management control	Foreign–primarily Japanese.	Foreign– primarily Japanese	Foreign–primarily Japanese	Korean	Mainly Turkish	Iranian
Level of import duties in on passenger cars (late 1970s)	Total ban on finished cars; 80% tariff on Complete Knock Down (CKD)	65% import duties on finished cars	Total ban on import of finished cars	High level tariff and occasional ban on imports of finished cars	High level tariff and occasional ban on imports of finished cars	200%–237% for imports of finished cars

Source: Wad (2009); Doner (1991); Jomo (2003); Aswicahyono et al (1999); Amsden (1989); Yuzal and Sari (2008); UN Comtrade; Alizadeh (1985)

companies. Again the scale of domestic production was quite small and production was geared towards the domestic market.

In all countries discussed here the domestic content of locally produced cars/ CVs remained limited in relation to government targets although there was variation between these countries. It appears that Indonesia was the least successful case, followed by Thailand, Malaysia, Turkey and Iran (Table 6.4). This was primarily due to market fragmentation by different brands and hence the small size of the domestic market making the production of several auto firms' components uneconomical in view of high economies of scale involved in the production of parts and components.

Economic reforms in the auto industry since the 1980s

As was mentioned earlier, with the exception of Korea the scale of production in Thailand, Indonesia and Turkey remained small up to the late 1970s. Also the proliferation of models and brands led to substantial fragmentation of market impeding vertical integration of the industry. These countries opted for market-oriented reforms including the provision of export subsidies and selective import liberalization in the early 1980s although their industries remained protected until the mid-1990s, when substantial deregulations were introduced. Since the mid-1990s, trade liberalization has also been accompanied by the formation of regional trade agreements.

Table 6.5 shows the form of rationalization undertaken by the selected countries.

Malaysia responded to fragmentation by opting for a national car project to rationalize the industry and also to increase the influence of *bumiputera,* the Muslim Malays who did not have much stake in the auto sector in contrast to the Japanese shareholders and Chinese-Malay who dominated the vehicle market (Jomo, 2003). The first national automotive company, Proton, that started to produce the Proton Saga in 1985, was 70 per cent owned by the government; the remaining shares were taken up by Mitsubishi Corporation of Japan. The company also made collaborative agreements with other foreign companies later on. Although in 1992 the company was listed on the Kuala Lumpur Stock Exchange, it is still mainly owned by the state. Porton enjoyed a considerable protection and was insulated from competition. High import duties of 140–300 per cent were imposed on CBU imported cars and also Proton enjoyed special government promotion in the form of tax incentives.[5] The second national car project, Perodua, was a smaller car and it was launched in 1994 through technical collaboration agreements with several Japanese and Western companies.[6]

Nevertheless, the national car projects have faced a severe challenge following the formation of the ASEAN Free Trade Area (AFTA). Malaysia, with its emphasis on the national car project, has been far less successful in competing in export markets compared to other members of AFTA, which includes Thailand and Indonesia (see the next section on their trade performances). All these countries have reduced import barriers to enhance competition and efficiency by eliminating intra-regional tariffs and non-tariff barriers.

Table 6.5 Development of the auto industry since the 1990s in selected countries

	Iran	Malaysia	Indonesia	Thailand	Turkey	South Korea
Rationalization of the industry	National car project Samand 2005	National car project Proton 1984; Perudoa 1992	Expansion into the export markets	Expansion into the export markets	Expansion into the export markets	Merger of national and foreign capital
Trading agreements	Not yet a member of WTO	Member of WTO January 1995. ASEAN Free Trade Area Mid 1990s	Member of WTO January 1995. ASEAN Free Trade Area Mid 1990s	Member of WTO January 1995 ASEAN Free Trade Area Mid 1990s	Member of WTO January 1995 Joining EU Customs Union Mid 1990s	Member of WTO January 1995
Production 2006 (passenger cars)	817,200	603,580	306,008	1,296,060	987,780	3,699,350
Production in 1997 (Passenger cars)	80,000	266,162	234,397	360,303	343,704	2,818,275
Average annual change (1997–2006)	33.6%	16.9%	24.4%	23.4%	16.6%	4.8%

Source: As in Table 6.4 and Abedini and Peridy (2009).

Indonesia's attempt at rationalization was through reinforcement of the local content project in the 1980s. In spite of government attempts to increase the domestic content to 50–70 per cent by 1984 the local content of the industry remained limited due to the prevalence of many models and brands and the lack of EOS. The overall production, for instance in the case of 17 brands in 1997, was less than 100,000 and the local content for passenger cars was around 20 per cent (Aswicahyono *et al.*, 1999). As a member of AFTA Indonesia also opted for substantial deregulation of the industry after the mid-1990s and has since subjected its automotive sector which is dominated by Japanese and Indonesian firms to stiff competition.

The automotive industry in Turkey also tried to reinforce the local content regulations without much success. Furthermore, Turkey faced severe financial crises in the 1980s which led to the stagnation of domestic demand throughout the 1980s. The industry is dominated mainly by the majority owned subsidiaries of Fiat, Renault, Ford, Toyota, Honda and a few other auto firms. The major policy change in the industry was initiated in 1996 in response to the Custom Union with the EU. Turkish industry has become far more globalized since joining the Custom Union with the EU which required compliance with EU quality regulations and standards. However, the Turkish market has been also subject to increasing import penetration.

Since 1990 Korea has emerged as a world producer although Korean ambitions for mass production and exports have evolved significantly over time.[7] Korean firms have moved up the ladder of comparative advantage by upgrading their products. Their success since the 1990s is based on a reputation for quality rather than on price alone, similar to that of Japanese cars. However, the ownership structure of the industry has been significantly globalized since the financial crisis of the late 1990s (Ravenhill, 2001). Close to 100 foreign companies either increased their presence or entered the market since the mid-1990s taking majority or complete control of previous joint-ventures. Heavy indebtedness of Korean auto companies like Kia, Daewoo and Samsung Motors influenced the speed of foreign ownership and mergers in the industry. Also DaimlerChrysler acquired around a 10 per cent share in Hyundai, which is still mainly owned by the Koreans.

Another successful exporter that has emerged among the countries in this study is Thailand (Wad, 2009). Thailand's market structure and management controls were similar to Malaysia up to 1980; however, since then Thailand has implemented a successful export-oriented strategy. The Thai auto industry is dominated by foreign capital led by Japan's leading auto companies exporting successfully to Japan and the global markets. Thailand is one of the main automotive export hubs among emerging markets.

As mentioned earlier, Iran opted for the national car project but is not yet a member of the WTO (partly due to the international sanctions). However, as is clear from Table 6.5, the average annual growth of passenger car production over the period 1997 to 2006 was 33.6 per cent – much higher than the other countries discussed here.

Performance

We now discuss the competitiveness and export performance of the industry in this section.

Trade performance

Table 6.6 shows the trade performance of the countries in this study over the period 2004 to 2007.

It is clear that, with the exception of Korea and Thailand, the remaining countries –including Iran, Malaysia, Indonesia and Turkey – all have a trade deficit in the auto sector. Korea and Thailand have succeeded in capturing a significant share of the global markets while Malaysia, Indonesia and Turkey have struggled with the competitive pressures arising from trade liberalization.

Table 6.6 Exports and imports in auto industry: Iran and selected countries (millions of US dollars)

	2004	2005	2006	2007
Iran				
Exports	NA	NA	277.4	NA
Imports	1,934.8	1,110.2	617.4	
Indonesia				
Exports	964.9	1355.3	1700.2	2144.1
Imports	2,395.4	3,033.8	2,421.7	2,739.6
S. Korea				
Exports	31,959.9	37,310.9	42,418.4	48,958.5
Imports	3,360.3	3,963.0	5,044.2	6,419.2
Malaysia				
Exports	655.5	827.4	974.0	1,307.8
Imports	2,542.6	3,066.5	3,093.2	3,168.0
Thailand				
Exports	5,331.4	8,116.7	10,055.8	12,759.2
Imports	3,551.1	3,849.5	3,664.7	4,143.8
Turkey				
Exports	8,147.9	9,428.9	1,679.5	3,105.5
Imports	101,107.9	10,378.8	5,367.2	4,985.5

Source: UN Comtrade. Auto sector includes both CBU passenger cars and commercial vehicles as well as their parts and components. Auto sector corresponds to 78 in SITC. Rev3.

Iran, a market that is still closed to foreign competition, also has a net trade deficit. Hence the national car project has remained dependent on imports. Furthermore, the share of both exports and imports has remained particularly low in the case of Iran (Abedini and Peridy 2009). A better indication is presented in Table 6.7 that reflects on a very low trade openness ratio for Iran regarding international trade in cars – 0.06 for Iran. This is almost half the openness ratio for cars in Indonesia, another country with a very small trade openness ratio. The trade openness ratio in cars is 10 times smaller for Iran than for Malaysia. The data in Table 6.7 includes only cars and not the whole auto sector and hence they differ from the data in Table 6.6. Nevertheless, they reinforce the evidence of the limited integration of the Iranian auto industry in the global market. In fact both export GDP ratios as well as import GDP ratios for cars are quite insignificant for Iran. They are 0.02 and 0.04 respectively in contrast to 0.93 for the world. This is despite a fast growth rate of production in Iran as mentioned earlier (Table 6.5).

In a study of the Iranian auto industry, Abedini and Peridy (2009), using gravity models, estimated the Iranian export potential towards Russia, Turkey, countries of North and Central Asia and North African countries concluding that the actual Iranian exports are 100 times less than they should be given Iran's high production capacity and proximity to these markets.

The gap between production and exports can be explained in part by the presence of a large population, replacement of old cars and import protection.

Table 6.7 International trade in car industry

	Exports (million US)	EX/IM ratio	EX/ GDP ratio	IM/GDP ratio	Openness ratio
Iran	112	0.53	0.02	0.04	0.06
Indonesia	366	0.80	0.05	0.06	0.11
Malaysia	151	0.11	0.06	0.54	0.60
Thailand	1950	5.93	0.38	0.06	0.45
Turkey	401	0.18	0.07	0.40	0.47
South Korea	21796	14.05	2.42	0.17	2.59
World	509,535	1.00	0.93	0.93	1.89

Source: Abedini and Peridy (2009).

In a country with more than 70 million population and high demand for replacing old cars (over 15 years old), which constitute more than 40 per cent of the total fleet, domestic demand can absorb most of the domestic production. Widening gaps between domestic production and exports are also reinforced by high import restrictions and tariffs. As high import tariffs and restrictions on imported vehicles limit consumer choice to domestic production and also reduce incentives to improve product design, standards and products' exportability by domestic producers. Despite a rapid growth of vehicle production in Iran, the safety and quality of domestic production appears to be in need of upgrading and improvement (BBC Persian, 2012).

However, the structure of incentives for the implementation of a national car project which operates under state ownership and is subject to a soft budget can mitigate economic efficiency and hence export performance. Korean success with the national car project in the mid-1970s was not subject to a soft budget constraint. Not only was the auto industry in Korea privately-owned but the main government objective for the industry was also expansion into the international market. By contrast, the main objective behind the implementation of a national car project in Iran and Malaysia has been to reduce import dependence and to increase self-reliance. However, by adopting a techno-nationalist strategy, the Korean objective has been to expand into global markets. Although Korea started with exports to Ecuador in 1976, the Hyundai Excel became the best-selling import model in the US market in 1987 (Ravenhill, 2001). This is in sharp contrast to the limited export performance of the Iranian auto producers.

Furthermore, with intense competition, substantial overcapacity and frantic merger activities in a globalized industry, it is doubtful whether the Korean experience of the 1970s can be repeated in the twenty-first century. As has been pointed out by Peter Wad:

With the exception of countries with huge potential markets like China and India the dominant academic view on establishing and sustaining viable

national automobile projects in Asian developing countries is pessimistic . . .
(particularly) at a time of a new global financial crisis emanating in the US
and a downturn of the global economy.

(2009: 172)

Conclusion

The Iranian auto industry has experienced a remarkable expansion since the mid-
1990s. However, this industry is much too closed to international trade. The future
development of the industry depends on its willingness and ability to expand
beyond the national boundaries. As things stand, its current export activities and
turnkey projects in Syria and some neighbouring countries are too limited.

It is time for the Iranian national automobile project either to produce exportable
brands targeting less competitive markets in, for example, neighbouring countries,
or to re-link with the leading auto firms. The latter policy requires not only moving
beyond Iranian automobile nationalism but also a different relationship with the
international economy and the removal of the sanctions.

Notes

* An earlier version of this chapter was presented at the conference 'Iranian Economy at
  a Crossroads: Domestic and Global Challenges' that was held at University of Southern
  California, Dornsife College, 18–19 September 2009. I am grateful to the conference
  organizers as well as participants for their comments and encouragement. The usual
  disclaimer applies.
1 It has been suggested that with the introduction of flexible production line in the 1980s
  the importance of economies of scale has been reduced in the auto industry (Kaplinsky,
  1984). Nevertheless there is ample evidence that without sufficient EOS high levels of
  flexibility cannot translate into competitiveness in the global market (Husan, 1997).
  For one thing despite the introduction of flexibility most parts and components are not
  standardized. There are few generic parts that can be used in several brands of motor
  vehicles without extensive customization. Instead parts and components are specific to
  particular models and these tie component producers to major terminal producers or
  head firms.
2 See: http://www.ikco.com/en/.
3 This has turned out to be a success within the semi-luxury category. Saipa also plans to
  boost exports by setting up assembly lines in target markets so as to ensure continuous
  exports of its products in the form of CKDs. Iran Khodro and Saipa have concluded a
  contract with the French car maker, Renault, to produce L90 passenger cars – an Iranian
  version of the French Logan.
4 The FT also cites Mohammad Bayatian, a member of the Parliament's industries
  committee that the total losses of Iran Khodro and Saipa had 'reached 10tn Rials
  ($407m) due to a 'fivefold rise' in prices of raw materials' (Ibid).
5 This made Proton prices 20–30 per cent cheaper than similar cars produced by other
  local producers. Market share of Porton increased to 73 per cent in 1988 from 47 per
  cent in 1986.
6 The second car project was more successful in terms of consumer demand and market
  shares.

7 The Hyundai Excel became the best selling import model in the US market in 1987. Korean companies have also a large number of subsidiaries around the world. Vehicle production increased from 120,000 in 1980 to 2.85 million in 1996 (Ravenhill 2001).

References

Abedini J. and Peridy, N., The emergence of Iran in the world car industry: an estimation of its export potential, *World Economy*, 32 (5): 790–818, 2009.

Alizadeh, P., *The process of import substitution industrialization in Iran (1960–78)*, Unpublished DPhil dissertation, Institute of Development studies (IDS), Sussex University, Falmer, Brighton, UK, 1985.

Amsden, A., *Asia's next giant: South Korea and late industrialization*, New York: Oxford University Press, 1989.

Aswicahyono, H., Tilik, A. and Rizal, Y., 'The development of the Indonesian auto industry', Centre for Strategic and International Studies, Economic working paper series WRE 051, Jakarta, Indonesia: http://www.csis.or.id/papers/wpe051, 1999.

Bahar, A., 'Reports on Iran's automotive sector,' Atieh Bahar Consulting Firm, Tehran, Iran: www.atiehbahar.com, 2005.

BBC Persian, 'Iran comes top in the number of global road accident deaths', 10 May 2012: http://www.bbc.co.uk/news/world-middle-east-18023809, 2012.

Doner, R. F., *Driving a bargain: automobile industrialization and Japanese firms in southeast Asia*, Berkeley, California: University of California Press, 1991.

Doner, R. F., Noble, G. and Ravenhill, J., *Industrial competitiveness of the auto parts industries in four Asian countries*, World Bank Policy Research Working Paper No. 4106, Washington DC, 2006.

Foreign Trade Statistics of Iran, Islamic Republic of Iran, Tehran: various issues 1969–77.

FT, Iran's car industry output falls sharply, *Financial Times*, 23 January, 2013.

Hansen, J.R., 'Iran: economies of scale and tariff levels in the motor vehicle industry', International Bank of Reconstruction and Development, Development Economies Department, 1973.

Humphery J. and Memedovic, O., 'The global automotive industry value chain: what prospects for upgrading by developing countries?', Sectoral studies series, Vienna: United Nations Industrial Development Organization (UNIDO), 2003.

Husan, R., The continuing importance of economies of scale in the automotive industry, *European Business Review,* 97 (1): 38–42, 1997.

Iran Khodro Industrial Group: http://www.ikco.com/en/.

Industrial and Mining Development Bank of Iran (IMDBI): 'Reports to the Executive Committee on Component Producers', various years; Centre for the Attraction and Protection of Foreign Investment, List of Foreign Investors up to March, Industrial and Mining Development Bank of Iran, Tehran, *mimeo*, 1978.

IMDBI, 'Annual reports to the board of directors for the general assembly of shareholders', Industrial and Mining Development Bank of Iran, various issues, 1959–78, Tehran.

Jenkins, R. O., *Dependent Industrialization in Latin America*, New York: Praeger publishers, 1977.

Jomo, K. S., 'Mahathir's flawed economic policy legacy', Forum: Kuala Lumpur: http://www.jomoks.org/research/other/rp003.htm, 2003.

Kaplinsky, R., *Automation: The Technology and Society*, London: Longman, 1984.

Nag B., Banerjee, S. and Chatterjee, R., 'Changing features of the automobile industry in

Asia': Comparison of Production, Trade and Market Structure in Selected Countries, Asia-Pacific Research and Training Network on Trade, Working Paper, No. 37, India, 2007.

OICA statistics, various years; www.OICA.net/catagory/production_statistics/

Pratten, C., *Economics of Scale in Manufacturing Industry,* Cambridge, MA: Harvard University Press, 1971.

Rahnema, S., 'Continuity and change in industrial policy' in Rahnema, S. and Behdad, S., eds, *Iran after the revolution, Crisis Of an Islamic State,* Publisher; I.B. Tauris, 1996.

Rasiah R., Sadoi, R. and Busser, R., *Multinationals, Technology and Localization in Automotive Firms in Asia,* London: Routledge, 2008.

Ravenhill, J., 'From national champions to global partnership: the Korean Auto industry, financial crisis and globalization', Centre for International Studies, Massachusetts Institute of Technology, MIT Japan Program, Working Paper series, 0.1.04, 2001.

Rhys, D. G., *The Motor Industry: An Economic Survey,* London: Butterworths, 1972.

Sturgeon, T. J. and Lester, R. K., 'The new global supply base: new challenges for local suppliers in East Asia', in Shahid, Y., Anjum, A. M. and Nabesshima, K., eds, *Global Production Networking and Technological Change in East Asia,* Oxford University Press, 2004.

Sturgeon, T. J., Memedovic, O., Biesebroeck, J. Van and Gereffi, G., Globalisation of the automotive industry: main features and trends, *International Journal of Technological Learning, Innovation and Development, 2 (1/2),* 2009.

UN Comtrade, Country Sectoral Data.

UNIDO, 'Establishment and Development of Automotive Industries in Developing Countries,' ID/36, Vol.2, 1971, Appendix A, 1971.

Wad, P., 'The automobile industry in Southeast Asia: Malaysia and Thailand', *Journal of the Asia Pacific Economy,* 14 (2): 172–93, 2009.

White, L. J., *The Automobile Industry since 1945,* Cambridge, MA: Harvard University Press, 1971.

Yuzal, S. and Sari, A., 'Automotive and auto parts industries in Turkey', Ankara: Export Promotion Centre, 2008.

7 The Iranian economy in the shadow of sanctions

Nader Habibi

Introduction

The economy of Iran has faced various types of sanctions ever since the 1979 Revolution. These sanctions were initially imposed by the United States, which was Iran's dominant trade partner before the Revolution. The first spark for the sanctions was the Iran hostage crisis. Then, in the 1980s, sanctions were part of the US dual containment policy adopted against Iran and Iraq. They were also intended to punish Iran for its anti-Western policies in the Middle East, such as its support for Hizbollah in Lebanon. A new and more important rationale was added in the 1990s, when the United States became alarmed about Iran's nuclear programme. In the 2000s, while the US-sponsored sanctions became more intense, additional sanctions were also imposed by the European Union (EU) and the United Nations (UN) at later stages.

The purpose of this chapter is to assess the impact of the evolving sanction regimes on Iran's economy. As will be demonstrated, the impact has been profound and has evolved with regard to the severity and forms of sanctions. Most research on the impact of sanctions in the West is focused on whether the sanctions are causing enough economic pressure to alter the behaviour of government. A number of econometric studies have also looked at the impact of sanctions on the volume of trade and aggregate economic output (Torbat, 2005). Instead of focusing on the quantitative cost of sanctions on Iran's economic output and foreign trade, my analysis looks at the structural and institutional changes that have been caused either directly or indirectly by more than three decades of sanctions. Furthermore, econometric studies will not be able to shed light on the impact of the most recent sanctions in 2012, which are far more intrusive than previous ones, due to lack of data. My analysis, on the other hand, pays more attention to the most recent sanctions. As will be demonstrated, the burden of the 2012 sanctions is far more serious than the limited sanctions of the past three decades.

The evolution of sanctions since 1979

Table 7.1 offers an overview of the various sanctions that Iran has faced since the 1979 Revolution. The history of sanctions against Iran can be divided into three

Table 7.1 Iran Sanctions Timeline (1979–2012)

Year	Scope	Cause	Initiated by
Nov-79	US freezes $10 billion in Iran Assets (A portion was released after American hostages were freed in 1981).	Hostage crisis	USA
Apr-80	Ban on commercial trade with Iran except for export of food and medical supply. Prohibits financial transactions in support of travel to Iran	Hostage crisis	USA
Jun-84	Prohibition of weapons sales to Iran	Concern about containment of Iran-Iraq war and Iran's alleged support for terrorism	USA
Oct-87	Ban on import and export of any goods and services from Iran	Concern about Iran's involvement in terrorism and attacks on ships in the Persian Gulf during Iran-Iraq war.	USA
Jun-92	Ban on export of arms to Iran; allows US president to impose sanctions against any country or entity that transfers sensitive materials to Iran	Concern about Iran's support for terrorism, nuclear programme	USA
Mar-95	Ban o US trade in Iran oil industry	Concern about Iran's support for terrorism, nuclear programme	USA
May-95	Prohibits the re-export of US goods to Iran and Investment in entities that are owned or controlled by the government of Iran	Concern about Iran's support for terrorism, nuclear programme	USA
Aug-96	Iran-Libya Sanctions Act 1996: Gave the US President the power to levy sanctions against any entity that invested more than $20 million in Iran's energy sector	Nuclear programme	USA
Apr-99	Partial easing of US sanctions as a goodwill gesture towards Iran's President Khatami and the reformists.	Nuclear programme	USA
Mar-00	Partial easing of US sanctions as a goodwill gesture towards Iran's President Khatami and the reformists.	Nuclear programme	USA
Aug-01	Iran-Libya Sanctions Act extended for an additional five years	Nuclear programme	USA
Sep-06	Prohibiting Bank Saderaat Iran from dealing with US financial institutions wither directly or indirectly. This sanction was extended to five other Iranian banks in November 2007.	Nuclear programme	USA

(Continued)

Table 7.1 (Continued)

Year	Scope	Cause	Initiated by
Dec-06	Ban on supplying nuclear related materials and technology to Iran; called for freezing the assets of Iranian persons and companies involved in the nuclear programme.	Nuclear programme	UNSC Resolution 1737
Mar-07	Arms embargo, list of frozen Iranian assets were expanded.	Nuclear programme	UNSC Resolution 1747
Mar-08	Further extension of the asset freeze, asked UN members to monitor a) the activities of Iranian banks, b) travels of persons associated with Iran's nuclear programme, c) cargos of Iranian ships and airplanes.	Nuclear programme	UNSC Resolution 1803
Jun-10	Called for freezing the assets of Iran Revolutionary Guards and Iranian Shipping lanes, called for denial of financial services for activities related to Iran's nuclear programme (Includes denial of banking services), Stricter inspection of Iranian cargo	Nuclear programme	UNSC Resolution 1929
Jul-10	Comprehensive Iran Sanctions, Accountability and Divestment Act of 2010: Bars the US government from awarding contracts and limit access to US market to companies that do business with Iran with focus on Iran's energy and banking sectors.	Nuclear programme	USA
Jul-10	Ban on sales of energy related goods and services, Ban on medium and long tern trade financing and financial guarantees, Bans EU companies from investing in Iran's energy sector,	Nuclear programme	European Union
Nov-11	US imposes penalties on companies that are involved in Iran's upstream (oil and gas) activities and petrochemical industry.	Nuclear programme	USA
Dec-11	The FY 2012 Defence Authorization Act: Sanctions again Iran's Central Bank	Nuclear programme	USA
Jan-12	Sanction against the Central Bank of Iran	Nuclear programme	USA
Jan-12	Froze the assets of Iranian Central Bank, approved an oil embargo effective July 2012	Nuclear programme	European Union
Mar-12	EU instructed SWIFT to deny financial transaction services to Iranian Banks	Nuclear programme	European Union
Jul-12	EU imposes a complete embargo on import of Iranian oil. It also imposes a ban on insurance services for Iranian oil shipments.	Nuclear programme	European Union

Source: Compiled by the author.

distinct periods. Phase one began in 1979 and lasted until August 1996. During this period Iran faced unilateral sanctions by the United States, but these sanctions did not interfere with other countries' trade with Iran. During this period, the United States imposed varying restrictions on trade and investment between US entities and Iran.

The second phase began with the Iran-Libya Sanctions Act 1996 (ISLA) and lasted until December 2006. With this act, the United States tried to restrict and reduce the economic relations of other countries with Iran. ISLA authorized the US government to impose sanctions on any domestic or foreign firm that invested more than $20 million in Iran's energy sector. At this stage, European countries were still reluctant to impose any sanctions against Iran because of their strong economic and trade ties with her. Instead, they were trying to resolve the disputes through dialogue and negotiations.

The third phase of sanctions against Iran began in December 2006 when the UN Security Council (UNSC) approved the first UN-sponsored sanctions against Iran. Resolution 1737 banned all member countries from sale of nuclear related materials and technology to Iran. It also called on members to freeze the assets of persons and companies that were active in Iran's nuclear programme. This third phase of sanctions was characterized by multinational efforts and more intensive unilateral sanctions by several countries other than the United States.

With the strong support of the United States and the EU, the UNSC approved three more sanctions resolutions against Iran during the period of 2007–10 (Resolutions 1747, 1803 and 1929). These resolutions called for freezing the assets of Iran's Revolutionary Guards and Iranian shipping lanes. They also called for increasing the inspections of Iran-bound cargo and denying financial/banking services for activities related to Iran's nuclear programme. These UN sanctions were followed by the first round of unilateral sanctions by the EU in July 2010. The EU imposed a ban on medium and long term trade financing and financial guarantees that are instrumental in trade facilitation. It also prohibited EU companies from investing in Iran's energy sector.

These EU sanctions coincided with a new round of unilateral US sanctions labelled the Comprehensive Iran Sanctions, Accountability and Divestment Act (CISADA). The CISADA imposed additional restrictions on international investment in Iran's energy sector. In particular, it threatened severe punishment for firms that invested in Iran's petroleum refinement industry to constrain the domestic production of refined products such as gasoline. It also imposed sanctions on the sale of refined petroleum products worth more than $5 million dollars in each 12 months. It further threatened sanctions against companies that offered transportation, financing and insurance for import of refined products.

The EU took additional steps in December 2011 and January 2012 when it adopted sanctions against Iran's central bank and approved an oil embargo (effective from 1 July 2012). In order to make the financial sanctions even more effective, in January 2012 the EU instructed the Society for Worldwide Interbank Financial Telecommunication (SWIFT, which is the inter-bank financial transactions clearinghouse based in Belgium) to stop its services to Iranian banks.

Similar sanctions against the Iranian central bank were also enacted by the United States in the same month. As a result, the focus of the sanctions against Iran shifted toward the financial and banking sector in the third phase as more countries joined the sanctions. Targeting the financial sector in effect has led to a comprehensive sanction against the entire economy. Many sectors of the economy, which depend on international banking transactions to facilitate imports and exports, have been affected adversely by these financial sanctions.

The impact of sanctions on Iran's international trade

Limited impact in early stages

The process of industrialization in Iran has led to a high degree of trade dependency in many economic sectors. By the time of the Revolution in 1979, the Iranian economy had experienced more than two decades of industrialization in the context of import substitution and protected domestic industries. Many of these industries, particularly in the manufacturing sector, were heavily dependent on international trade for machinery and materials. These industries included oil and petrochemicals, auto manufacturing (assembly), textiles and light electronic consumer goods manufacturing. There was also a sharp increase in imports of consumer goods and agricultural products during the 1960s and 1970s thanks to the rising oil revenues and the Pahlavi regime's desire to spend a portion of these revenues on consumer subsidies. By the late 1970s, the United States and Western Europe were Iran's largest trade partners.

This trade dependency would have increased Iran's vulnerability to comprehensive trade sanctions but the unilateral US trade sanctions that were introduced in the 1980s and 1990s had a limited impact on the Iranian economy for several reasons. First, they targeted US-Iran trade on specific products, which affected some sectors of Iran's economy without significant impact on others. Second, since many industrial countries were willing to trade with Iran, Iranian businesses were able to find alternative sources for many American products though not all of them. In some cases costs were higher and quality was poorer but nevertheless substitute products were found.

Third, the sanctions did not directly target Iran's oil exports and oil revenues. Iran lost the United States as an oil client but it retained many European and Asian clients. Similarly the US prohibition of investment in Iran's oil and gas sector in those decades had only a partial impact, as Iran was able to obtain investment and technology from European and Asian oil companies.[1] Fourth, Iran was able to obtain some American products such as spare parts for US made machinery and aircrafts in international black markets. This indirect procurement was more expensive and on occasions unreliable but it helped Iran reduce the adverse effects of the sanctions. Faced with a weapons embargo during the war with Iraq war, the Islamic government developed a large network of front companies and middlemen to purchase arms and dual use products from international dealers. These covert arm deals were unavoidable because most of Iran's weapon systems such as jet fighters were purchased from American arms manufacturers before the Revolution in the 1960s and 1970s.

Sizable trade diversion since 2000

In more recent years, the US and international trade sanctions have resulted in a significant amount of trade diversion on Iran's side. In a dynamic process, the United States has continuously identified Iran's top trade partners and used its economic and diplomatic leverage to force them into cutting back their economic ties with Iran. Iran has responded to the withdrawal of each partner by expanding its ties with other partners and sometimes finding new partners. This dynamic process has been repeated several times in the past two decades but more so in more recent years. First Iran switched to European partners when American firms enforced the sanctions in the 1990s. Then it switched to the UAE (mainly Dubai) as a re-export partner when European countries joined the sanctions in the 2000s. The growth of Iran-UAE trade did not go unnoticed by the US as it used its diplomatic and economic leverage with the UAE to reduce that country's trade with Iran. Iran has since responded by shifting some of its trade from the UAE to Turkey and China. As the United States put pressure on the UAE to cut back its ties with Iranian businesses, Iran has switched to Turkey and China. The impact of this process is visible in the frequent change of the list of Iran's major trade partners at demonstrated in Tables 7.2 and 7.3.

Since Iran's commodity exports are dominated by oil and refined oil products, which were not subject to sanctions until very recently, we observe relative stability in the position of most of Iran's export partners since 1977 with the exception of China. Since 2000 China's share of Iran's oil and gas exports has steadily increased and it has replaced the EU as the largest importer of Iranian products since 2011. As trade with Western nations became more difficult, Iran viewed China as a potential long-term oil customer and the two countries signed a long-term 25-year oil and gas cooperation contract worth $75 billion in 2004, which led to a sharp increase in China's purchase of Iranian crude oil. Iran also made a commitment to export natural gas to China in return for Chinese oil firms' participation in the development of several oil and gas fields in Iran.[2]

The impact of sanctions is more visible in Table 7.3, which shows how the list of leading exporters to Iran has changed over time. A visible trend is the falling rank of Iran's major European partners. Germany, which was Iran's largest source of imports for several years, fell from number one in 2000 to number four in 2011 after the UAE, China and South Korea. The UK, France and Italy also moved further down the list while China, the UAE and South Korea were able to increase their shares in Iran's import market. Among the European countries, France, Germany, Italy and the UK have gradually joined the international sanctions and adopted unilateral sanctions of their own against Iran in recent years. As a result the combined share of these four countries in Iran's merchandise imports has been on a downtrend in the last decade. While the decline was slow up until 2005, we see in Figure 7.1 that it has accelerated ever since. This figure also shows that after

Table 7.2 Iran's Top Ten Export Destinations (Based on value of exports in US dollars)

1977	1985	1990	2000	2005	2011
Japan	European Union	European Union	European Union	European Union	China
Italy	Japan	Japan	Japan	Japan	European Union
Turkey	Italy	Germany	South Korea	China	India
Singapore	Turkey	Italy	Italy	Italy	Japan
Netherlands	Singapore	United Kingdom	China	South Korea	Turkey
Spain	Netherlands	Switzerland	Singapore	Turkey	South Korea
Romania	Spain	Spain	Greece	Netherlands	Italy
France	Romania	France	Netherlands	France	Spain
United States	France	India	France	Spain	Greece
Syria	United States	South Korea	Spain	Greece	France
India	Syria	Turkey	Turkey	Singapore	Netherlands
Sri Lanka	India	Austria	Philippines	Philippines	Pakistan
Finland	Germany	United States	Germany	Syria	Syria
Pakistan	Sri Lanka	Singapore	India	India	Sri Lanka
Canada	Finland	Pakistan	Portugal	United Arab Emirates	United Arab Emirates

Source: Direction of Trade Statistics various years (trade date as reported by Iran). The rankings are calculated by the author.

Note: The table includes European Union as a block but many EU member countries are also included separately. Since EU countries have imposed several sanctions as a unified economic block it is helpful to see how this entire block has ranked as a trade partner for Iran.

2005, the share of China has sharply increased. The growing participation of European countries in the sanctions and China's willingness to fill the resulting gap is clearly visible. However, this trend is only partly due to sanctions. Iran is one of many developing countries that have witnessed a large increase in China's share in their imports.[3]

Sanctions have impacted Iran's economic relations with the United Arab Emirates (UAE) more than any other country. Because of geographic proximity and several waves of migrations Iran has had a long history of trade with Dubai, which in recent years has been home to a large Iranian community. Most of Iran's economic relations with the UAE are concentrated in the Emirate of Dubai while the relations with the federal government in Abu Dhabi have been adversely affected by a territorial dispute over three small islands in Persian Gulf and close geopolitical cooperation of the UAE Federal government and the United States.[4]

Sanctions have had three distinct effects on Iran-UAE relations. First, as sanctions made it more difficult for Iranian firms to trade with many European and Asian countries in recent years, many Iranian businesses tried to overcome the

Table 7.3 Iran's Top 15 Import Origins (Based on value of imports in US dollars)

1977	1990	2000	2005	2007	2009	2011
European Union	European Union	European Union	European Union	European Union	European Union	United Arab Emirates
Germany	Germany	Germany	United Arab Emirates	United Arab Emirates	United Arab Emirates	China
United States	Japan	United Arab Emirates	Germany	Germany	Germany	European Union
Japan	Developing Countries: Europe	Russia	France	China	China	South Korea
United Kingdom	Italy	Italy	China	Switzerland	South Korea	Germany
Italy	United Kingdom	South Korea	Italy	South Korea	Switzerland	Turkey
France	United Arab Emirates	Japan	South Korea	United Kingdom	Italy	Russia
Netherlands	Belgium & Luxembourg	France	Switzerland	France	Turkey	India
Switzerland	Turkey	China	Sweden	Italy	United Kingdom	Italy
Belgium & Luxembourg	South Korea	United Kingdom	Japan	India	France	France
U.S.S.R.	Netherlands	Canada	Russia	Japan	Japan	Japan
Australia	Switzerland	Belgium	United Kingdom	Turkey	India	Thailand
India	France	Australia	India	Austria	Russia	Spain
Sweden	Austria	Kazakhstan	Turkey	Russia	Singapore	Netherlands
Romania	Canada	Spain	Netherlands	Belgium	Netherlands	Ukraine

Source: Direction of Trade Statistics various years (trade date as reported by Iran). The rankings are calculated by the author.

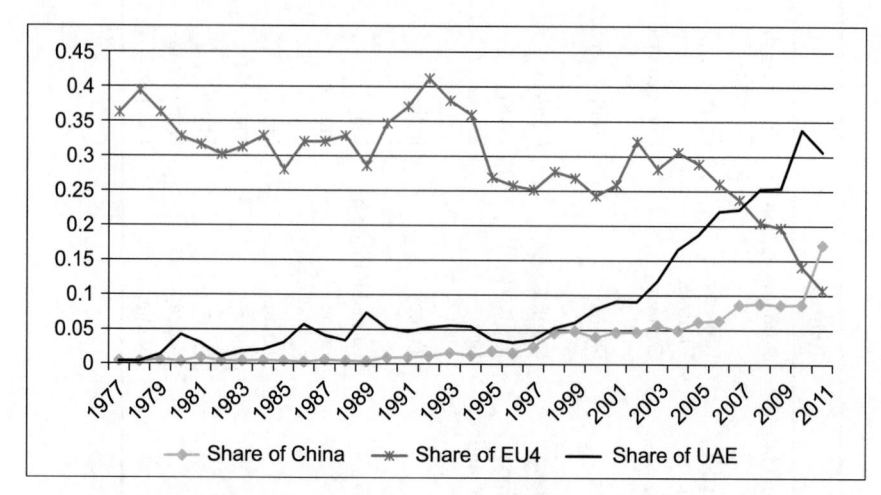

Figure 7.1 Relative Shares of EU4 (France, Germany, Italy, UK), China and UAE in Iran's Merchandise Imports

Source of data: Direction of Trade Statistics (IMF) 3012.

sanctions by establishing branches in the UAE (primarily in Dubai). This adaptation allowed them to deal with the global economy as UAE-based businesses. Consequently there was a rapid increase in the number of Iranian-owned businesses in the UAE during 2000s although, in compliance with the UAE business regulations, they had to find a local partner.

These businesses have played a crucial role in the expansion of trade between Iran and the UAE in recent years and they have facilitated the rapid expansion of the UAE exports to Iran as demonstrated in Figure 7.1. In 2011 the UAE emerged as the leading exporter to Iran with a record $29 billion which was 28 per cent larger than 2010. This sharp increase has been realized despite the US's efforts to reduce UAE's trade links with Iran.[5] Indeed the growth of Iran's imports from the UAE is mainly a result of the difficulties that it faces in trade with other exporters because of the sanctions. Most of the UAE's exports to Iran are re-exports of products that are either fully manufactured in other countries or marginally assembled in the UAE before being shipped to Iran. So Iran's trade with the UAE has mostly been an indirect trade with many other countries which cannot trade with Iran directly because of the sanctions. In addition to official trade, a large amount of goods are also smuggled to Iran from the UAE in small boats.[6] Some products also go to Iran indirectly through Iraq.

Second, as escalating sanctions made Iran's investment environment inhospitable Iranian households and businesses invested large sums in Dubai's booming real estate sector and other businesses. Hence the UAE became one of the main beneficiaries of capital flight from Iran, which has intensified in the past decade as a result of Iran's tensions with the West. Iranian investments in Dubai took a beating in 2009 when that city-state's housing market collapsed.

Third, the growing reliance of Iran on trade and investment relations with the UAE has not gone unnoticed by the United States. Starting in 2008, the United States used its diplomatic leverage in Abu Dhabi to reduce these economic ties. While the UAE has been reluctant to fully comply with the US demands it has taken some limited steps to show compliance. For example several banks in the UAE have cut back in their transactions with Iranian entities and some have refused to open lines of credit for trade between Iran and the UAE (Habibi, 2010). These steps increased the cost of trade between the two countries. More recently, the UAE government has also imposed new restrictions on residence visa renewals for Iranians. As a result of these pressures, some Iranian businessmen have relocated their businesses from Dubai to Turkey and Malaysia. Turkey in particular has seen a rapid increase in the number of new business investments by Iranian entities since 2008 (Habibi, 2012).

Sanctions and foreign investment in Iran since 1989

The impact of sanctions on Iran's ability to attract foreign investment for energy and manufacturing sectors was also minimal during the 1980s and 1990s. During the 1980s, Iran's business climate was considered high risk by international investors who were deterred by the xenophobic attitude and revolutionary rhetoric of the government toward foreign investment on one hand, and the ongoing Iran-Iraq war on the other. After the death of Ayatollah Khomeini and election of Akbar Hashemi Rafsanjani as Iran's President in 1989, the government tried to improve the business climate.

During the 1990s, President Rafsanjani initiated a number of market-oriented economic reforms. His attempt to introduce a new foreign investment law was blocked by his conservative opponents in the Parliament. President Khatami continued this quest and was able to gain parliamentary support for a revised foreign investment attraction law in 2000 but this law was blocked by the Guardian Council on the ground that it would compromise the country's economic independence. The Guardian Council rejected two more attempts of the Parliament to approve this law and finally it was referred to the Expediency Council for a final decision.[7] The former President Rafsanjani, who was the Head of the Expediency Council at the time, gained approval for the foreign investment law which was called 'the Foreign Investment Promotion and Protection Act' (FIPPA) in May 2002.[8]

Approval of FIPPA raised optimism about prospects of foreign investment in Iran but it saw considerable opposition and resistance by opponents of President Khatami and his economic policies in years that followed. Despite these uncertainties and obstacles, Iran was able to attract some limited amount of foreign investment. While investment in most economic sectors faced many difficulties, there was more agreement among the ruling elite on the need to attract foreign investment and foreign partners for development of Iran's oil and gas sector. Iran was able to attract several foreign partners to this sector although the American oil Companies stayed away because of the US sanctions. Frustrated by its inability to influence Iran's foreign policy, the United States launched its first extraterritorial sanction against Iran by adopting the Iran-Libya Sanction Act of 1996 (ILSA). As mentioned above, this law targeted international oil and gas companies that invested more than $20 million in Iran's energy sector.

The ILSA was enacted at a time when the Rafsanjani government was seeking international investment in several oil and gas development projects. Initially European governments did not pay much attention to ILSA as they continued to emphasize dialogue and economic engagement as best strategies for modifying Iran's foreign policy. Consequently, the European firms such as the French oil company, Total, showed interest in these projects.[9] They continued to sign long-term investment contracts with Iran's oil ministry under buyback arrangements in the following years but actual progress on these contracts was slow.[10] In addition to major European oil firms such as Shell, Statoil, ENI and Total, several Asian companies from Malaysia, China and South Korea also signed similar contracts with Iran during the 1990s. In 1998, the offshore SIRRI A oilfield came on-stream as the first buyback contract to become operational. The foreign operators in this contract were Total and Petronas (Malaysian).

After Mohammad Khatami was elected to Iran's presidency in 1997, the US and European governments were hopeful that he would be able to moderate Iran's foreign policy. For a brief period (1999–2000), during Khatami's first term, the tensions between Iran and the United States diminished. During this short interval, the United States relaxed some of the anti-Iran sanctions as a goodwill gesture. Unfortunately this attempt toward rapprochement failed and the United States extended ILSA for an additional five years in 2001.

Two developments in the late 1990s and early 2000s motivated Iran to intensify its efforts to attract foreign investment for its oil and gas industry. First, several large oil and natural gas fields such as Azadegan, Darkhovin and Dashte-Abadan (offshore) were discovered in this period which required substantial amount of financial capital and advanced technology. Second, after considerable debate and internal disagreement, the government of Iran approved a privatization plan for several sectors including parts of the oil and gas sector, in the context of the Third Socio-Economic Development Plan (2000–5). In addition the price of crude oil increased substantially after 1999 and created added incentive for the expansion of oil output.

Consequently Iran signed several contracts with European and Asian oil firms during the first half of 2000s. One of the most active European companies in Iran in that period was Shell. Shell Exploration (a subsidiary of Shell) signed a buyback contract to restore two offshore oil fields of Soroosh and Norouz in the Persian Gulf. These fields were badly damaged during the Iran–Iraq war in the 1980s. The contract was signed in 1999 and Shell Exploration completed its development by 2005. These fields produce approximately 190,000 barrels per day. Shell had several other projects in Iran during that period. Similar contracts were also signed with Total, Elf and ENI in this era.

While Iran was able to sign several contracts with the international oil companies in the 1990s and 2000s despite the US sanctions, sanctions had an impact on the terms and conditions of these contracts and their pace of progress. Since some international oil companies were deterred from competing for Iran's investment projects because of the sanctions, those who were willing to ignore the sanctions had a stronger bargaining power and were able to extract more favourable terms from the Iranian side than otherwise. The United States was also able to put sufficient pressure on some firms that signed deals with Iran to cause significant delays and slowdowns in the implementation of these contracts. [11] Nowhere have these delays been more visible than in Iran's attempts to develop the offshore South Pars gas field in the Persian Gulf. Iran shares this field with Qatar, which has rapidly expanded its production levels and is now a leading exporter of LNG. Iran has signed several contracts with foreign partners to develop this field but so far most of these projects remain in the developmental stage and progress has been slow.

At an aggregate level, it is difficult to isolate the impact of the sanctions on Iran's crude oil output from other factors in the 1990s. The Iran–Iraq war (1980–7) severely damaged Iran's production capacity and the government was eager to expand production as fast as possible in the post-war era. However, as shown in Figure 7.2, production has increased at a slow pace until 2011 and it has not reached the pre-Revolution level of 6 million b/d at any stage in the post-Revolutionary period. This is at least partly due to the maturity of many of Iran's oil fields whose yields are declining. Based on Iran's growing need for hard currency and statements by various government officials, expanding the crude oil production capacity has, however, been a continuous objective. Yet

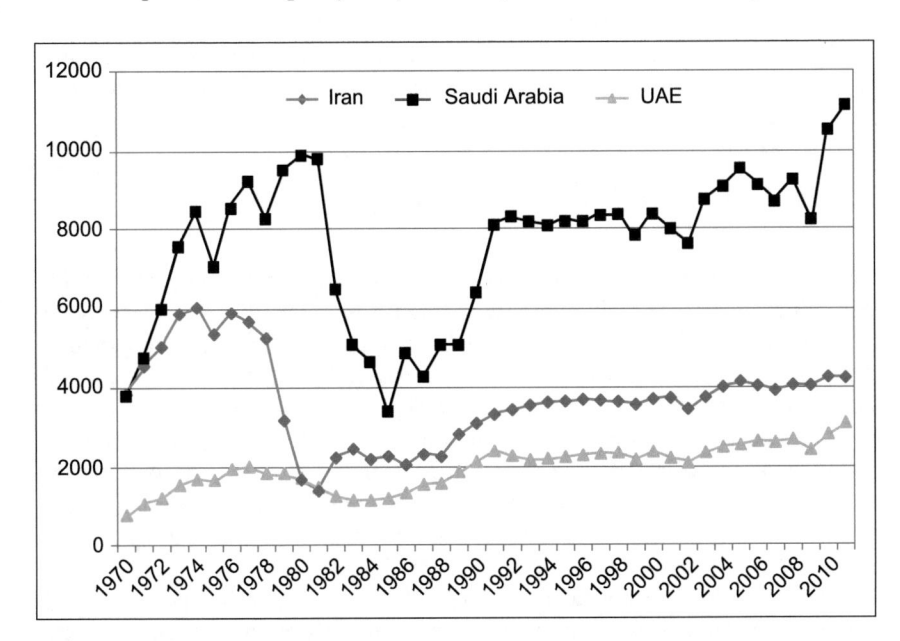

Figure 7.2 Crude Oil Production, 1970–2011 (Thousand Barrels Per Day)

Source: Energy Information Agency (2013).

Iran's production record so far should be viewed as a partial success. On the one hand, the Oil Ministry was able to maintain production in the 3.6–4 million barrels per day range since 1992. On the other hand, it has not been able to increase production above this range due to sanctions and domestic techno-logical constraints. More recently, however, as we shall see in the next section, the introduction of new financial and oil sanctions since July 2012 has led to a sharp decline in the demand for Iran's crude oil.

During the 1990s and the first half of the 2000s, the US sanctions did not have a direct effect on foreign investment flows into Iran's non-oil sectors such as manufacturing. Only those industries that required American-made inputs for which alternative sources did not exist were impacted on in the short run and even then it was possible for many firms to either purchase the products illegally or eventually find alternatives. Iran's auto industry in particular was able to expand its joint venture partnerships with several European and Asian auto-makers during 1990–2006. With the help of these partners, Iran was able to expand its passenger car production from 157,000 units in 1998 to an impressive 1,000,000 units in 2006.[12] The most active foreign automaker in Iran during this period was the French firm Peugeot, which partnered with Iran's largest auto firm, Iran Khodro. This partnership released several Peugeot models for Iran's domestic market. Other international firms that cooperated with Iranian auto firms in this period were Kia, Hyundai, Daewoo, Nissan, and Renault. In recent years all of these international firms have had to cut back or end their presence in Iran due to the most recent round of sanctions after 2006. Consequently, the sanctions began to take a toll on Iran's auto industry output by late 2011. The total number of automobiles produced during April 2012 was reportedly 32 per cent smaller than in April 2011. The decline was significantly larger in trucks and bus production.[13]

Impact of recent sanctions on oil exports and financial transactions

The United States' efforts to increase the economic pressure on Iran steadily intensified after 2006 as it was able to secure four rounds of UN economic sanctions (2006, 2007, 2008 and 2010) against Iran's nuclear programme (see Table 7.1). In addition, and as mentioned above, the US government approved the CISADA in July 2010. This received a significant boost in the same month, when European countries introduced bans on several areas of economic cooperation such as energy investment, trade finance guarantees, cargo transport, insurance and financial services. Nevertheless Iran was still able to partially deflect these pressures by diverting its trade to other countries such as Russia, China and Turkey that were willing to trade with Iran.

Realizing that it does not have enough leverage to secure the cooperation of all of Iran's trade partners with the trade and investment sanctions, the United States turned to a new strategy in late 2011 by focusing on Iran's international financial transactions. International trade in the modern global economy is highly dependent on global financial institutions that facilitate the flow of payments among trade partners. The US announced a ban on banking transactions with Iran's central bank (ICB), which applied to both American and non-American financial institutions. The measure was significant for two reasons: first, earlier sanctions on many of Iran's commercial banks had increased the role of the ICB in Iran's economy. Second, the ICB serves as the main financial institution for Iranian government's international transactions including the all-important payment for oil exports. The sanctioning of the ICB came as a significant disruption to Iran's ability to receive payment for its crude oil sales.

The United States also convinced the EU to adopt another severe set of financial sanctions. In March 2012, the EU ordered the Belgium-based financial clearinghouse SWIFT to stop its service to Iranian banks. SWIFT has come to play a crucial role in international transactions by facilitating a fast and efficient mechanism for transfer of funds among banking institutions worldwide. Lack of access to SWIFT has caused a noticeable slowdown in international transactions of Iranian businesses and government institutions. The government has been forced to switch from the US dollar to the national currencies of some of its oil customers such as Turkey, China and India.[14] Accepting payment in these currencies either limits Iran to using the oil revenues for purchasing goods in these specific countries (effectively compelling Iran into barter trade of oil for an equivalent value of imports from each oil consumer), or imposes large transaction costs for conversion into dollar or euro for international spending.[15] Both options have proven costly for the Iranian economy.

Iran tried to escape these financial limitations in some countries such as Turkey by selling its oil in local currency and then converting the revenues into gold. The gold then was being transferred from Turkey to Dubai and recorded as Turkish gold sold to the UAE. It was then re-exported to Iran or used for import purchases in that country. This strategy led to a sharp increase in gold exports to Turkey in the first half of 2012 and attracted US attention. The United States intensified its efforts to stop this indirect method of payment for Iranian oil. In late 2012 the US Congress introduced a bill to ban gold exports to Iran.[16]

Along with these financial measures, the EU also announced a sanction on Iran's crude oil on 23 January 2012 that came into effect on 1 July 2012. The combination of this oil embargo announcement and the financial sanctions resulted in a severe crisis of confidence in Iran during December 2011 and January 2012. Investors and ordinary households worried that sanctions would reduce Iran's oil revenues and the central bank would not be able to sustain the exchange rate, which had been more or less stable since 2001. Consequently there was a sharp increase in demand for hard currencies and precious metals as people and businesses tried to shield their savings against the likely depreciation of the national currency and the high inflation rates that would have followed. This was followed by a more severe depreciation in the second half of 2012 as the European oil embargo became effective. Consequently, the free market exchange value of the US dollar rose by 100 per cent in the second half of 2012 (Figure 7.3).

While this sharp and sudden depreciation in the value of Iran's national currency was triggered by sanction-related developments, the blame does not fall

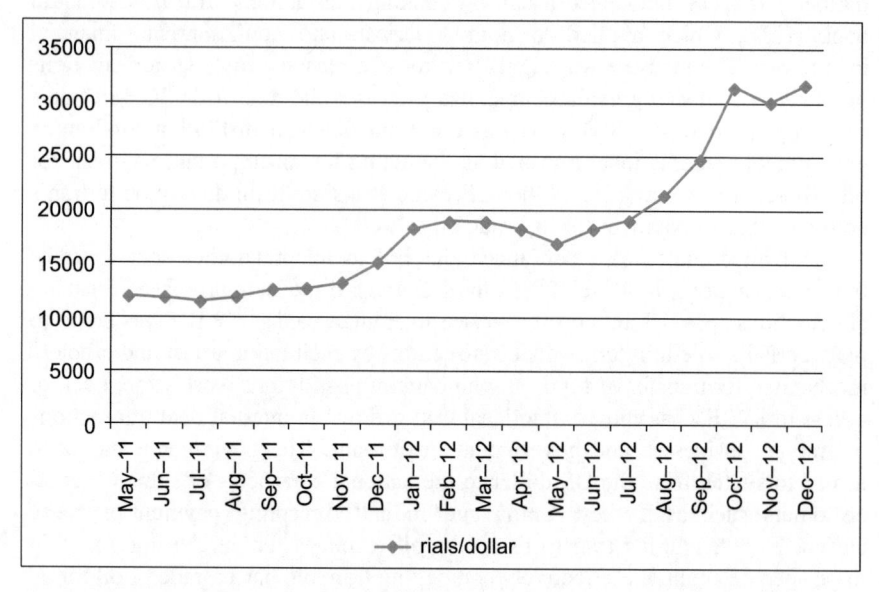

Figure 7.3 Iran, the Rial–Dollar Exchange Rate in the Free Market (End of the day price on 20th of each month)

Source: Daily rates as reported in Eghtesad Online Website (www.eghtesadonline.com)

Source: Eghtesad Online website. I looked at daily price for specific day of the month (first of farvardin, first of ordibehesht, ... In the archives.) Rial/$ free exchange rate (price on 20th day of the month)

entirely on sanctions. The relatively stable exchange value of the dollar against the Rial for nearly a decade until early 2011 was a result of deliberate government policy despite rapid increase in domestic liquidty and inflation. As a result of high domestic inflation and managed exchange rate, the Rial had become grossly over-valued and an adjustment in the exchage rate was inevitable in the long run. Had it not been for the psychological effect of the sanctions and public fear of a decline in future oil revenues, the government might have been able to postpone this adjustment even further or devaluate the Rial at a managed and gradual pace.

The rapid depreciation in late 2012 was also partly a result of the factional disagreements inside the government over economic policy and and the resulting economic mismanagement. When the crisis intensified in September and October 2012, it seemed that no single government agency was fully in charge of monetary and exchnage rate policy. The decision makers in the executive branch and Parliament (*Majlis*) pointed the finger of blame at each other. President Amadinejad was sharply criticized and his attempts to blame the crisis on Western sanctions was rejected by his conservative opponents in the Parliament.[17]

There are many other indications that the most recent sanctions (since the second half of 2011) have had a visible and adverse impact on all sectors of the Iranian economy through reductions in trade, foreign investment and business confidence. In addition to Iran's auto industry that was described above, other manufacturing activities have also been affected by shortages and higher cost of imported machinery and raw materials as well as the withdrawal of foreign partners in many cases. Iran's non-oil export industries have also been impacted by the financial sanctions and loss of markets due to sanctions.

The depreciation of the Rial in 2012 has had a profound impact on all segments of Iranian economy. Both producers and consumers have had to adjust to this unexpected exchange rate shock. It has led to a sharp increase in the cost of imports of raw materials and machinery for domestic producers. The direct impact on each industry depends on its degree of dependency on foreign inputs, which varies from industry to industry. A survey by the Association of Industrial Managers (*Anjoman Modiran Sanaye*) during the period 2005–9 has revealed that, on average, 16 per cent of the raw materials and intermediate inputs of the manufacturing sector were imported.[18]

This survey also found that in addition to supply materials these industrial units were also dependent on imported machinery and capital goods. According to this study, 20.6 per cent of the capital goods and machinery of the manufacturing units were imported from abroad during the same period. Consequently, the 100 per cent depreciation of the exchange rate in 2012 has resulted in significantly higher import procurement costs for the manufacturing sector. Furthermore sanctions have not only increased production costs through the depreciation of the Rial, but they have also interrupted the supply of some imported materials altogether in some cases.

The manufacturers try to overcome these interruptions by searching for substitute products from other countries that are wiling to ignore the sanctions. Some have also tried to obtain the products indirectly from the black market or smuggle it from neighbouring countries, sometimes helped by several government agencies.[19] While these steps have reduced shortages for some production inputs, they have resulted in much higher costs and lower quality of substitute products from domestic or alternative foreign sources. Consequently, as a result of the depreciation of the Rial and import disruptions some industries have suffered production declines (Table 7.4). At the same time, these developments have allowed some industries that produce domestic substitutes for more expensive and unavailable imports to increase their output.

Table 7.4 Industrial Sectors with Largest Percentage Change in Output during April-September 2012 compared to the same interval in 2011

Output Decline	%	Output Increase	%
Buses & Minibuses	78.6	Neopon	14
Cars and Vans	42.3	Electromotors	13.8
Small Trucks	39.9	Polyester Thread (PET)	10.2
Large Trucks (Trailers)	32.8	Glass	9.9
Monitors	20.3	Raw Steel	9.3
Air Conditioners	17.2	Machine-made carpet	8.3
Television	12	Copper bullion	7.9

Source: Ministry of Industry, Mine and Trade (2012).

Decline in oil exports

In 2012, the EU opened a new front in its anti-Iran sanctions stance by pressuring the international insurance companies to deny insurance for Iran's oil shipments. The United States put similar pressure on all international shipping insurers to deny insurance for transportation of Iran's oil shipments. Iran tried to offset this action by offering its own insurance or using its own tankers to deliver oil to its customers but these counterstrategies were not fully effective. This insurance sanction caused concern among Iran's Asian customers, who continued to buy oil from Iran. The combination of various sanctions had a significant impact on Iran's oil exports in 2012. After denying their adverse impact for several months, Iran's Oil Minister finally acknowledged that oil exports fell by 40 per cent in 2012 in comparison to 2011 (Gladstone, 2013). As a result, Iran reduced its daily oil output by almost one million barrels per day during the first half of 2012. Consequently, if the sanctions on oil exports continue in 2013 and beyond, Iran will experience a significant decline in oil revenues which will lead to fiscal contraction. This will force the government to re-examine many of its spending and subsidy priorities. It can also lead to visible structural changes in the economy that will be described below.

Until early 2012, Iranian officials operated under the assumption that since the reduction of Iran's crude exports will push up oil prices, Western nations will not resort to sanctioning Iran's oil exports. In 2012, they realized that the United States was in fact such sanctions. As speculation intensified, Iran threatened to close the Strait of Hormuz to all oil exports if it was not allowed to export its oil.[20] This threat never materialized and the United States focused on Iran's oil customers. The United States had asked Saudi Arabia to boost its output and offer additional crude oil to Iran's regular oil customers such as China. The Saudi government, which has experienced escalating tensions with the Iranian government over recent developments in Bahrain and Syria, complied with this request and supplied more oil to the global economy.[21] Iraq's oil output also increased in 2012 as it surpassed Iran to become the second largest producer in OPEC.[22] As a result, the oil importing countries that reduced their purchases of Iranian crude were able to find alternative supplies and the average price of crude oil in the second half of 2012 was no higher than in the first half.

The decline in Iran's oil exports has not only had profound effects on Iran's economy but it has also impacted the country's oil industry itself. Iran has responded by a partial reduction in its daily oil production and increased storage of unsold oil on land and sea.[23] Shutting off some of the older oil wells can cause long-term damage to them by reducing the pressure and allowing salt-water to penetrate into the oil reservoir.[24] That is why Iran has been reluctant to shut off too many oil wells and instead has tried to sell its excess oil at a discount in the open market to potential buyers who are willing to ignore the US and European sanctions (Ibid.). If the sanctions continue and enforcement proves effective, Iran will have no alternative but to shut off some oil wells.

The institutional and structural impact of sanctions

The international sanctions of the past three decades in general and the latest phase of US and EU unilateral sanctions since 2010 in particular have not only interrupted production and forced the economy of Iran to operate below potential but they have also led to significant institutional and structural changes. Some of these changes were brought about by the direct impact of the sanctions and some resulted from the countermeasures that the government of Iran implemented to neutralize these sanctions. Furthermore, in some cases the economic policies that were being implemented independently of sanctions had to be revised because of the sanctions and the underlying international tensions. These various ways that the sanctions have affected the structure of Iran's economy are explored in the next section.

Militarization of the economy

One of the most important impacts of the sanctions is that it has increased the economic role of the Islamic Revolutionary Guards Corp (IRGC). The IRGC's economic activities began during President Rafsanjani's reconstruction era in the late 1980s and early 1990s when he wanted to enhance the IRGC's sources of revenue outside of the fiscal framework. These involvements were partially rolled back during Khatami's presidency as he tried to attract foreign investment and create more opportunities for the private sector. Khatami's efforts to marginalize the IRGC and its former officers in the economic sphere resulted in a backlash and the IRGC prevented some public projects from being awarded to foreign contractors.[25]

President Ahmadinejad had a much more favourable attitude towards the economic activities of the IRGC. During his presidency, IRGC acquired many economic assets and was awarded hundreds of large-scale government contracts. The expansion of the IRGC's economic and commercial activities was partly facilitated by their penetration in key political positions during Ahmadinejad Presidency. As key supporters of Ahmadinejad during his presidential campaign in 2005 and 2009, the Guards enjoyed his political support for expanding their political influence. In July 2011 after the appointment of Rostam Qasemi, a high ranking Guards officer to the position of the Oil Minister, the number of former Revolutionary Guards officers in President Ahmadinejad's cabinet rose to twelve in an 18-member cabinet (Alfoneh, 2012). This militarization of the executive branch enjoyed the full support of the Supreme Leader and was partly justified by the Sanctions and other Western hostilities towards the Islamic Regime. The presence of the Guards in Ahmadinejad's cabinet, particularly at the helm of the Oil Ministry, in turn facilitated the expansion of their economic and commercial activities. On many occasions the sanctions indeed served as a direct or indirect excuse for increasing the IRGC's involvement. For example:

1. In some cases foreign investors abandoned a project because of the sanctions and IRGC moved in as a substitute contractor. This has been

the case with projects in oil, natural gas, transportation and construction sectors.[26]

2. In other cases, a domestic firm was going bankrupt because of sanctions-related adverse developments. The IRGC or its affiliated companies would step in and purchase the firm to prevent its bankruptcy. In a related scenario, IRGC or other semi-public organizations such as the religious foundations stepped in to purchase the shares of the firm during privatization because the offers from private sector were too low and would have amounted to the sale of the public assets. The low private offers, of course, were indirectly caused by the sanctions, which had deteriorated Iran's investment and business climate.

3. In a third group of cases, the IRGC took over a firm or entered into an industry because of its strategic significance. The best example of this category was the IRGC's 50 per cent purchase of Iran's mobile telecommunications corporation in 2009. The rationale (in addition to profitability) was that control over telecommunication would help with information gathering and neutralizing Western plots for covert operations and espionage. Another relevant example is the large number of IRGC-operated port authority managements in the Persian Gulf, which enable it to transfer banned goods with minimum risk of detection.

4. Logistic and procurement support: the IRGC and other government agencies have also assumed an active role in helping domestic producers and importers with purchase and transportation of products that are subject to international sanctions. Domestic producers for example receive assistance and guidelines on how to import these products indirectly by setting up import-export companies in neighbouring countries such as the UAE, Turkey and Turkmenistan.

It must be noted that in all of these activities, in addition to shielding the domestic economy against sanctions, other motivating factors were also involved such as revenue enhancement for the organization and profit opportunities for the IRGC officers and their private business interests. These are common motives for the participation of military in civilian economic activities, which, coincidentally, is not a unique phenomenon to Iran. It is observed in many countries where the armed forces enjoy a privileged position. The best-known case in the Middle East is Egypt where under Hosni Mubarak the military established a diverse range of industrial and retail businesses to enhance its revenues.

In general, militarization of the economy is costly and inefficient. It often results in non-competitive practices and unfair distribution of fiscal and financial resources in favour of military-owned industries. In the case of Iran, many independent private sector contractors have complained about the unfair advantages of the IRGC-affiliated businesses in competition for government contracts, subsidized hard currency for imports, and business loans. In the case of Iran, however, under current hostile international conditions and the intrusive nature of the sanctions, the economic activities of IRGC that are listed above, were perhaps inevitable and they have partially offset the adverse impact of sanctions on domestic economic activity.

Sanctions as rationale for subsidy reform

The escalation of Western sanctions in recent years gave the Iranian government an excuse to implement an important but unpopular economic reform, which would have faced significant domestic political resistance in the absence of sanctions. Price subsidies on many refined oil products and natural gas, which consumed a substantial share of the government's fiscal expenditures, were either removed or substantially reduced in December 2010. Iran's refining capacity for production of gasoline and other refined oil products has not kept up with the domestic demand in the past two decades. The sanctions and poor economic management prevented Iran from expanding and upgrading its refineries. At the same time, highly subsidized domestic fuel prices led to a sharp increase in demand for gasoline, which was made worse by the unprecedented growth in automobile ownership. These developments forced Iran to import nearly one third of its annual gasoline consumption by 2009.

Several administrations in Iran entertained the possibility of raising fuel prices to address this rising demand but they moved very cautiously to avoid political backlash and social unrest (like in most oil exporting countries, urban citizens of Iran consider themselves entitled to cheap gasoline and refined oil products). It was only after there were some indications that the United States was putting pressure on international gasoline suppliers to Iran that government officials worried about supply disruptions and used this concern to accelerate the removal of price subsidies on several fuel products.[27] A major step in the rationalization of fuel and utility prices was taken in December 2010 which led to a significant reduction of price subsidies and after a few months resulted in a reduction of demand for gasoline, diesel fuel and natural gas.[28] While these price increases raised the cost of living and production costs, they forced the consumers and producers to become more efficient. These subsidy reforms were later praised by the IMF, which has consistently encouraged member nations to reduce their fuel subsidies.[29]

Unfortunately, the latest round of sanctions has indirectly eroded the efficiency gains of the subsidy reforms. Instead of allowing the fuel and energy prices to float, the government reduced the subsidies by simply raising the prices to a higher fixed price that was still regulated by the government. This adjustment resulted in a higher real price for these products in 2011. However, in light of the recent depreciation of the Rial and domestic price inflation for all other commodities, the fixed nominal price of energy products (utilities included) resulted in a decline in their relative prices. This development in effect increased the amount of implicit price subsidies that the government was offering on these products. Attempts by the Ahmadinejad government to adjust these prices again in 2012 were frustrated by its conservative opponents in the Parliament. These opponents, under the leadership of Ali Larijani, speaker of the house, were concerned that Ahmadinejad was trying to gain political popularity by increasing the direct cash payment that would have accompanied any price increases for energy products.

Prolonged sanctions and industrial investment

In Iranian year 1388 (2009–10), the (non-oil) industrial sector accounted for 20 per cent of GDP compared to 18 per cent in 1385 (2006–7) and 15.2 per cent in 1379 (2000–1).[30] The US sanctions and international hostilities since 1979 have motivated the government of Iran to focus on technological and industrial self-reliance. This policy has been consistently pursued until today and it has resulted in domestic production of a wide range of products. Torbat (2010) offers a detailed account of Iran's technological achievements over the past three decades. The most visible examples of these achievements are found in military technology and weapons developments. Another good example is Iran's auto industry, which enjoyed rapid expansion after 2000 and by 2008 production level was comparable to Turkey and higher than any Arab country. This industrial expansion reduced Iran's import dependency on many finished industrial products but the industrial units were still dependent on imports of advanced machinery and some input materials. For any country that wishes to maintain a modern and efficient industrial sector this supply chain, dependency is inevitable. Up until 2011, the sanctions caused partial disruption in this supply chain but Iran was able to partly neutralize the supply disruptions by a dynamic trade policy that was described earlier. It is arguable that before 2011 the sanctions had a mixed impact on Iran's industrialization. On the one hand, they encouraged industrial self-reliance in some industries with active government support. On the other hand, they partially disrupted the supply chain of some industries and increased the investment risk for the private sector. The most recent sanctions, however, have had a severe adverse effect on industrial activity.

The latest sanctions have not only affected industrial output as was explained above but they have also affected the investment climate of industrial activity. Most industrial units are under stress and investors have become cautious about the profitability of such units under current and potentially worsening sanctions. The government has tried to counter these high risks and encourage domestic industrial investment by offering low interest loans through state-owned banking system (see Chapter 5 of this book). During President Ahmadinejad's presidency, these loans were directed toward smaller industrial units with shorter construction time (*Sanaye Zood Bazdeh*). Unfortunately the hostile business climate and import procurement difficulties have prevented many of these projects from achieving profitability and the banking system is facing a high rate of default on these industrial loans.

As shown in Table 7.5 the number of permits issued and the estimated value of investment in the industrial sector was stagnant in 2011, which marks the beginning of the more severe recent round of sanctions. The available data for March to September 2012 also suggests that further decline in industrial investment is

Table 7.5 Investment in the Industrial Sector

Year (Iranian Calendar)	Number of Permits for Industrial Units.	Projected Volume of Investment Based on the # of Permits Issued. (billion rials)
1388 (2009–10)	13,383	836,806
1389 (2010–11)	15,941	863,336
1390 (2011–12)	15,805	807,484
1391 (2012–13)	12,752	457,776

Source: Ministry of Industry, Mine and Trade (2012).

Note: The 2012–13 figures are the author's estimations based on data available for the first six months of the year.

expected in 2012. If the sanctions continue and intensify in the coming years, the impact on industrial activity and industrial investment will become more visible. In a January 2013 speech, Iran's Minister of Industry, Mine and Trade acknowledged that sanctions had taken a heavy toll on industrial activity.

> The sanctions put so much pressure on the nation's economy that we were unable to procure the materials needed for various [economic] sectors. This was because we had no hard currency, the Central Bank was unable to transfer its funds from abroad and there was no access to international transportation to bring the goods to [our] country.
>
> Mehdi Ghazanfari, Minister of Industry, Mine and Trade,
> January 10, 2013[31] (Translated by the author)

The Minister's statement indicates that Iran's industrial sector is still highly dependent on international supplies and international markets despite the Iranian government's stated objective of achieving self-reliance.

Concluding remarks

Iran has been subject to one type of sanction or another ever since the 1979 Revolution. These sanctions began as unilateral sanctions by the United States and with limited aims but they have become much more comprehensive and multinational in the past three years. In the earlier stages of sanctions, their impact on Iran's economy was limited to effects on imports and investment because the international community was reluctant to disrupt is oil exports. Determined to stop Iran's programme at all costs but reluctant to resort to military action, the United States focused on intensifying the economic sanctions. Through intense diplomatic efforts, it was able to bring the EU on board in the mid-2000s as it broadened the scope of sanctions. The joint efforts of the United States and the EU resulted in several sanctions resolutions against Iran in the UN Security Council. These resolutions, however, were partially watered down by Russia and China, which have maintained warm economic and diplomatic relations with Iran.

As the Iranian government remained defiant despite these sanctions, the United States and the EU introduced several new sanctions that went far beyond those approved by the UN. These new sanctions have disrupted all aspects of Iran's trade and relationships with the international community (including its oil exports).

Prior to these new rounds, Iran was able to evade the sanctions through flexible and dynamic trade diplomacy. It involved switching to a new trade partner as soon as an existing trade partner was forced to sever its ties with Iran. As a result, the impact of sanctions on Iran was somewhat limited. High oil revenues allowed the government to import consumer goods and provide for the basic needs of the population. Furthermore despite the sanctions (and because of their limited scope) Iran's economy was able to enjoy moderate economic growth as it registered an average growth rate of 4.7 per cent per annum during the period 2000–10. While this record is better than economic decline, it has remained below potential in part because of the sanctions. Given Iran's oil revenues and skilled human capital, one can argue that it could have achieved six to eight per cent annual growth in the absence of sanctions.

However, in the new round since 2011, the sanctions introduced have been different and are having a more severe and adverse effect on Iran's economy. Sanctions on oil exports, financial transactions, the central bank, and cargo insurance have caused severe disruptions on Iran's oil revenues and trade. It is now clear that the West is no longer interested in pressuring the regime without causing humanitarian suffering. The mentioned sanctions have affected the entire economy of Iran and ordinary citizens are suffering as a result of them. The exchange rate depreciated by more than 75 per cent in 2012 while domestic inflation reached record high levels. Industrial activity has declined by up to 40 per cent according government officials and has resulted in the loss of thousands of jobs. Even more concerning for the general population is the shortage of medicine for which funds are available but the transactions cannot be completed because of the financial sanctions which effectively render international banking inaccessible for Iranian businesses.

As bad as the 2012 round of sanctions were, it is likely that if Iran does not offer significant concessions on its nuclear programme the United States and the EU are planning even more severe sanctions which could effectively amount to a complete trade embargo.

In addition to economic hardship for the population, sanctions have also caused some deep transformations in Iran's economy. These changes have come about as intended and unintended consequences of the measures that Iranian government has implemented to counter the sanctions. As we have seen, these have led to the militarization of the Iranian economy. The Revolutionary Guards have acquired a large number of economic assets as sole owners or partners, in part to shield them from the sanctions. This development could prove very costly and politically very difficult to reverse in the long run.

Similarly, the sanctions and international hostility have been used as partial justification for appointing former and current guard members to key political positions in the executive branch. The government also used the sanctions and the danger of (imported) fuel shortages to introduce a subsidy reform programme that many other oil-exporting countries have not dared to implement. To the extent that such reforms were necessary to reduce the massive waste of heavily subsidized energy products, sanctions have served as catalysts for positive – albeit inadvertent – changes.

Overall, the adverse impact of sanctions on the economy and people of Iran has sharply intensified since early 2012. Western governments that were concerned about the humanitarian effect of sanctions in the past now seem indifferent toward the hardship that the sanctions might cause for the civilian population. What matters to them is whether the sanctions will cause enough pain and headache for the ruling regime to force it to accept the Western demands on its nuclear programme.

Notes

1   For a detailed account of how other countries undermined US sanctions against Iran see Kozhanov (2011).
2   The 2004 agreement was followed by several other long-term energy agreements in 2005, 2009 and 2011. In each of these agreements, Chinese firms agreed to invest in the development of Iran's oil and natural gas fields in return for long-term oil and gas sales commitment by Iran.
3   For a discussion of the rising Chinese market share in the Arab countries, see Habibi (2011).
4   The UAE federal system gives each of the seven emirates that make up the country considerable control over their economic policies although the wealthiest Emirate, Abu Dhabi enjoys some leverage over others because of its oil wealth. For a detailed account of Iran's economic relations with the UAE, see: Jahani (2011).
5   In its latest macroeconomic assessment of the UAE economy, the IMF takes notice of the rise of UAE trade with Iran in 2011 in spite of the sanctions but argues that the latest financial restrictions have led to a reduction of trade in the final quarter of 2011 and predicts that the sanctions will have a more visible adverse effect on Iran-UAE trade in 2012 (see, IMF, 2012).
6   Boat smuggling either originates directly in the Dubai port or indirectly via the Omani port city of Khasab at the Strait of Hormuz, which is only a 45 minute boat ride to Qeshm Island in Iran (Habibi, 2010: 9).
7   According to Iran's constitution when the Guardian Council rejects a parliamentary decision three times the dispute is referred to a council of appointed politicians called the Expediency Council for a final decision.
8   For a detailed account of the 2002 foreign investment law, see Pesaran (2011).
9   For a detailed account of European early response to ILSA, see Clawson (1997).
10 Since Iran's constitution forbids foreign ownership of oil and gas assets, the government has opted for buyback service contracts in its efforts to attract foreign investment to the energy sector. The buyback arrangements are regulated under Iran's 1987 Petroleum Law. For a detailed account of Iran's use of buyback contracts see: Shiravi and Ebrahimi (2006).
11 For example the American Oil Company Conoco signed a contract for the development of an offshore field for Iran but it was forced to cancel this contract under pressure from the US government (See, Richter and Wright, 1995).

12 For a detailed account of the performance of Iran's automotive industry during this period see Alizadeh (2009) and Chapter 6 of this book.

13 'Khordosaaz Chini Jaigozine Hyundai dar Bazaar Iran Shod,' (Chinese Automaker Replaced Hyudai in Iran Market), BBC-Farsi, May 18, 2012. http://www.bbc.co.uk/persian/business/2012/05/120518_l25_iran_hyundai_market.shtml?print=1 (accessed online on 21 May 2012)

14 'India and China Skirt Sanctions with Junk for Oil,' Bloomberg, March 30, 2012, http://www.bloomberg.com/news/2012-03-29/india-and-china-skirt-iran-sanctions-with-junk-for-oil-.html, (accessed online on 27 April 2012).

15 Keeping large amounts of money in local currency of a trade partner can also cause new headaches. In August 2012 Iran filed a complaint with the Korean government against the Woori Bank and the Industrial Bank of Korea for offering extremely low interest rates on its 5 trillion Won ($4.4 billion) deposit with these institutions. See Korea Herald, 6 August 2012, http://view.koreaherald.com/kh/view.php?ud=20120816001050&cpv=0; accessed online on 9 March 2013).

16 See Parkinson and Soloman (2012).

17 One of the most vocal critics of the government's handling of the currency crisis was the MP Ahmad Tavakoli. See: 'Enteghad-e Tavakoli be dolat, vaziyat-e arz va tala eghtesad ra be varshekastegi mikeshaanad.' (Tavakoli's criticism of the government, the currency and gold situation will push the economy towards bankruptcy), Hamshahri, 24 January 2012, http://www.hamshahrionline.ir/news-158132.aspx (accessed online on 26 April 2012)

18 Only production units with 10 or more employees were included in this study. See: 'Asaar Afzayesh Gheimat Arz ba Sanaye Karkhane-ei' (The impact of exchange rate depreciation on manufacturing industries), Association of Industry Managers, January 3, 2013, http://www.donya-e-eqtesad.com/Default_view.asp?@=338462; accessed online on 5 January 2013.

19 For an account of the Revolutionary Guards' role in supporting smuggling activities in the Persian Gulf, see: Dehghanpisheh (2010).

20 David Blair, 'Iran threatens to close Strait of Hormuz over EU oil sanctions', *Telegraph*, http://www.telegraph.co.uk/news/worldnews/middleeast/iran/9032948/Iran-threatens-to-close-Strait-of-Hormuz-over-EU-oil-sanctions.html, 23 January 2012; accessed online on 26 February 2013.

21 Aside from concern about Iran's involvement in Arab countries, Saudi Arabia is itself opposed to Iran's nuclear programme because it views Iran as a strategic rival in the Persian Gulf.

22 'OPEC output rises, offsets more Iran shrinkage: survey', *Fox Business*: http://www.foxbusiness.com/news/2012/10/31/opec-output-rises-offsets-more-iran-shrinkage-survey943263/, 31 October 2012; accessed online on 25 February 2013.

23 In summer 2012, oil industry observers reported that Iran was using its large fleet of tankers as floating storage for crude oil as it searched for potential buyers. Most of these tankers were seen circling in the Persian Gulf near or inside Iranian waters. See: 'Oil backed up, Iranians put it on idled ships', *New York Times*, http://www.nytimes.com/2012/07/05/world/middleeast/oil-embargo-leads-iran-to-disguise-tankers.html?pagewanted=all&_r=0, 4 July 2012; accessed online on 24 February 2013.

24 'Iran Just can't Stop Pumping Oil', www.CNNMoney.com, http://money.cnn.com/2012/07/10/news/economy/Iran-oil/index.htm, 10 July 2012; accessed online on 22 February 2013.

25 The best example of this IRGC intervention took place in May 2004 when IRGC forced the government of President Khatami to cancel the license of a Turkish-Austrian company (TAV) to manage the customs and security services of the newly inaugurated Imam Khomeini Airport. The IRGC made this demand on the grounds that the presence of foreign employees in the new airport posed a national security risk. Consequently, the Revolutionary Guards took direct control of the airport's operations and security.

See: Sepehr, Vahid, 'Tehran Airport Closure Becomes National Embarrassment', www.Payvand.com, http://www.payvand.com/news/04/may/1115.html, 18 May 2004; accessed online on 19 February 2013.
26 For a detailed account of the IRGPs network of economic holding companies and diverse economic activities, see Nader (2009).
27 The US attempts to limit the supply of gasoline exports to Iran intensified after December 2009 when the US house approved a law to impose penalties on foreign firms that supplied gasoline to Iran. See: 'House Passes Iran Gasoline Sanctions Bill', *Reuters*, 15 December 2009, http://www.reuters.com/article/2009/12/16/us-usa-iran-sanctions-idUSTRE5BE61K20091216; accessed online on 5 May 2012.
28 'Kahesh-e 1.6 dar sadi masraf benzin dar saal navad' (A 1.6 per cent reduction in gasoline consumption during April 2011-March 2012), Khabarkhodro, 5 May 2012, http://khabarkhodro.com/Detail.asp?id=178111; accessed online on 20 May 2012.
29 The IMF assessment of Iran's subsidy reform programme appeared in Guillaume *el al.* (2011).
30 'Barrasi Vaziyat Bakhsh Sanaat va Ma'dan' (A Review of the Conditions of the Industry and Mines Sector), 2010, Ministry of Economy and Finance, http://www.econo.ir/pdf/sanatomadan.pdf; accessed online on 8 January 2013.
31 'Vazir-e Sanat va Ma'dan: Tahrimha Falaj Konandeh Ast', (Ministry of Industry and Mine: The Sanctions are Crippling), BBC News Farsi Section: http://www.bbc.co.uk/persian/business/2013/01/130110_ka_ghazanfari_sanction.shtml, 10 January 2013; accessed online on 12 January 2013.

References

Alfoneh, A., 'Iran's Revolutionary Guards strike oil', *Middle East Quarterly*, 10739467, Winter, 19 (1), 2012.

Alizadeh, P., 'The Iranian auto industry in a comparative perspective' presented at the Conference titled Iranian Economy at a Crossroads, USC, September 2009, http://dornsife.usc.edu/conferences/iran/documents/Theautoindustry-revisedversion.pdf; (cited online 27 April 2012).

Clawson, P., 'ILSA's first year: what effect on Iran & on allied policy towards Iran?', Hearing Before the House International Relations Committee, 23 July 1997: http://www.iranwatch.org/government/US/Congress/Hearings/hirc-072397/us-hirc-clawson-072397.htm, (cited online 13 May 2012).

Dehganpisheh, B., Smuggling for the state, *Newsweek*, 19 July 2010, 152 (3): 42–3, 2010.

Direction of Trade Statistics, International Monetary Fund, various years.

Eghtesad Online Website: www.eghtesadonline.com.

Energy Information Agency, International Energy Statistics: http://www.eia.gov/cfapps/ipdbproject/iedindex3.cfm?tid=5&pid=53&aid=1&cid=AG,BA,EG,IR,IZ,IS,JO,KU,LE,LY,MO,MU,QA,SA,SU,SY,TS,TC,YM,&syid=2005&eyid=2011&unit=TBPD, (cited online 9 March 2013).

Gladstone, R., 'Iranian Foreign Minister concedes sanctions have hurt exports', *The New York Times*, January 7, 2013.

Guillaume, D., Zytek, R. and Farzin, M. R., 'Iran – The chronicles of the subsidy reform', IMF Working Paper No 11/167, Washington: International Monetary Fund, 2011.

Habibi, N., 'The impact of sanctions on Iran-GCC economic relations', Middle East Brief Series, Crown Center for Middle East Studies, November, No 45: http://www.brandeis.edu/crown/publications/meb/meb45.html, 2010.

Habibi, N., 'GCC States' import demand: the effects of geopolitics', Crown Center for Middle East Studies, Crown Paper No 6, June: http://www.brandeis.edu/crown/publications/cp/cp6.html, 2011.

Habibi, N., 'Turkey and Iran: growing economic relations despite western sanctions', Middle East Brief Series, Crown Center for Middle East Studies, May, No 62: http://www.brandeis.edu/crown/publications/meb/meb62.html, 2012.

IMF, 'United Arab Emirate, 2012 Article IV Consultation', page 8: http://www.imf.org/external/pubs/ft/scr/2012/cr12116.pdf (cited online 20 May 2012)

Jahani, K., 'Sanctioning Iran: the view from the United Arab Emirates', *al-Nakhleh,* Spring 2011, http://fletcher.tufts.edu/Al-Nakhlah/~/media/E71692D3A02E4FA7AD 849519B30749E8.pdf, (Cited online, 6 May 2012).

Kozhanov, N. A., Economic sanctions against Iran undermined by external factors, *Middle East Policy*, 18 (3): 144–60, 2011.

Ministry of Industry, Mine and Trade, Islamic Republic of Iran, *Namaagar*, No 12, October, 2012a.

Ministry of Industry, Mine and Trade, *Monthly Statistical Report,* No 12, September, 2012b.

Wehrey, F., Green, J. D., Nichiporuk, B., Nader, A., Hansell, L., Nafisi, R. and Bohandy, S. R., 'The rise of Pasdaran: assessing the domestic role of Iran's Islamic Revolutionary Guards Corps', Rand Corporation, 2009.

Parkinson, J. and Soloman, J., 'The US bears down on Turkish gold link with Iran', 30 November: http://online.wsj.com/article/SB10001424127887323751104578150803 540506358.html, (Cited online on 22 December 2012).

Pesaran, E., *Iran's Struggle for Economic Independence: Reform and Counter-Reform in the Post-Revolutionary Era,* London and New York: Routledge, 2011.

Richter, P. and Wright, R., 'Clinton kills Iran-Conoco oil deal', *Los Angeles Times*, March 15: http://articles.latimes.com/1995-03-15/business/fi-43080_1_clinton-administration-officials; accessed on 9 March 2013, 1995.

Shiravi, A., and Ebrahimi, S. N., 'Exploration and development of Iran's oilfields through buyback,' *Natural Resources Forum, 30* (3): 199–206, 2006.

Torbat, A. E., Impacts of the US trade and financial sanctions on Iran, *The World Economy*, 28 (3): 407–34, 2005.

Torbat, A. E., 'Industrialization and dependency: the case of Iran', *ECO Economic Journal*, http://www.ecosecretariat.org, Economic Cooperation Organization, October, 2010.

8 Wage discrimination against women in Iran

Moaven Razavi and Nader Habibi

Introduction

Despite significant progress toward gender equality worldwide, numerous empirical studies have revealed that women still face noticeable wage differentials and wage discrimination in many developing and industrial countries.[1] A woman that performs the same tasks as a man and has a similar level of education and work experience is still likely to earn less. This gender wage differential has narrowed in many countries but it still persists.[2]

In this article we investigate the magnitude of wage discrimination against women in the Iranian labour market by decomposing the male–female wage differential into differences in human capital and discrimination. Economic and social discrimination against women is an important issue that affects the lives of millions of women and households. Many urban households now depend on incomes of both spouses to meet their expenses. A number of social and economic developments in recent years make it more imperative to investigate gender wage inequality. First, in light of the recent increase in the ratio of divorced and never married women in Iranian society, wage and employment discrimination against women takes on added significance. For women who have to support themselves, wage discrimination will lead to a lower standard of living than otherwise they could have achieved. Second, the unprecedented decline in fertility has reduced the burden of child-bearing on many women and provided them with enough free time to seek part-time or even full-time employment. The total fertility rate of Iranian women declined from an average of 6.9 during 1980–5 to 2.3 in 1995–2000. It further declined to under two births per woman by 2005 (Abbassi-Shivazi *et al.*, 2009).

Third, another important development that raises the social cost of wage discrimination in Iran is the growing number of educated women who are seeking employment. Unlike earlier decades, when most Iranian women chose (or were forced by their male relatives) to marry after graduation from high school and become homemakers afterward, they are now eager to educate themselves and join the labour market whenever opportunities are available.

Fourth, the number of female university graduates in Iran has sharply increased. Prior to the Islamic revolution many conservative religious families did not allow the female members of their households to pursue higher education, fearing that a university environment might have a corrupting Westernizing influence on young women. Islamization of the universities and the universal imposition of *hijab* (the Islamic veil) have alleviated some of these fears and now conservative families are less worried about the presence of women in universities. On the contrary, many conservative families now encourage and support their daughters' pursuit of higher education. It is well documented that women currently make up well over 50 per cent of college students and every year thousands of well-qualified educated women enter the labour force.[3] As demonstrated by Bahramitash and Esfahani (2009) female labour force participation and employment in Iran has undergone a fundamental transformation after the Islamic revolution. Women are moving beyond traditional female dominated jobs such as carpet weaving and handicraft. Instead they are entering the labour force with high levels of education and seeking more skilled job opportunities as professionals and specialists. Many of these specialist and skilled women are now working in various service sectors such as education, healthcare and social services. In 2006, women accounted for 48.6 per cent of the total workforce in these three categories (Bahramitash and Esfahani, 2009: Table 3.6).

According to the aggregate employment data of the Statistical Center of Iran, the share of women in the labour force, as measured by the labour force participation rate (LFPR), stood at 18.5 per cent in 2006. Although this is a significant improvement in comparison to 1986 when it was only 10.2 per cent, it is still smaller than women's share of the labour force in industrial countries.[4] Most of this increase in LFPR during the period 1986–2006 is attributable to younger women aged 15–34. Women's employment rate has also increased during this period but unfortunately employment opportunities for women have not kept pace with their increasing participation rate. The share of the working-age female population that was employed rose from 7.8 per cent in 1986 to 14.7 per cent in 2006. Consequently, the unemployment rate for women remained high as it declined modestly from 25.5 per cent in 1986 to 23.3 per cent in 2006. It must be mentioned that initially female unemployment declined between 1986 and 1996 as the economy recovered from the devastation of the Iran–Iraq war but as a growing number of educated women entered the labour force after 1996 it rose again to the higher level that was mentioned above.[5]

Fifth, since wage discrimination against women is more significant in the private sector, in light of the recent privatization of Iranian economy and growing deregulation of the labour market, there is added concern regarding the vulnerability of women to wage discrimination. Evidence shows that women have become more vulnerable to wage discrimination in privatized industries. While in the public sector the uniform wage and benefit policy has shielded female employees against overt wage discrimination, lack of regulation in the private sector and in the underground economy has created an unfavourable work environment for women (Mortazayi Langaroudi *et al.*, 2011).

An overview of the literature on gender wage discrimination

With the rapid increase in education and labour force participation of women in developing countries since the 1970s, labour economists have conducted numerous studies on gender wage gap in these countries.[6] These studies have revealed that the portion of the gender wage gap that can be attributed to wage discrimination varied considerably from one developing country to another. In some countries, such as the Philippines, it was as high as 68 per cent while in others, such as Tanzania and Senegal, it was very close to zero (Arabsheibani, 2000: 129).

Empirical studies of wage discrimination in Middle Eastern countries are rather limited. An early analysis was conducted by Hosni and Al-Qudsi (1988) on Kuwait's labour market. This study reported that an estimated 32 per cent of the wage gap between male and female employees was due to wage discrimination. A follow-up study on wage discrimination in Kuwait was conducted by Shah *et al.* (1990). They found that wage discrimination against women varied by female employees' ethnicity. Non-Arab women faced the highest level of wage discrimination followed by Arab non-Kuwaiti women and Kuwaiti women respectively.

In another more recent study, El-Hamidi (2008) investigates the impact of trade liberalization on gender wage discrimination in Egypt. She finds that during 1998–2006 wage discrimination against women increased in the tradable sector and decreased in the non-tradable sector. She concluded that trade liberalization during this period led to increased competition in the labour market which resulted in larger wage discrimination against women.

There have been several empirical studies of gender wage discrimination in Turkey in recent years as well. Cudeville *et al.* (2010) use data from a 2003 survey and report the gender wage gap in that country at 38 per cent. They further estimate that 63 per cent of this gap can be attributed to wage discrimination. These findings are comparable to wage discrimination estimates for several European countries such as Spain and Greece.

Methodology

We use the Oaxaca (1973) decomposition model to measure the portion of the gender wage gap in Iranian labour market that is due to wage discrimination. The Oaxaca technique allows us to separate the average wage difference between men and women into a portion that is attributable to differences in human capital and experience (H) and a portion that is attributable to discrimination (D). Let w_m and w_f be the annual wages of men and women, respectively. Each individual's wage is a function of his or her level of education, years of experience and other characteristics that are expected to affect productivity. We consider a separate wage function for each gender and generate two wage functions:

$$\ln w_m = \Sigma \beta_{mi} \cdot X_{mi} + u_m \qquad (1)$$

$$\ln w_f = \Sigma \beta_{fi} \cdot X_{fi} + u_f \tag{2}$$

where: X_m and X_f = Human capital characteristics of males and females
   β_m and β_f = Coefficients of human capital characteristics for males and females; and
   u_m and u_f are the error terms.
   $I = 1, 2, \ldots, n$ represents the list of human capital characteristics such as education and experience that affect the wage level of an employee.
   Estimation of equations (1) and (2) will give us:

$$ln\overline{W}_m = \Sigma\hat{\beta}_{mi}.\overline{X}_{mi} = \hat{\beta}_m.\overline{X}_m \tag{3}$$

$$ln\overline{W}_f = \Sigma\hat{\beta}_{fi}.\overline{X}_{fi} = \hat{\beta}_f.\overline{X}_f \tag{4}$$

Equations (3) and (4) give the mean values of salaries as a function of the mean value of human capital traits and the estimated coefficients. We then estimate the wage differential between men and women as:

$$ln\overline{W}_m - ln\overline{W}_f = \hat{\beta}_m.\overline{X}_m - \hat{\beta}_f.\overline{X}_f \tag{5}$$

In order to partition this wage gap into attributions to human capital (H) and Discrimination (D) we add and subtract $\hat{\beta}_m.\overline{X}_f$ from equation (5).

$$ln\overline{W}_m - ln\overline{W}_f = \hat{\beta}_m.\overline{X}_m - \hat{\beta}_m.\overline{X}_f + \hat{\beta}_m.\overline{X}_f - \hat{\beta}_f.\overline{X}_f$$

$$= \hat{\beta}_m.(\overline{X}_m - \overline{X}_f) + (\hat{\beta}_m - \hat{\beta}_f).\overline{X}_f = H + D \tag{6}$$

In equation (6) we have decomposed the difference in logarithm of the average wages of men and women into two components, The first component $H = \hat{\beta}_m.(\overline{X}_m - \overline{X}_f)$ shows the portion of the difference that is explained by differences in human capital and productivity of men and women. The second component $D = (\hat{\beta}_m - \hat{\beta}_f).\overline{X}_f$ is the portion of the wage differential that is not caused by differences in human capital and skill characteristics of men and women. Hence, D is viewed as a measure of wage difference between men and women that is attributed mainly to discrimination. We use equation (6) in our statistical estimation that follows.

Data

We have used data from Iran's 2005 Household Income and Expenditure Survey (HIES) in our statistical analysis.[7] The HIES is conducted annually by the Statistical Center of Iran. The sample size varies from year to year to reflect demographic and population changes. Household is the basic sampling unit in HIES but data is collected at individual level for all members of the households that are included in the sample. The HIES uses a two-step (cluster) sampling approach. First the optimum number of city blocks (urban neighburhoods) and villages that must be sampled in each province is determined to meet the precision requirements of the sample. Then the city blocks and villages are randomly selected. In the second step, five rural households in each selected village and 100 urban households in each city block are randomly selected (Statistical Center of Iran, 2005).

In HIES 2005 a total number of 26,895 households (with 120,639 household members) were surveyed. In this sample 102,278 household members were above ten years old. The sample included 5,305 employees in the public sector and 14,522 in the private sector. The profile of active population over ten years old (Table 8.1) clearly shows that female participation in the labour force is significantly smaller than male participation. In comparison to the 2002 HIES survey, which is not reported here, the female participation rate has increased by three percentage points to 14 per cent in 2005.

Findings

Table 8.2 summarizes the main characteristics of public and private employees in the 2005 HIES survey. As we can see in this table, women are highly under-represented in both private and public sector employment. The share of women employees in the private and public sectors were approximately ten per cent and 19 per cent, respectively. The share of female public sector employees that lived in rural areas was 16.7 per cent. Table 8.2 also indicates that the education level of private sector employees was much lower than public sector employees. We further notice that female public sector employees were on average more educated than their male counterparts although the education levels of both male and female workers in private sector were very low.

In spite of a relatively small number of female employees in the public sector, a large proportion of women who have a chance to work in governmental organizations are in the category of scientists and specialists. In this HIES sample

Table 8.1 Household activities of the active population (older than 10 years)

Activities	Male (%)	Female (%)	Total (%)
Employed	59	14	36
Unemployed	8	3	5
Pensioned and Others	9	8	9
Student	24	23	23
Homemaker	0	53	27
Total	**100**	**100**	**100**

Source: calculated by authors based on HIES 2005.

Table 8.2 Characteristics of male and female employees in public and private sectors (2005 sample)

Characteristics	Public Sector		Private Sector	
	Men	Women	Men	Women
Sex Ratio (%)	80.36	19.64	90.30	9.70
Logarithm of Hourly Wage	9.18	9.3823	8.432	7.59
Hourly Wage (in Rial)	9,701	11,876	4,592	1,978
Share living in rural area (%)	30.77	16.45	55.03	58.68
Share living in province of Tehran (%)	11.94	9.47	8.46	8.13
Share of unskilled workers (%)	32.77	3.39	55.43	43.52
Share of skilled workers (%)	35.89	23.13	42.17	46.74
Share of managers and specialists (%)	31.34	73.48	2.39	9.74
Age	37.80	35.01	32.86	30.78
Age squared	1529.68	1295.09	1235.78	1087.23
Level of education in years (quantified)	12.78	15.99	5.90	6.30
Share of ever married (%)	85.82	77.17	68.15	56.14
Sample size	4,104	1,003	10,988	1,181

Source: Calculated by authors based on the HIES 2005, Statistical Center of Iran.

about 73.44 per cent of all female employees belonged to this category in public sector compared to 30.65 per cent of all male employees; in the private sectors these ratios are 8.36 and 2.14 per cent respectively. At the same time the absolute number of men in the scientists and specialists category is still much larger than women (1,589 men compared to 874 women).

In terms of wage differences between men and women in the public sector, we observe a 22 per cent gap in hourly wage in favour of women. This gap reflects the higher salaries of specialist jobs and the larger participation of female public sector employees in these occupations in comparison to male public sector employees. The average hourly wage of men in private sector, on the other hand, is 132 per cent larger than women's. This larger gender wage gap in the private sector can also be partly explained by the difference in types of jobs that are occupied by women in the private sector. Most women working in the private sector are employed in low-skill, low-paid jobs.[8] With respect to demographic characteristics, female workers on average are younger than men and are also less likely to be married.

Wage equations by gender

Table 8.3 presents the wage equations that we have used in the first stage of the Oaxaca decomposition. We run separate regressions for men and women in

Table 8.3 Estimation results for male and female workers in public and private sectors

Independent Variables	Public Sector		Private Sector	
	Men	Women	Men	Women
Intercept	3.70***	5.12***	6.36***	6.21***
Living in rural area	–0.02 NS	–0.01 NS	–0.11***	–0.37***
Living in province of Tehran	–0.21***	0.03 NS	0.08***	0.37***
Skilled workers	0.30***	0.35**	0.15***	–0.01 NS
Managers and specialists	0.48***	0.76***	0.59***	0.32**
Age	0.20***	0.16***	0.09***	0.06***
Age squared	–0.00***	–0.00***	–0.00***	–0.00***
Level of education (quantified)	0.03***	0.02***	0.02***	0.06***
Ever married	0.84***	0.21***	0.21***	0.16*
Sample size	4,104	1,003	10,988	1,181
Adj. R-Squared	0.53	0.33	0.22	0.27

Notes: The significance of the estimated coefficients are reported as:
*indicates $p<.05$,
**indicates $p<.01$,
***indicates $p<.001$

private and public sectors. In each model the logarithm of individual hourly wages was regressed against the following explanatory variables: education level, age, age squared, rural/urban residential status, a dummy variable for residence in Tehran, two dummy variables for skill levels and a dummy variable for marital status. In order to capture the effect of the variations in skill sets, we define three major skill categories; a) scientists and specialists, b) skilled workers, and c) unskilled workers. Accordingly we include two dummy variables for the first and second categories while treating the unskilled workers as the reference category.

We used the OLS regression method to estimate each equation. In this equation we have used the employee's age as a proxy for experience. Since the marginal improvement in skills and productivity, that is often associated with experience, is higher in earlier years of employment we have added age-squared to the model to capture the diminishing marginal contribution of age (experience) to productivity and annual wage.

The results of estimations in Table 8.3 are consistent with mainstream empirical studies on determinants of wages and salaries in developing countries. As expected, higher skills make a positive contribution to women's wages in both private and public sector wage equations for women.

In the private sector wage equations the positive impact of being a manager or specialist is larger and more significant for men than women. The contribution of being a skilled worker to hourly wages is positive and significant for men but remains insignificant for women (in both cases the reference category is unskilled workers). Another consistent result across sectors is the inverted U-shape relation between wage and age (as a proxy for experience). As is generally expected, hourly wage increases with age until a certain age, beyond which it gradually declines. The wage equations also show a positive return to education but some gender differences are visible. First we observe that return to education is higher for women than men in the private sector but the opposite is true in the public sector. Second, while the return to education for men is higher in the public sector, for women it is higher in the private sector.

We observe that men's salary levels in the public sector are lower in Tehran, when compared to other provinces, in comparison to other locations. This result which might seem counterintuitive is due to the additional salary that is offered to public employees who are willing to serve in government offices outside of capital (kharej-az-markaz). Table 8.3 results for private sector employees show higher wages for both men and women in Tehran province, which is well in line with our expectations. Tehran is the largest centre of industrial and commercial activity in the country and as such it has higher wage and price levels than other parts of Iran. We also observe a gender gap in terms of marital status: The ever-married employees earn higher salaries than those who have never been married. This is true for both male and female employees in both sectors but the extra earnings are largest for the ever-married men in the public sector.

Decomposition of gender wage differentials

Based on the Oaxaca technique that was described in Equations 1 to 6 we can use the wage equation estimates to decompose the total male–female wage differential into the human-capital (explained) and the discrimination (unexplained) components. By inserting the estimates from wage equations and mean value of explanatory variables in equation 6 we decompose the total gender wage gap as reported in Table 8.4.

Decomposition figures in Table 8.4 reveal that discrimination is a significant cause of the gender wage gap (the lower hourly wages for women) in both sectors.

Table 8.4 Oaxaca decomposition results for male–female wage gap in public and private sectors

2005 Survey	Public Sector		Private Sector	
	Difference in Log (Wage)	Ratio (%)	Difference in Log (Wage)	Ratio (%)
Human Capital Differences (H)	−0.14	70.71	0.0117	1.39
Discrimination (D)	−0.058	29.29	0.828	98.57
Total Gender Gap	−0.198	100.00	0.84	100.00

Note: The results are estimated by authors based on the figures in Tables 8.2 and 8.3.

Results show that gender wage discrimination is more severe in the private sector in comparison to the public sector. In the public sector discrimination is responsible for 29 per cent of the wage gap while 71 per cent is explained by male employees' higher level of human capital (education plus experience). In the private sector, on the other hand, almost the entire wage gap (99 per cent) is due to gender wage discrimination (Figure 8.1).

The wage discrimination estimates that we have found above might be prone to the self-selection bias effect. This bias arises from the fact that a significant segment of female population does not participate in the labour force (women who stay at home and take care of their family). Women who work are not a random sub-sample of all women. Rather, they have self-selected themselves into the labour force, therefore their characteristics might be different from women who are not working (i.e. different motivation structures). Hence the non-random selection of these women could be a source of potential bias in our estimates.[9] Several empirical studies have shown that the self-selection bias can be a significant component of total gender wage discrimination.[10] A recent study on gender wage discrimination in Iran by Alavian (2012) reveals that selection bias distorts the Oaxaca decomposition results. By correcting the model for selection bias Alavian obtains larger discrimination components in every annual estimate from 2005 to 2009. The upward adjustments that he obtained were relatively small in 2005 and 2009 but more significant in the remaining years.

In general there are three ways to address the selection bias problem. One approach is to apply the Heckman selection bias model (Heckman, 1979). The

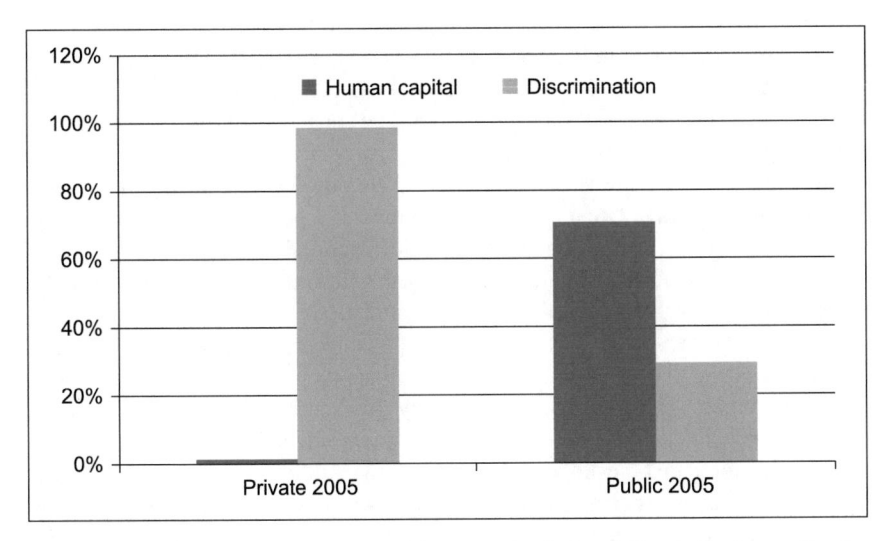

Figure 8.1 The Relative Contributions of Human Capital and Discrimination to Gender Wage Gap

Source: Table 8.4.

second approach is to find a matched sample among male employees with characteristics similar to self-selected females. The third approach is a variation of the second approach in which an organic stratum of the labour force which is less prone to self-selection bias is chosen for analysis. We will use the third approach below to reexamine the gender wage discrimination in Iran.

One group of workers with a significantly lower possibility of self-selection bias is the highly skilled labour force. In the skill category of scientists and specialists, both men and women are equally motivated to participate in the labour force. Women who have selected to spend several years studying in universities and developing highly specialized skills are very unlikely not to participate in the labour force. Hence the ratio of non-participant females in this category is almost as small as males which would mean that the female self-selection bias is no longer a concern. In the following section we will estimate the Oaxaca decomposition model for the scientists and specialists employment category.[11] We will further extend this analysis to two other groups with lower skill sets for comparison.

Wage gap and skill level

In order to develop a better understanding of the dynamics of wage discrimination in Iran we repeated the Oaxaca decomposition estimates for three types of employees: a) scientists and specialists, b) skilled industrial workers, c) unskilled workers in service sector. We use the same HIES sample for this analysis and apply the decomposition model separately to each skill category.[12]

In order to ensure that our findings are consistent and comparable across three skill categories we use the same wage equation model in the first stage of the Oaxaca estimation. The independent variables of the wage equation are: Rural resident dummy variable (Rural = 1, Urban = 0), Resident of Tehran province dummy variable (Tehran = 1, other = 0), Age, Age squared, Education, and Public sector employment dummy variable (pubic = 1, private = 0).

The dependent variable is the logarithm of the hourly wage of the employee. We estimated six wage equations (one equation for men and one for women in each job category). The regression estimates are reported in Table 8.5.

Using these equations' estimates and the mean values of variables (not reported) we estimate the total wage gap and its components for each skill category. The results appear in Table 8.6 and Figure 8.2. The results show that the gender wage gap among specialists and scientists is significantly smaller than skilled and unskilled workers. This could be explained by the fact that highly skilled women are better able to negotiate the terms of their employment contracts. Another important factor is that most of these jobs are in the public sector in which salaries are regulated and employers have less room to discriminate on the basis of gender among employees of equal rank.[13] Most of the gender discrimination in the public sector appears in the shape of discrimination in promotion and delegation of top managerial responsibilities. In other words women enter with equal compensation but gradually they face a glass ceiling that limits their upward career growth.

Table 8.5 Wage equation estimates for men and women in three skill categories in 2005

Skill Category	Gender	Intercept	Living in rural area	Living in province of Tehran	Age	Age squared	Level of education in years (quantified)	Ever married	Public Sector	Sample Size	Adj. R-Square
							Independent variables				
Scientists and Specialists	Men	5.85 ***	−0.02 NS	0.04 NS	0.14 ***	0.00 ***	0.02 ***	0.23 ***	0.21 ***	1190	0.25
	Women	5.47 ***	0.09 NS	0.10 NS	0.14 ***	0.00 ***	0.02 ***	0.18 **	0.66 ***	776	0.30
Industrial Workers	Men	5.35 ***	−0.04 NS	0.06 NS	0.15 ***	0.00 ***	0.02 ***	0.22 ***	0.30 ***	2824	0.35
	Women	6.40 ***	−0.23 **	0.56 NS	0.05 **	0.00 *	0.02 NS	−0.07 NS	1.10 ***	389	0.10
Unskilled Workers	Men	7.17 ***	−0.17 ***	0.02 NS	0.06 ***	0.00 ***	0.00 NS	0.14 ***	0.44 ***	5464	0.14
	Women	6.72 ***	−0.50 ***	0.45 NS	0.04 *	0.00 NS	0.03 NS	0.27 NS	0.63 *	458	0.13

Source: Authors' estimates based on HIES 2005.
Notes: The significance of the estimated coefficients are reported as:
 * indicates p<.05,
** indicates p<.01,
*** indicates p<.001. (NS: not significant).

Table 8.6 Oaxaca decomposition results for gender wage gap in various skill categories

2005 HIES Survey	Component	Human Capital Differences (H)	Discrimination (D)	Total Gender Gap
Scientists & Specialists	**Difference in Log (Hourly Wage)**	0.149	0.092	0.241
	Ratio	61.83%	38.17%	100.00%
Industrial Workers	**Difference in Log (Hourly Wage)**	0.235	1.071	1.307
	Ratio	17.98%	81.94%	100.00%
Unskilled Workers in Service Sector	**Difference in Log (Hourly Wage)**	0.03	0.881	0.911
	Ratio	3.29%	96.71%	100.00%

Source: Authors' estimates based on HIES 2005.

Converting the logarithm values of the total gender wage gap in Table 8.6 to wage ratio percentages we find that for the scientists and specialists category, male employees earn 24 per cent more than female employees on average. The comparable wage gap percentages for industrial workers and unskilled workers are 249 per cent and 88 per cent respectively.

The decomposition data in Table 8.6 shows that the contribution of wage discrimination to gender wage gap is relatively smaller for scientists and specialists. While discrimination accounts for 38 per cent of the wage gap in this skill

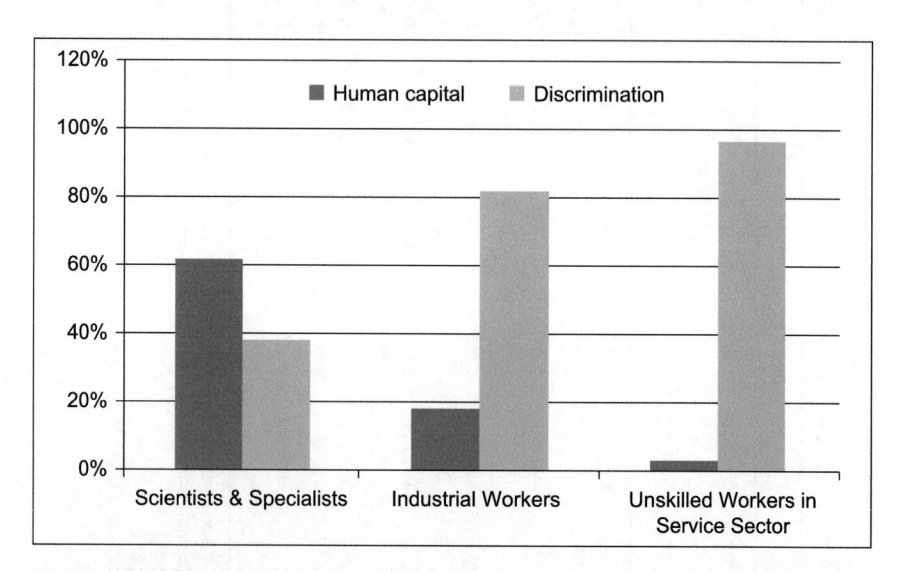

Figure 8.2 Relative Contributions of Human Capital and Discrimination to Gender Wage Gap (Male Preferred) for Three Skill Categories

Source: Table 8.6.

category, its contributions to the wage gap for industrial and unskilled workers are 82 per cent and 97 per cent respectively. Based on these results we can conclude that specialization and pursuit of scientific activities propels women into job environments with relatively smaller wage discrimination. Nevertheless, the magnitude of wage discrimination is still significant and appears to be an important cause of the gender wage gap in all three skill categories, as shown in Figure 8.2.

The findings of our empirical analysis are broadly consistent with the findings of a detailed multi-year analysis of gender wage discrimination in Iran by Alavian (2012). Alavian finds that if gender discrimination against women was eliminated, their salaries would be approximately 17 per cent higher (p. 53). Repeating the estimation for different skill categories based on the 2009 HEIS data, Alavian finds no wage discrimination against women in professional jobs, 23 per cent in technical (Semi-professional) jobs, 98.4 per cent for industrial jobs and 93 per cent for unskilled jobs (page 55, diagram 5.1). The main divergence between the findings of Alavian and ours is related to the professional and specialist category for which we obtain 38 per cent wage discrimination against women whereas Alavian obtains 12 per cent discrimination against men. This difference could be partly due to the selection of observations for this subsample. His sample is also limited to urban households while ours includes both urban and rural.

The presence of gender wage discrimination among industrial workers in Iran has been investigated in an interview survey study by Oreyzi (2006). Based on a sample of 98 male industrial workers in an automobile manufacturing firm in Tehran and 98 female industrial workers in a textile firm in Isfahan, Oreyzi finds that women and men at equal wage categories have unequal skills and abilities. Survey shows that in these wage equivalency situations women, on average, have more knowledge, skill and ability (KSA). This inequality is an indirect indicator of gender wage discrimination and is consistent with our findings.

Conclusions

In recent years, despite many adverse conditions, Iranian women have enjoyed a significant improvement in university education and acquisition of productive skills. Yet, unfortunately, they still face many barriers in the labour market. First, they face employment and promotion discrimination which leads to higher unemployment rates for women in comparison to men. Second, as suggested by our empirical findings, they also face a sizable wage discrimination which is noticeable in both private and public sectors. The prevalence of wage discrimination could further discourage some women from entering the labour force.

Applying the Oaxaca decomposition method and using the 2005 HIES of Iran, we found that the gender wage gap in public sector jobs is significantly smaller than private sector. Furthermore, the decomposition of this gap into contributions of human capital and discrimination revealed that gender wage discrimination was more severe in the private sector. Female public sector employees were mostly specialists and skilled workers with significantly higher education than female workers in the private sector. We further repeated the Oaxaca decomposition for specific skill categories and found that there was a negative correlation between skills and wage discrimination. Female employees in the category of scientists and specialists faced less wage discrimination than those in lower skilled categories. The absolute size of the gender wage gap was also smaller for more skilled employment categories. This could be partly explained by the fact that most of the specialist and scientist jobs are found in the public sector and government regulations prevent wage and benefit discrimination among public sector employees. As a result there is little room for discretion by individual managers. Another possible explanation is that highly skilled and specialist female workers have more bargaining power.

The high level of wage discrimination in the unskilled service sector is partly due to the fact that in recent years it has become culturally acceptable for young women in larger cities to work in low pay retail jobs. These female employees, who often live with their parents, are willing to accept part- and full-time low wage jobs because a portion of their living expenses is covered by their immediate family.

Yet an even more significant explanation for the prevalence of gender wage discrimination among industrial workers and unskilled workers is that most of these jobs are in the private sector and government regulations against wage discrimination in the private sector are poorly enforced. This is a significant problem that will become even more severe as Iran continues its privatization and deregulation reforms.

The Islamic government of Iran initiated a series of privatization and market liberalization reforms during the presidency of Ali Akbar Hashemi Rafsanjani, which have gradually moved forward despite periodic setbacks. Many public enterprises have been privatized and in the remaining public organizations thousands of jobs have been replaced with service contracts as cost reducing measures. Often the employees whose public employment was terminated were reemployed by the companies that offered the services of those employees to the government (in most cases these companies were created by high ranking government officials and their relatives). This was most visible in the case of administrative, cleaning and custodial jobs. The transition often resulted in deregulation of the labour contracts and loss of public sector benefits for the affected employees. This transition has also made female employees more vulnerable to wage and employment discrimination.

This study and a handful of other studies also suggest that in Iran, the main concerns of gender discrimination in the economic domain is shifting from educational and human capital inequities to wage and employment discrimination in the labour market. As demonstrated in our study, male–female wage differences are mainly due to discrimination, and appropriate social policies are needed to confront these discriminatory practices. With the ongoing market-oriented reforms that are shifting job opportunities from the public sector to the private sector, there is a strong need for better regulation and monitoring of employment conditions in the private sector. Strong legislation against gender discrimination in the labour market is needed and enforcement mechanisms must be strengthened.

Another important step required is to address the underlying cultural bias and the predominant patriarchal culture that tolerates various forms of work-related discrimination against women. This culture still sees men as the main breadwinners for the family and views womens' earnings as of secondary significance. Such an attitude often makes it easy for an employer to bypass a qualified woman in favour of a male employee for promotion and wage increase opportunities. Prevalence of such discriminatory attitudes sometimes discourages female employees from fighting for their rights and pushes some of them to leave their job altogether. Yet in light of the growing number of female college graduates and skilled female professionals that have entered the labour market in recent years, there is a strong need to confront these cultural biases through education and regulation.

Finally, the prevalence of wage discrimination in private sector and limited opportunities in the public sector have led many women to withdraw from the labour force but these conditions might also lead to a different outcome in the coming decade. The number of well-educated women in urban areas is rapidly increasing and some of them who fail to find well paying suitable jobs as paid employees are likely to become entrepreneurs and establish their own businesses. These female-owned businesses will not only provide income for their owners but they are also more likely to create jobs for other women and pay more equitable wages to their female employees.

Notes

1 For example an online survey of more than 400,000 respondents in 12 countries revealed a wage gap in the range of 13 to 23 per cent. This survey was conducted by www.wageindicator.org. For details see: http://www.ituc-csi.org/IMG/pdf/gap-1.pdf, Global Gender Pay Gap, International Trade Union Confederation, February 2008, Belgium.
2 Said and El-Hamidi (2005) estimate the wage gap in Morocco and Egypt based on the 1990s data. They find that gender wage gap due to discrimination declined in Egypt but increased in Morocco during this period.
3 In 2010 women accounted for 60 per cent of total enrollment in public universities in Iran (Aryan 2012: 46).
4 The average share of women in labour forces of 23 Western industrial countries was reported as 43.9 per cent in 2005 (International Labor Organization, 2009: Table A15).
5 In addition to the recent rise in female LFPR that has been reported by Iran Statistical Center, there is also some evidence that women's labour force participation is significantly undercounted in the official statistics (Moghadam, 2009).
6 Some of the earlier studies are: Boulier and Pineda (1975) on the Philippines; Shields (1980) on Tanzania; House (1983) on Cyprus; Svejnar (1984) on Senegal and Jamison and van der Gaag (1978) on China. In the 1990s, Gilek and Sahn (1997), Rogers (1998) and Appleton *et al.* (1999) analyzed the gender wage gap in Guinea, South Korea and Ethiopia, respectively.
7 HIES is collected on an annual basis by the Statistical Center of Iran (SCI) as a component of the System of National Accounts (SNA).
8 In recent years it has become culturally acceptable for women to work in the retail sector and a growing number of young women are employed in low-wage sales positions. These women are mostly single and live with their parents. As a result they are willing to accept low-pay jobs which help them feel independent and earn small

amounts of income for personal expenses. For more details see Mortezayi Langaroudi *et al.* (2011).

9 Although this type of self selection can happen among men as well, there is evidence in the literature and in our sample that it is much smaller than among women.

10 The significance of self-selection bias in gender wage discrimination in Bangladesh was reported by Ahmed and Maitra (2010).

11 In our sample this category also includes high ranking bureaucrats and politicians.

12 The sample size for the three skill categories that we have selected are as follows: Scientists and Specialists: 1,221 men and 798 women; Industrial Workers: 3,241 men and 445 women; and Unskilled Workers in the Service Sector: 6,753 men and 649 women.

13 Iran has adopted a uniform public sector pay schedule in 1973. According to this law public organizations and state enterprises are prohibited from wage discrimination on the basis of gender.

References

Abbasi-Shivazi, M. J., McDonald, P. and Hosseini-Chavoshi, M., *The Fertility Transition in Iran: Revolution and Reproduction*, Springer, 2009.

Ahmed, S. and Pushkar, M., Gender wage discrimination in rural and urban labour markets of Bangladesh, *Oxford Development Studies*, March, 38 (1): 83–112, 2010.

Alavian-Ghavanini, A., 'Barrasi shekaaf jensiyati dar manategh shahri Iran' (An analysis of gender wage gap in urban areas of Iran), Master's Thesis, Dean of Management and Economics, Sharif Technical University, 2012.

Appleton, S., Hoddinott, J. and Krishnan, P., 'The gender wage gap in three African countries', *Economic Development and Cultural Change*, 47: 289–312, 1999.

Arabsheibani, R. A., Male-Female earnings differentials among the highly educated Egyptians, *Education Economics*, 8 (2), 2000.

Aryan, K., 'The Boom in Women's Education' in Povey & Rostami-Povey, eds, *Women, Power and Politics in 21st Century Iran*. London, Ashgate: 35–52, 2012.

Bahramitash, R. and Esfahani, H. S., 'Nimble fingers no longer! Women's employment in Iran', chapter in *Contemporary Iran* by Gheissari, A., Oxford University Press, 2009.

Boulier, B. L. and Pinada, L. P., Determinants of Male-Female Wage Differentials in Government Agencies, *Philippine Economic Journal*, October 1975.

Cudeville, E. and Gurbuzer, L. Y., Gender wage discrimination in the Turkish labour market: Can Turkey be part of Europe?, *Comparative Economic Studies*, September, 52 (3): 429–63, 2010.

El-Hamidi, F., 'Trade liberalization, gender segmentation, and wage discrimination: evidence from Egypt', *Cairo: Economic Research Forum*, Working Paper 414, 2008.

Glick, P. and Sahn, D. E., Gender and educational impacts on employment and earnings in West Arica: evidence from Guinea, *Economic Development and Cultural Change*, 45: 793–823, 1997.

Heckman, J. J., Sample selection bias as a specification error, *Econometrica* 47 (1): 153–61, 1979.

Hosni, D. J. and Al-Qudsi, S. S., Sex discrimination in the labour market of Kuwait, *International Journal of Manpower*, 9: 10–22, 1988.

House, W. J., Occupational Segregation and Discriminatory Pay:The Position of Women in the Cyprus Labor Market, *International Labor Review*, 122, 75–93, 1983.

International Labor Organization, 'Global employment trends for women', Geneva: http://www.ilo.org/public/libdoc/ilo/P/09275/09275%282009%29.pdf, 2009.

International Trade Union Confederation, 'The global gender pay gap', ITUC, 2008.

Jamison, D. T. and vander Gaag, J., Education and earnings in People's Republic of China, *Education Economics*, 6: 161–6, 1987.

Moghadam, F. E., Undercounting women's work in Iran, *Iranian Studies*, 42 (1), 2009.

Mortazayi L. M., Safarzadeh, H., Keshavarz, N. and Far, E. H., 'An analysis of working women's wages and the proposal for remote work: a round table discussion'; July, Accessed at: http://www.ofros.com/zanan/kmhk_bdzsh.htm in September 2012.

Oaxaca, R., Male-female wage differentials in urban labour markets, *International Economic Review*, 14: 693–709, 1973.

Oreyzi, H., 'Barrasi-e tajrobi-e shekaaf dastmozdi mobtani bar jensiyat dar sanat-e Iran' (An empirical analysis of gender wage gap in Iran's industrial sector), in Farsi, *Quarterly Journal of Research in Social Welfare* (Faslnameye elmi pajuheshi refah ejtemaie), 1385, 5 (21): 73–97, 2006.

Poulier, B. L. and Pineda, L.P., Male-female wage differential in a Philippine government agency, *The Philippine Economic Journal*, 14: 436–48, 1975.

Rogers, Y., A reversal of fortunes for Korean women: explaining the 1983 upward turn in relative earnings, *Economic Development and Cultural Change*, 46: 727–48, 1998.

Said, M. and El-Hamidi, F., 'Wage inequality by education and gender in MENA: Contrasting the Egyptian and Moroccan experiences in 1990s', Cairo: Economic Research Forum, Working Paper 122005013, http://www.erf.org.eg/cms.php?id= publication_details&publication_id=506, 2005.

Shah, N. M, and Al-Qudsi, S. S., Female work roles in a traditional oil economy: Kuwait, *Research in Human capital and Development*, 6: 213–46, 1990.

Shields, N., *Women in the Urban Labor Market of Africa: The Case of Tanzania*. World Bank, 1980.

Statistical Center of Iran, 'Records complex-household expenditure and income survey in urban and rural areas.' Tehran: The Management Planning and Organization of Iran, 2005.

Svejnar, J., The Determinants of Industrial Sector Earnings in Senegal, *Journal of Development Economics*, Elsevier, Vol. 15 (1–3), 289–311, 1984.

Index